Metacognition

Metacognition

Knowing about Knowing

edited by Janet Metcalfe and Arthur P. Shimamura

A Bradford Book
The MIT Press
Cambridge, Massachusetts
London, England

First MIT Press paperback edition, 1996
© 1994 Massachusetts Institute of Technology

This book was set in Baskerville by DEKR Corporation and was printed and bound in the United States of America.

Library of Congress Cataloging-in-Publication Data

Metacognition : knowing about knowing / edited by Janet Metcalfe and
  Arthur P. Shimamura.
    p. cm.
  "A Bradford book."
  Includes bibliographical references and index.
  ISBN 0-262-13298-2 (HB), 0-262-63169-5 (PB)
  1. Metacognition. 2. Cognition. I. Metcalfe, Janet.
II. Shimamura, Arthur P.
BF311.M4489   1994
153—dc20   93-37597
                                                                  CIP

Contents

Foreword

For more than a hundred years cognitive psychologists, along with other students of the brain/mind, have been busy studying how people know things. The most conspicuous result that has emerged from these efforts is the growing awareness that the more we know about knowledge the more we know how little we know. Problems of cognition are complicated and seem to be becoming increasingly so. Part of the complexity turns out to reside in the fact — only recently "discovered" — that we can identify many more different kinds of knowledge, and many more different forms of knowing, than anyone ever suspected. The problem of organizing the extant evidence concerning kinds of knowledge into empirically valid classificatory schemes is going to occupy many good minds in the future. There exists an even more recent insight, however, which seems to be on its way of becoming a part of the Zeitgeist. This one concerns the realization that there is no direct correlation between kinds of knowledge and forms of knowing, between representation and process. What we regard as a particular kind of knowledge can be known in many ways, and a particular form of knowing may have as its object many different kinds of knowledge. A 5-year-old knows the grammar of the language she speaks in that she speaks it according to a complex set of rules, but she cannot verbally describe her knowledge in the same way as she can 10 years later. A college student can form the image of an apple as readily as she can form the image of a triangle, even though the two kinds of knowledge — concerning concrete objects and abstract ideas — have little in common. When the

reality of the dissociation between knowledge and knowing is acknowledged, a powerful impetus will exist for an intensive and systematic exploration of the manifold of relations between these two
concepts and what they represent.

The research activity that has recently burgeoned under the general rubric of metacognition, a rich sample of which is assembled in
the present volume, is one of several manifestations of the turmoil
surrounding the issue of the relation between knowledge and knowing. The beginning of metacognition as a separate research topic,
one that is perceived as somehow different from "plain" cognition,
can be traced back to Hart's Ph.D. thesis at Stanford in 1965 on
feeling of knowing, even if the official appellation, by Wellman and
Flavell, of the general category into which Hart's work fitted came
some 10 years later.

With the wisdom of hindsight, and the historian's prerogative of
interpreting the past in terms of the past's future, it is possible to see
the growth of the field of metacognition as an (unconscious?) rebellion against behavioral or behavioralist orientation of the then
prevailing orientation in psychology. Although the information-processing paradigm was already well on its way in 1965, it had not
brought much relief from behaviorism's stranglehold on consciousness, the historical, true subject matter of psychology. The mental
processes with which the newly emerging cognitive scientists began
filling the "black box" were the observer's abstractions rather than
the individual's conscious experiences. It was the study of the mind
from the point of view of the "third" person, and in that sense did
not differ greatly from the basic orienting attitudes of behaviorists.

Although Hart's pioneering paradigm clearly served the purpose
of capturing his subjects' first-person awareness of categories of
knowledge that could not be discriminated in terms of the standard
behavioral performance, Hart himself did not evoke the concept of
consciousness or awareness in his work. In the middle of the 1960s
that was a wise and politic thing to do for a young investigator who
wanted to publish in the establishment's journals. But even without
the banner carrying the big "C" word, Hart's rebellion's consequences were far-reaching. The present volume is only the latest to
a long string of testimonials to its success.

What is a bit more puzzling is why most of the students of meta-cognition and metamemory today still use behavioralistically safe expressions, such as memory "monitoring," mnemonic "behavior,'" memory "search," tip-of-the tongue "states," and tip-of-the-tongue and feeling-of-knowing "experience." Do they use these expressions deliberately in order to avoid the big bad "C" word? Or do they take it for granted that when they refer to monitoring, and judgments, and experience, everyone understands that they are indeed talking about conscious monitoring, conscious judgments, conscious experience? But if so, and if it is true that consciousness is a necessary condition of metacognitive judgments and metacognitive experiences, why not claim explicitly that conscious awareness is one of the defining attributes of the domain of metacognition?

Some scientists today remain dubious about consciousness as a fit topic for scientific study, declaring it to be an epiphenomenon. They claim that consciousness cannot be operationally defined, or its existence cannot be objectively verified, or it cannot be measured, or it does not help us to predict anything, or some or all of the above. These critics have not paid attention to what is happening around them. The many interesting and reliable empirical facts about metacognition of the kind reported in this volume have gone a long way toward answering the old queries of the sceptics. Thus, is there any evidence that consciousness plays a critical rather than an epiphenomenal role in the workings of the brain/mind? Yes there is: Machines without consciousness, and animals whose consciousness is different from that of human beings, could not perform many of the tasks that human subjects in metacognitive experiments, and others of the same general kind, can and do perform. If in doubt, make a machine think creative but plausible thoughts about its own future. The ability of a human being to reflect on his or her conscious awareness of the world represents an evolved skill that serves important biological functions. Once we realize this fact it becomes worth our while to search for the biological utility of metacognition. Some investigators are indeed already asking pertinent questions.

Some other recent work in cognitive psychology and cognitive neuroscience of memory has revealed that people can make many complex judgments both consciously and nonconsciously. The behavioral outcome may be identical — the subject declares that a name belongs to a famous person, that A — AS — N represents the same thing as ASSASSIN, or that an event happened in a particular place at a particular time — but metacognitive judgments reveal clear differences in their underlying processes. When the facts of meta-cognition are added to these other recently discovered facts concerning phenomena of conscious awareness, the question must be raised as to whether the time has come to change the rules of our science. Things that are known to exist and to behave lawfully in the natural world — such as phenomena of consciousness and awareness — must be admissible as a legitimate objective of scientific study even if the standards first created at the time when Descartes was struggling with the problem of the localization of soul may not fit exactly.

Our own awareness of what, who, and where we are, and what we experience, is a fact of nature more certain than any observations we can make, or any measures we can take, of other existences, relations, and happenings beyond the reach of our immediate experience. A science of the brain/mind that does not capture or even acknowledge these basic facts, is out of touch with reality. One can ignore the scientific problem of consciousness only if one is deliberately willing to profess lack of interest in the most fascinating invention of evolution.

Endel Tulving
Rotman Research Institute of Baycrest Centre

Preface

Cogito ergo sum.
— *Descartes, 1628*

The ability to reflect upon our thoughts and behaviors is taken, by some, to be at the core of what makes us distinctively human. Indeed, self reflection and personal knowledge form the basis of human consciousness. Of course, even without conscious awareness, humans can learn, change, and adapt as a function of the events and contingencies in the social and physical environment. Such plasticity, though, can be ascribed to a variety of other living organisms, from plants, to invertebrates, to mammals, and even to non-living machinery. What appears unique to humans and what has fascinated the minds of countless philosophers and scientists is the self-reflective nature of human thought. Humans are able to monitor what is perceived, to judge what is learned or what requires learning, and to predict the consequences of future actions. Moreover, we can distinguish reality from imagination, evaluate the quality of our own responses, and make plans for the future.

The term *metacognition* has been used to describe our knowledge about how we perceive, remember, think, and act — that is, what we know about what we know. The term was originally developed to characterize changes in self reflection during early development (Brown, 1978; Flavell & Wellman, 1977). In recent years, this area of study has surged forward, progressing from a field in which the emphasis was once the mere characterization of the phenomenon to one in which a wide variety of scientific questions are being analyzed and answered. In particular, recent psychological studies have evaluated the role of metacognition in learning, memory, thinking, problem solving, and decision making. Theoretical models of the causes and functions of metacognition have been proposed and tested against one another. In addition, the application of metacognitive research to real world settings has been useful in diverse domains, such as education, eyewitness testimony, problem solving, aging, and neuropsychology.

The current study of metacognition was foreshadowed (though some might say impeded) by intense interest in introspectionism during the turn of the century. The method of reporting the contents of perceptions, memories, and thoughts was as much rooted in philosophy as it was in science. Ultimately, this method was scientifically intractable. Much later, psychological analyses of behavior suggested that people's reports about their mental processes, abilities, and knowledge were often spurious and ill-founded. Based on these analyses, it was suggested that a great deal of our knowledge is inferential or heuristic in nature. That is, we often base metacognitive knowledge — such as "feelings of knowing" — on inferential information, which may be correlated with the target information itself (e.g., "I know many things about space travel, so I must know the code name for the first space module to land on the moon"). Such inferences may be made without having any knowledge of the target information (the answer is *Eagle*). Thus, the basis of metacognitive judgments may not always be ascribable to *privileged access* to our own mental states and knowledge. The issue of whether individuals have direct privileged access to mental information — and the circumstances under which such access occurs — is controversial and a central issue in psychological studies of metacognition.

The quality and accuracy of people's beliefs about their own knowledge can be addressed in a variety of circumstances. Although metacognitive beliefs are rarely taken to be entirely valid, it is nevertheless the case that normal human beings frequently act upon such beliefs. The student who believes that he knows the material for the upcoming examination is liable to go to a Grateful Dead concert (or worse) rather than to the library. The eyewitness to a crime scene is liable to be a convincing witness on the stand, though his or her knowledge about the crime may be based on spurious misperceptions and memories. The would-be scientist who believes that certain problems are intractable is liable to choose a different field of research. The mathematician who believes he is on the verge of proving a new theorem is liable to devote boundless energy to the task. Such examples demonstrate that our metacognitive beliefs, though often spurious, are indisputably motivating. The manner in which cognition and metacognition interact is another central theme in empirical and theoretical analyses of metacognition.

In this volume, the authors describe psychological research on metacognition and the conditions under which metacognitive beliefs are either veridical, spurious, or biased. They explore how self-reflective processes are used in perception, memory, and problem solving, and how these processes are affected by subject variables such as developmental changes or neurological impairment. Finally, they identify methodological and theoretical issues important for this kind of research. In the preparation of this volume, we would like to thank Tom Nelson for spurring our interest in metacognition and, in particular, the completion of this project, Endel Tulving for fostering our thoughts about this and other scientific issues, and Teri Mendelsohn and her colleagues at MIT Press for their support and efficiency in putting this volume to print. Finally, we would like to thank our families and friends — without them, self reflections would be much less satisfying.

Metacognition

1

Why Investigate Metacognition?

Thomas O. Nelson and Louis Narens

Why should researchers of cognition investigate metacognition? This chapter constitutes one answer to that question.

Metacognition is simultaneously a topic of interest in its own right and a bridge between areas, e.g., between decision making and memory, between learning and motivation, and between learning and cognitive development. Although the focus of this chapter is on the metacognitive aspects of learning and memory — which throughout the chapter will be called *metamemory* — both the overall approach and many of the points apply as well to other aspects of cognition. Emphasis is placed on some shortcomings in previous research on memory that have been commented on by several prominent investigators. It is to those investigators' credit that they stepped back from their specific investigations to take stock of the overall progress in the field and to highlight problems. We believe those problems can be solved, with research on metacognition playing a major role in that solution.

Previous Research

In a well-known book, Kuhn (1962) wrote that science proceeds by alternating between periods of "normal science" (during which investigators do research within a commonly accepted paradigm) and "crises" (during which investigators seek a new paradigm due to problems with the old one). This account of science has been attacked strongly (e.g., Shapere, 1971; Suppe, 1977), but it may nevertheless be useful here as a heuristic conceptualization. Although no single paradigm has completely dominated the research on human learning and memory during the past 50 years, there have been identifiable frameworks that large numbers of researchers have investigated in unison.

Prior to the 1950s, the aim was to unify psychology via a science of all behavior. Learning and motivation were investigated as interconnected phenomena. During subsequent decades, a shift occurred away from animal research and toward research on human memory via information processing; learning became deemphasized, and motivation became "assumed" and was no longer investigated. The next few paragraphs expand some on that shift.

In the 1950s and early 1960s, researchers focused on topics such as multiple-list learning that were important within the framework of interference theory (Underwood & Postman, 1960), but that focus of research waned during the later 1960s. For instance, Postman (1975) concluded that "interference theory today is in a state of ferment if not disarray" (p. 327).

During the 1960s and early 1970s, the emphasis changed from learning to memory, and researchers focused on topics such as serial-position curves in single-trial recall, which were important within the framework of the rehearsal-buffer model of memory (Atkinson & Shiffrin, 1968). That focus was later replaced by investigations of various kinds of orienting tasks during incidental memory. Within the levels-of-processing framework of Craik and Lockhart (1972), memory was construed as a byproduct of perceptual activity rather than as a deliberate consequence of rehearsal. However, by 1980, Wickelgren concluded, "The levels of processing fad is over in the field of learning and memory" (p. 40).

During the 1980s, the field became even more fragmented into isolated pockets of research on various aspects of learning and memory, with no dominating theory or framework that most researchers are working on in unison.[1] Interest increased in taxonomic distinctions (e.g., explicit memory versus implicit memory) and in neuropsychological factors (Shimamura, 1989). There has also been a renewed interest in the topic of consciousness, with an especially compelling case having been made recently by Flanagan (1992, pp. 11–13 ff) for a three-pronged approach to investigating con-

sciousness via phenomenological reports, behavioral data, and research on the brain (e.g., neuropsychological research). However, it
is not so much that the substantive problems researched in earlier
years have been solved and that their solutions have been integrated
into a growing body of knowledge; rather, the previous problems
have been left unsolved, and new problems have became the focus
of subsequent research.

Thus the net result of 50 years of research on learning and memory
has been a particularly rapid series of Kuhnian alternations of "normal science" and "revolutions," with the effects of prior research on
subsequent research being remarkably shortlasting. Although this
series has produced rich and varied sets of empirical findings, experimental paradigms, and modeling techniques, it has not produced
dominant theories or frameworks that expand on their predecessors.
This failure to produce theories and frameworks that encompass the
findings of prior decades is undoubtedly an important factor for the
relatively slow rate of *cumulative* progress[2] in learning and memory
when compared to, for example, major subfields of physics, biology,
and chemistry. We believe that this failure and the lack of cumulative
progress in human learning and memory are due at least partly to
the following three shortcomings that have been commented on by
several prominent investigators. Those comments are brought together here, and the major goal of the remainder of this chapter is
to offer the beginnings of a foundation designed to facilitate cumulative progress.

Three Shortcomings of Previous Research

There are three shortcomings that are from our (and several other
investigators') perspective undesirable. These shortcomings are interrelated, and each tends to give rise to the next.

First Shortcoming: Lack of a Target for Research

The bulk of laboratory research on human memory lacks concrete
targets. A target for research should be defined in terms of some to-
be-explained behavior of a specific category of organism in a specific
kind of environmental situation (cf. Neisser, 1976). Scientific fields

typically make the most progress when they have targets outside the laboratory on which to focus (e.g., planetary motion in astronomy, earthquakes in geology, tornadoes in meteorology). Gruneberg, Morris, and Sykes (1991) concluded, "In general terms, it seems to us self-evident that everyday phenomena are the starting point for many questions for all sciences, and that all sciences progress by refining and controlling variables within the laboratory. . . . Compared with the successes of the other sciences, the successes of psychology in general, and memory research in particular, are pretty small beer" (p. 74). Thus the hope is that such naturalistic targets will give the successive programs of research a common goal to continue investigating, so that progress can be cumulative. Although there are exceptions (e.g., Bahrick, 1984), most laboratory research on memory is oriented more toward esoteric laboratory phenomena that are of interest primarily to researchers (i.e., *fachgeist*[3]) rather than toward a concrete target *outside the laboratory* that the laboratory investigations are attempting to illuminate. Similarly in the domain of theoretical models, Morris (1987) concluded, "The choice and development of models of human cognition seems to depend very much upon the personal interests of the modellers and very little upon the empirical and practical demands of the world" (p. xv).

Some people have reacted so strongly against these trends as to suggest that laboratory experiments are no longer appropriate as a research strategy for human memory (e.g., Wertheimer, 1984). By contrast, we believe with Neisser (1976) that our goal should be "to understand cognition in the context of natural purposeful activity. This would not mean an end to laboratory experiments, but a commitment to the study of variables that are ecologically important rather than those that are easily manageable" (p. 7). Similarly, Roediger (1991) wrote, "The traditional role of naturalistic observation is to draw attention to significant phenomena and to suggest interesting ideas. Researchers will then typically create a laboratory analog of the natural situation in which potentially relevant variables can be brought under control and studied" (p. 39). Such laboratory research could then serve as the basis for an integrative theory that has obvious relevance to at least one naturalistic situation.

A similar plea for a naturalistic target has been echoed by Parducci and Sarris (1984):

The desire for ecological validity, expressed in a number of the chapters, cannot be separated from the concern to make psychology more practical. . . . Scientists continue to study psychological problems without apparent concern for practical applications. . . . There do seem to be strong forces pushing even traditional areas of psychological research in practical directions. Granting agencies, particularly in the U.S., have recently been favoring "mission" research. (pp. 10–11)

Although the remarks of these researchers are useful in telling us what we should not be doing (namely, studying a laboratory phenomenon for its own sake), they do not offer a specific suggestion for what we should be doing. Before researchers can focus on specific kinds of ecologically valid situations, it may be desirable to specify the categories of people and the kinds of naturalistic situations that will be the target of the research. This is rarely done, as pointed out by Estes (1975):

The entire array of conceptual systems — association theory, functionalism, and behavior theory — which dominated research on both human and animal learning over the first half of the century had in common a view of a hypothetical ageless organism. . . . The tendency to theorize in terms of an abstract organism may seem unnecessarily sterile, making cognitive psychology both autistic relative to other disciplines and remote from practical affairs. (p. 6)

Estes' opinion was recently echoed by two well-known psychologists this year. Shepard (1992) wrote, "The experimental tasks used in the 1950s by Estes and others (including myself!) continued the existing tradition in American psychology of designing stimuli and tasks on the basis of prevailing theoretical ideas, with little regard to what types of problems the species was adapted to solve in its natural environment" (p. 420). Similarly, the reviewer Boneau (1990) concluded:

Psychological research is too faddish. Movements in research are tied too much to the development of a paradigm or methodology. The problem should be the driving force and the paradigms and methodologies developed for it. The problem should be one that is closely tied to the natural world. Experimental psychology has had too much tendency to go off into the lab and forget all contact with reality. (p. 1594)

Thus there is a need to make explicit both the specific categories of people and the specific environmental situations that are to be the targets of research on human learning and memory. So what would be a good target on which investigators can focus? Although various targets[4] are possible, the one emphasized in our research is the following: *To explain (and eventually improve) the mnemonic behavior of a college student who is studying for and taking an examination.* We chose this target in part for the following reasons: It is relevant (who spends more time memorizing for and taking examinations than college students?), naturalistic, practical, concrete, and challenging in terms of theory.

Investigators of human memory already do the bulk of their research on college students, but usually only for reasons of convenience (e.g., because such people are easily accessible as subjects for experiments). Rather than trying to understand college students per se, the target of most investigators is, as pointed out in the previous quotation from Estes, vague and typically consists of little more than a hope that the results will generalize to some unspecified target population. By contrast, if we began explicitly to define the population of college students as a target population of interest rather than merely being the population that is handy, the design of our experiments on memory would likely change accordingly (examples are given below). Further, such an approach would help to make explicit some potentially interesting mnemonic processes that previously have been implicit and unexplored.

Second Shortcoming: Overemphasis on a Nonreflective-Organism Approach

In most previous and current research, human memory is conceptualized narrowly, almost in *tabula-rasa* fashion analogous to a computer storing new input on a disk. Although people can be regarded as encoding and retrieving information (perhaps analogously to what occurs in a computer), those activities have been assumed to be *nonreflective.* Indeed, nothing approaching consciousness is evident in any available computer (Searle, 1992). To our knowledge, *none* of the currently available computerized learning/memory algorithms contains a model of itself and its monitoring and control capabilities (ramifications of this can be seen in the discussion of Conant & Ashby below); instead, only the programmer has a model of the computerized learning algorithm and its processes.[5] Ramifications of this point have been elaborated by Searle (1992). Moreover, *computers do not have the imperfect retrieval of stored information that is so characteristic of humans* (Tulving & Pearlstone, 1966; Bahrick, 1970). Whereas current theories of human learning and memory typically construe people as automatic systems, sound theories need to be developed that construe people as *systems containing self-reflective mechanisms for evaluating (and reevaluating) their progress and for changing their on-going processing;* such mechanisms do occur in the domain of metacognition, as discussed below.

One way in which the nonreflective-organism approach manifests itself is exemplified by research on different orienting processes during incidental memory, where the assumption is made that researchers can discover what is automatically stored in memory whenever a subject makes a given orienting response. Although this assumption may sometimes be valid, it certainly cannot capture the fact that a college student studying for an examination is a conscious, self-directed organism who is continually making memory-relevant decisions about how difficult it will be to memorize a given item or set of items, about what kind of processing to employ during that memorization, about how much longer to study this or that item, and so on. No current theory of memory sheds light on (or even attempts to explain) that fact.

Thirty years ago, Miller, Galanter, and Pribram (1960) remarked about the focus of research on human learning and memory: "The usual approach to the study of memorization is to ask how the material is *engraved* on the nervous system . . . an important part of the memorizing process seems to have been largely ignored" (p. 125, italics added). Later, Reitman (1970) expanded on that view, saying, "Memory is not a simple decoupleable system; it is more like a complex interconnected collection of structures, processes, strategies, and controls. Memory behavior does not depend solely upon a memory subsystem; it reflects the activity of the human cognitive system as a whole" (p. 490). Still later, Estes (1975) discussed the importance of "the formulation of the conception of 'control processes' (Atkinson & Shiffrin, 1968) in human memory and the recognition that learned voluntary strategies play a major part in virtually all aspects of human learning" (p. 7).

Viewing people as self-directed seems most compatible with the conception of people as steering their own acquisition and retrieval. We are suggesting not that studies of experimenter-directed learning and memory should cease but rather that substantial research is also warranted on self-directed learning and on the self-reflective mechanisms that people do/could use to facilitate acquisition and retrieval. Some progress has already been made (e.g., Johnson & Hirst, 1991; Nelson & Narens, 1990), and early steps toward such a theory will be discussed below.

Third Shortcoming: Short-Circuiting via Experimental Control

Another potential shortcoming of previous research is a methodological ramification of investigators construing their subjects as non-reflective. Ironically, although the self-directed processes are not explicitly acknowledged in most theories of memory, there is an implicit acknowledgment on the part of investigators concerning the importance of such processes. The evidence for this is that investigators go to such great lengths to design experiments that eliminate or hold those self-directed processes constant via experimental control! Two examples serve to illustrate.

First, instead of investigating how and why a subject distributes his study time, most investigators present every item for the same amount of time, typically with instructions to the subject to focus on only the current item. This was noticed by Miller et al. (1960) when they remarked, "People tend to master the material in chunks organized as units. This fact tends to become obscured by the mechanical methods of presentation used in most experiments on rote learning, because such methods do not enable the subject to spend his time as he wishes" (p. 130). Similarly, Carlson (1992) wrote about the "elaborate efforts to hide from subjects such information as that certain items are repeated in studies of memory or learning. Such efforts are, of course, a backhanded acknowledgment of the powerful causal role of consciousness in determining behavior" (p. 599). By contrast, newer approaches have explored how subjects distribute their study time and what the consequences of those activities are (Hall, 1992; Mazzoni & Cornoldi, 1993; Nelson, 1993; Nelson & Leonesio, 1988; Zacks, 1969).

Second, instead of investigating the strategies that a subject spontaneously uses to memorize a given set of items (note: compelling evidence for such strategies comes from the now-classic findings of subjective organization by Bousfield, Bower, Tulving, and others during the 1950s and 1960s), most investigators tell the subject what strategy to use. If the investigator were not concerned that the subject might spontaneously use a strategy different from the instructed one, then the investigator would not bother instructing the subject about which strategy to use!

Others have also noticed this research style of trying to minimize the learner's self-directed processing. For instance, Butterfield and Belmont (1977) concluded:

In spite of the recent emergence of the executive function as a general theoretical construct, there has been very little effort to study it. Indeed, because of its very complexity, Reitman (1970) advocated a method of minimizing the executive by systematically instructing subjects to use highly specific sequences of control processes. This procedure assigns the executive function to the experimenter, rather than to the subject, in an effort to reduce unexplained variability in dependent measures resulting from spontaneous executive decisions by the subjects. (p. 282)

Thus investigators attempt to eliminate or reduce their subjects' variations in self-directed processing because (1) such processing on the part of the subject is typically construed mainly as a source of noise (as discussed below), and (2) until recently, there have not been theoretical frameworks within which to systematically explore the subjects' self-directed processing. Although the research strategy of attempting to minimize variations in self-directed processing (e.g., via giving instructions to the subject about how to rehearse the items) is legitimate for investigating the main effects of such instructions, there is also a need for a research strategy that investigates self-directed processing.

Sometimes the person's role in directing his or her own processing is not even acknowledged. For instance, "instructions to use imagery" may degenerate into "the person's use of imagery yielded." Moreover, people do not necessarily follow the experimenter's instructions to use a particular encoding strategy. Eagle (1967) found that subsequent recall was uncorrelated with strategy instructions per se but was correlated with people's reported strategies; strategy instructions served only to shift the number of people who reported using one or another strategy (for additional confirmation, see Paivio & Yuille, 1969). Although the investigator can instruct the person to use imagery, if the person believes that imagery should not be used, the result may be quite different from that of another person who receives the identical instructions but who believes that imagery should be used (cf. MacLeod, Hunt, & Mathews, 1978).

The approach of trying to minimize variations in self-directed processing also prevents the investigator from discovering what kind of strategy the subject would spontaneously use in the situation under investigation. In contrast to the approach to research that minimizes or disregards self-directed processing, research on metacognition emphasizes the potential importance of self-directed processing.

Toward a Theory of Metacognition

Twenty years ago, Tulving and Madigan concluded in the *Annual Review of Psychology:*

What is the solution to the problem of lack of genuine progress in understanding memory? It is not for us to say because we do not know. But one possibility does suggest itself: why not start looking for ways of experimentally studying, and incorporating into theories and models of memory, one of the truly unique characteristics of human memory: its knowledge of its own knowledge. (1970, p. 477).

Some investigators have begun to explore this possibility under the label of "metacognition" (Flavell, 1979; for prototypes of research on metacognition, see Nelson, 1992). These investigations have been fruitful, indicating that such an approach may indeed yield the kind of progress that Tulving and Madigan called for but could not find in 1970.

Critical Features of Metacognition

Conant and Ashby (1970) proposed and interpreted a theorem that "the living brain, so far as it is to be successful and efficient as a regulator for survival *must* proceed, in learning, by the formation of a model (or models) of its environment" (p. 89, their italics). They

not necessarily

concluded, "There can no longer be any question about *whether* the brain models its environment: it must" (p. 97, their italics). This idea has important implications for psychology (e.g., Yates, 1985; Johnson-Laird, 1983; Rouse & Morris, 1986).

In addition to a model of itself, two additional critical features are needed so as to have a metacognitive system, and they are summarized in figure 1.1. The first is the splitting of cognitive processes into two or more specifically interrelated levels. Figure 1.1 shows a simple metacognitive system containing two interrelated levels that we will call the "meta-level" and the "object-level." (Generalizations to more than two levels are given below.) The second critical feature of a metacognitive system is also a kind of dominance relation, defined in terms of the direction of the flow of information. This flow — analogous to a telephone handset — gives rise to a distinction between what we will call "control" (cf. Miller et al., 1960) versus "monitoring" (cf. Hart, 1965). When taken together with the aforementioned idea that the meta-level contains a model of the object-level, these two abstract features, splitting into two interrelated levels (meta-level versus object-level) and two kinds of dominance relations (control versus monitoring), comprise the core of metacognition as we use the term. These two features are interpreted in the following way.

also not always (handwritten margin note)

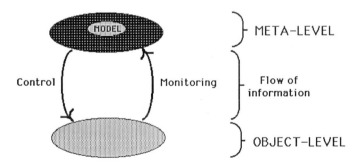

Figure 1.1
Nelson and Narens' (1990) formulation of a meta-level/object-level theoretical mechanism consisting of two structures (meta-level and object-level) and two relations in terms of the direction of the flow of information between the two levels. (Note: The meta-level contains an imperfect model of the object-level.) Adapted from Nelson and Narens (1990).

Control is interpreted as follows:

The fundamental notion underlying control — analogous to speaking into a telephone handset — is that the meta-level *modifies* the object-level, but not vice versa. In particular, the information flowing from the meta-level to the object-level either changes the state of the object-level process or changes the object-level process itself. This produces some kind of action at the object-level, which could be: (1) to initiate an action; (2) to continue an action (not necessarily the same as what had been occurring because time has passed and the total progress has changed, e.g., a game-player missing an easy shot as the pressure increases after a long series of successful shots); or (3) to terminate an action. However, because control per se does not yield any information from the object-level, a monitoring component is needed that is logically (even if not psychologically) independent of the control component. (Nelson & Narens, 1990, p. 127)

Monitoring is interpreted as follows:

The fundamental notion underlying monitoring — analogous to listening to the telephone handset — is that the meta-level *is informed by* the object-level. This changes the state of the meta-level's model of the situation, including "no change in state" (except perhaps for a notation of the time of entry, because the rate of progress may be expected to change as time passes, e.g., positively-accelerated or negatively-accelerated returns). However, the opposite does not occur, i.e., the object-level has no model of the meta-level. (Nelson & Narens, 1990, p. 127)

More Than Two Levels

The distinction between meta-level and object-level can easily be generalized to more than two levels. The development here will be given for monitoring; a similar development, except in the opposite direction (cf. figure 1.1), could occur for control.

During monitoring, the meta-level uses information about the object-level — and perhaps[6] about the relationship between the object-level and still other levels for which that level is in turn a meta-level. This information is used to update the meta-level's model of what is occurring at the object-level. This multilevel idea of processing extends naturally to finitely[7] many levels, $L_0,...L_i,...,L_j,...L_N$, where the first level, L_0, processes information about only the object, and L_j processes information about lower level L_i (where $i < j$) and perhaps about interrelationships between this lower level L_i and other levels for which L_i is a meta-level (e.g., level L_h for which $h < i$). Then level L_j is acting as a "meta-level" and all the aforementioned levels (i.e., L_0, L_h, L_i) as "object-levels." Simultaneous with that, L_i is acting as an "object-level" for L_j and for perhaps still higher levels.[8]

Thus the critical concern of our analysis of metacognitive monitoring is not the absolute levels in the sequence but rather is the relational aspect, wherein some processes dominate others via control and monitoring. The boundary between object-level versus meta-level (e.g., recalling an answer versus reporting that an answer was recalled, respectively) is sometimes sharp and at other times may be more fuzzy.

The overall system can process information by using all of the various levels, with each level being concerned about different aspects of the situation (cf. Minsky, 1985). In contrast to the view that memory is dissociated from higher level strategies, our view is that almost all memory situations intimately involve some monitoring and control, which are important heuristic categories of organization for our framework. The members of those two categories are defined denotatively (i.e., ostensively), using the general guidelines elaborated earlier (viz. "control" refers to affecting behavior, whereas "monitoring" refers to obtaining information about what is occurring at the lower levels). Next, we will describe some subdivisions of each of these two categories for the area of metamemory.

Control Processes in Metamemory

An early formulation of control processes was illustrated by servomechanisms such as a thermostat that controlled the onset and offset of a furnace so as to yield a desired temperature (Bateson, 1972; Wiener, 1948). Servomechanisms were investigated by psychologists during the 1950s in human-factors research, especially on the role of feedback during motor learning. The formulations of self-directed control in human verbal learning were called "control elements" (Estes, 1972), "control processes" (Atkinson & Shiffrin, 1968), or "executive processes" (Greeno & Bjork, 1973).

However, there are some important differences between those formulations and the one in Nelson and Narens (1990). In the latter, the input stemming from the meta-level is to the object-level mechanism itself, such that the meta-level can modify the object-level mechanism. In the aforementioned formulations, by contrast, the control process merely provided input that the object-level mechanism worked on.

This distinction can be illustrated by looking more closely at the thermostat example. In the earlier formulations, the thermostat was conceptualized merely as an on-off switch that provided input to activate or deactivate the furnace; the thermostat never changed the internal workings of the furnace in any way. By contrast, if the Nelson-Narens formulation were applied to a temperature-regulation situation, the control processes could be conceptualized not only in terms of starting and stopping the furnace but also in terms of altering the way in which the furnace worked (e.g., the input might cause the fan belt on the furnace motor to tighten so as to change the speed at which the blower dispenses air into the vents).

Another difference between the Nelson-Narens formulation (versus most previous formulations) is that the meta-level is assumed to be operating simultaneously with the object-level, not sequentially as in most (but of course, not all) computers. The meta-level and object-level processes are assumed to be operating simultaneously on different aspects of the situation and perhaps working at different temporal rates. This departure from previous formulations was made by Broadbent (1977; who in turn cites the earlier views of Kenneth Craik and Bartlett) when he wrote:

There are two concepts which have been current recently, and which might be used to explain the classic findings. . . . First, there is the notion of separate stages in the nervous system. In this notion, information about an event is processed in one way in one place and then passed on to another place where different operations are performed. The second notion is that of transfer of control, where a single processor is supposed to carry out one operation, store the result, and then carry out a different set of operations, in response to instructions from a different region of the program. These two notions . . . do not include the idea of a simultaneous operation over different time-scales; and above all they do not include the idea of one processor altering the operation of another. . . . When therefore a [production-system] program such as those of Newell and Simon is operating so as to produce hierarchically organized behavior, this does not mean that there is a hierarchy of processes, like the organization chart of the Civil Service. It only means that there is a hierarchy of rules in long-term memory, much as books in a library are divided into large sections. . . . *The dominant feature is that one process alters the nature of another process, rather than merely supplying it with input . . . the upper level is concerned with modifiability.* . . . To revert to the concepts of Newell and Simon, we do not merely need the processor to manipulate the outside world and its own short-term memory, under the control of various productions; we also need rules in long-term memory for the writing or deletion of rules in long-term memory. (pp. 185–200, italics added)

Thus control processes are not conceptualized as being limited to the starting and stopping of object-level processes, although this is one important function of control processes (e.g., see Logan & Cowan, 1984). Control processes can also modify the object-level processes, e.g., new rehearsal strategies (cf. learning to learn, or, in more computer-oriented jargon, "Higher organisms do not appear to have fixed software — they can implement new programs to meet unexpected contingencies"; Johnson-Laird, 1983, p. 503).

Besides exploring the role of control processes in modifying people's rehearsal strategies, research on metacognition also explores the role of control processes in other aspects of memory performance (e.g., search strategies, the allocation of study time to various items, search termination — see the Framework section below).

Monitoring Processes in Metamemory

For the control processes to regulate the system effectively, information is needed about the current state of the system. The monitoring processes in human memory were initially referred to by Hart (1967) as the "memory monitoring system."

The person's reported monitoring may, on the one hand, miss some aspects of the input and may, on the other hand, add other aspects that are not actually present (cf. Nisbett & Wilson, 1977). Although the accuracy of reported monitoring may vary across different situations, we expect that the reported monitoring seldom gives a veridical (i.e., nothing missing and nothing added) account of the input. This is not unlike one of the traditional views of perception, where what is perceived is different from what is sensed (i.e., perception conceptualized as sensation plus inference), except that what is analogous to the objects being sensed here is the object-level memory components.

A distinction should be drawn between retrospective monitoring (e.g., a confidence judgment about a *previous* recall response) and prospective monitoring (e.g., a judgment about *future* responding). Prospective monitoring is further subdivided by Nelson and Narens (1990, p. 130) into three categories in terms of the state of the to-be-monitored items:

1. *Ease-of-learning (EOL) judgments* occur *in advance of acquisition,* are largely inferential, and pertain to items that have not yet been learned. These judgments are predictions about what will be easy/difficult to learn, either in terms of which items will be easiest (Underwood, 1966) or in terms of which strategies will make learning easiest (Seamon & Virostek, 1978).

2. *Judgments of learning (JOL)* occur *during or after acquisition* and are predictions about future test performance on *currently recallable* items [but see below].

3. *Feeling-of-knowing (FOK) judgments* occur *during or after acquisition* (e.g., during a retention session) *and* are judgments about whether a given *currently nonrecallable* item is known and/or will be remembered on a subsequent retention test. [Empirical investigations of the accuracy of FOK judgments usually have the subsequent retention test be a recognition test (e.g., Hart, 1965), although several other kinds of retention tests have been used (for reviews, see Nelson, Gerler, & Narens, 1984; Nelson, 1988).]

Perhaps surprisingly, EOL, JOL, and FOK are not themselves highly correlated (Leonesio & Nelson, 1988). Therefore, these three kinds of judgments may be monitoring somewhat different aspects of memory, and whatever structure underlies these monitoring judgments is likely to be multidimensional (speculations about several possible dimensions occur in Krinsky & Nelson, 1985, and Nelson et al., 1984).

We now believe, in contrast to the above, that JOL should be defined as follows:

Judgments of learning (JOL) occur *during or soon after acquisition* and are predictions about future test performance on recently studied items. These recently studied items may be items for which there has not been a recall test or for which a recall test occurred (irrespective of the correctness/ incorrectness of answer).

This newer formulation of JOL, although in some cases yielding overlap with the above formulation of FOK, appears to be more

wrong approximate theories

useful (e.g., see Dunlosky & Nelson, 1992; Nelson & Dunlosky, 1991) than the earlier formulation.

There are at least two important questions about a person's reported monitoring. The first question is, *What factors affect the person's judgments* (e.g., what factors increase the degree to which people feel that they will recognize a nonrecalled answer)? For instance, Krinsky and Nelson (1985) found that people report having a greater FOK for items to which they were informed that they had made an incorrect recall response (i.e., commission-error items) than for items to which they had omitted making a recall response (i.e., omission-error items). This question pertains to the basis for the judgment and is not concerned with the accuracy of that judgment (e.g., people may or may not be correct in predicting better subsequent recognition on commission-error items than on omission-error items).

The second question is, *What factors affect the accuracy of the person's judgments* (e.g., when are FOK judgments most accurate)? For instance, FOK accuracy for predicting subsequent recognition of non-recalled answers is greater for items that previously had been overlearned than for items that previously had been learned to a criterion of only one correct recall (Nelson, Leonesio, Shimamura, Landwehr, & Narens, 1982). Also, the aforementioned variable of type of recall error (commission versus omission) tends to reduce FOK accuracy because subsequent recognition is usually equivalent on those two types of items.

Subjective Reports as a Methodological Tool for Investigating Monitoring and Control Processes
Long ago, William James (1890) emphasized the use of (nonanalytic) introspection:

Introspective Observation is what we have to rely on first and foremost and always. . . . I regard this belief as the most fundamental of all the postulates of Psychology. (p. 185, his italics)

Around the same time, the structuralist psychologists used a form of subjective reports in which trained introspectors (who participated in approximately 10,000 trials before being allowed to contribute data) attempted to discover the elements of the generalized normal human mind. However, because that form of subjective reports yielded too many unstable empirical generalizations, turn-of-the-century psychologists rejected it (e.g., Watson, 1913). Moreover, the structuralists "had no theory of cognitive development, . . . there was no theory of unconscious processes, . . . there was no serious theory of behavior. Even perception and memory were interpreted in ways that made little contact with everyday experience" (Neisser, 1976, p. 3).

Subjective reports have reemerged in a form that avoids the problems in the version of analytic introspection used by the structuralists. In his state-of-the-field chapter, Estes (1975) concluded,

Only in the very last few years have we seen a major release from inhibition and the appearance in the experimental literature on a large scale of studies reporting the introspections of subjects undergoing memory searches, manipulations of images, and the like. This disinhibition appears to be a consequence of a combination of factors. Among these are new developments in methodology. (p. 5)

In the new approach, people are construed as *imperfect* measuring devices of their own internal processes:

This distinction in our use of subjective reports is critical and can be highlighted by noticing an analogy between the use of introspection and the use of a telescope. One use of a telescope (e.g., by early astronomers and analogous to the early use of introspection) is to assume that it yields a perfectly valid view of whatever is being observed. However, another use (e.g., by someone in the field of optics who studies telescopes) is to examine a telescope in an attempt to characterize both its distortions and its valid output. Analogously, introspection can be examined as a type of behavior so as to characterize both its correlations with some objective behavior (e.g., likelihood of being correct on a test) and its systematic deviations — i.e., its distortions. (Nelson & Narens, 1990, p. 128)

As the methodological foundation evolves for determining when the tool (either the telescope or introspection) is or is not accurate, the content-area researchers (either astronomers or investigators of human memory) can use that methodological foundation to improve the accuracy of their conclusions, using the tool where it is accurate and/or adjusting their conclusions to correct for known distortions. For instance, in terms of theoretical formulations, Ericsson and Simon (1980) regard subjective reports as more accurate for short-term memory than for long-term memory (but see the *delayed-JOL effect* in Nelson & Dunlosky, 1991). In terms of methodology, improvements have been made in the accuracy of conclusions drawn from subjective reports about the FOK, both in terms of new techniques of data collection (for rationale, see Nelson & Narens, 1980, 1990) and in terms of better ways of analyzing FOK data (Nelson, 1984).

Thus the new approach to using subjective reports both recognizes and avoids the potential shortcomings of introspection (e.g., Nisbett & Wilson, 1977) while capitalizing on its strengths (e.g., Ericsson & Simon, 1980, 1984). This view, which is fundamentally different from the ones used at the turn of the century, opens the way for several broad questions that are empirically tractable and that are important both for theory and for practical applications: Can we develop an adequate characterization of introspective distortions? Can anything be done to reduce those distortions (e.g., see Koriat, Lichtenstein, & Fischhoff, 1980)? Can we characterize the way in which introspections — even with their distortions — are used by the person to affect other aspects of the system?

With regard to the last question, even if a person's behavior (e.g., subsequent recognition of nonrecalled items) is predicted no more accurately by the person's own subjective reports than by predictions derived from other people's performance (Nelson et al., 1986a), this does not reduce the importance of our studying the person's subjective reports as related to his or her own control processes (e.g., Nelson & Leonesio, 1988). As long as the person's subjective reports are *reliable* (and the evidence indicates that they are — Nelson et al., 1986a; Butterfield, Nelson, & Peck, 1988), then something is being tapped, and it may be a subsystem that interacts in important ways with other aspects of the system.

Furthermore, monitoring that is less than perfectly accurate is still useful to the individual as an approximation, as pointed out by Fodor (1983): "The world often isn't the way it looks to be or the way that people say it is. But, equally of course, input systems don't have to deliver apodictic truths in order to deliver quite useful information" (p. 46). Although previous writers such as Nisbett and Wilson (1977) have highlighted the possibility of distortions in introspective monitoring, they have not emphasized its potential role in affecting control processes. A system that monitors itself can use its own introspections as input to alter the system's behavior. One of our primary assumptions is that in spite of its imperfect validity and in spite of its being regarded by some researchers as only an isolated topic of curiosity, introspective monitoring is an important component of the overall memory system, because most memory activities are self-directed on the basis of introspectively obtained information.

Researchers attempting to understand that system can tap the person's introspections so as to have some idea about the input that the person is using. The present chapter attempts to shift the spotlight of researchers' attention toward self-directed memory and attendant processes such as introspection. This should help correct the "drunkard's search" that began when Watson (1913) rightly emphasized investigations of behavior but wrongly asserted that introspection had no critical role to play in those investigations. As Neisser (1976) remarked, "The realistic study of memory is much harder than the work we have been accustomed to . . . the legendary drunk who kept looking for his money under the streetlamp although he had dropped it ten yards away in the dark" (p. 17).

Our Own Approach to Research Metamemory

In our own research on learning and memory, we have striven to avoid the above mentioned three shortcomings and have focused on metacognition.

Framework

Consistent with the idea that "the two great functions of theory are (1) to serve as a tool whereby direct empirical investigation is facilitated and guided, and (2) to organize and order empirical knowledge" (Marx, 1963), we developed a framework that integrated a wide variety of previously isolated findings and that highlighted empirically tractable questions about metamemory for future research to explore.

The master view of our framework is shown in figure 1.2. The three major stages of acquisition, retention, and retrieval (cf. Melton, 1963), along with several substages, are listed between the two horizontal lines. Monitoring processes are listed above the time line, and

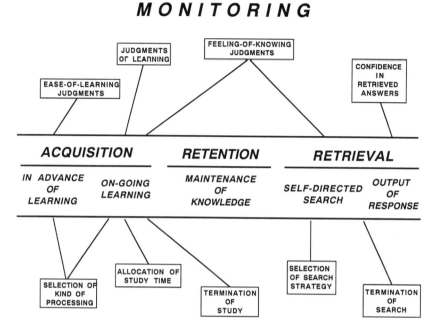

Figure 1.2
Master view of the Nelson-Narens (1990) framework. Memory stages (shown inside the horizontal bars) and some examples of monitoring components (shown above the horizontal bars) and control components (shown below the horizontal bars). Adapted from Nelson and Narens (1990).

control processes are listed below the time line. Figure 1.2 brings those constructs together via a morphological approach (Cummins, 1983). (Note: *Morphological* theories are theories that give a specification of structure — e.g., an explanation of how a cup holds water — in contrast to *systematic* theories, which additionally include the idea of organized interaction; other aspects of our framework not shown in figure 1.2 are systematic, e.g., figures 4 and 5 in Nelson & Narens, 1990.) The details of our framework will not be discussed here, but expositions of it are given in Nelson and Narens (1990; reprinted in part in Nelson, 1992).

Target of the Research

Although the Nelson-Narens framework described above and other theoretical frameworks may try to explain the same sets of data, they do so by emphasizing different aspects of human memory. Many of the important phenomena for metamemory are important to other frameworks only in that they must be neutralized ("short-circuited") experimentally; and many of the important phenomena for the other frameworks are inconsequential for the Nelson-Narens framework because they are not relevant to natural settings and/or do not bear on the concepts used by our framework. This leads to a version of the metaphorical idea of "throwing the baby out with the bathwater" in which one framework's baby is the other framework's bathwater. Because we utilize naturalistic targets, our preference is to let the naturalistic target determine which is the baby and which is the bathwater. We find this approach — letting a target (naturalistic or otherwise) determine basic memory concepts and issues — to be preferable to relying on theorists' guesses about the fundamental mechanisms underlying human memory, because the history of learning/memory research has shown that the overall confidence of one's peers about such guesses reliably fades, and often quickly.

Renewed Emphasis on Learning

We know too little about people's *mastery* of new information during multitrial learning (compared with the kind of memory that remains after a single study trial). In many naturalistic situations, the person's goal is to master a new body of information, e.g., a list of foreign-language vocabulary or new text material. Metacognitive mechanisms can facilitate that goal. The delayed-JOL effect (Nelson & Dunlosky, 1991) illustrates how the accuracy of monitoring one's own learning of new items can be greatly improved. A promising next step is to use the improved monitoring to facilitate mastery through more effective metacognitive control, for example, using delayed JOLs to guide the allocation of study time (Graf & Payne, 1992; Nelson, Dunlosky, & Narens, 1992). Human learning is itself an important topic that has received renewed emphasis recently from the interest in PDP models and that seems to us to contain an especially rich set of metacognitive components (Vesonder & Voss, 1985). Those components include people's goals, models of how to achieve those goals, and metacognitive monitoring/control mechanisms to be used for that achievement. Although PDP (and other computer-simulation) models focus on object-level memory processes, there is nothing to prevent those models from being conjoined with metacognitive processes. Moreover, the latter may help to solve a formidable shortcoming of computer-simulation models of cognition that has been pointed out by Searle (1992, pp. 212–214 and his summary point no. 7 on p. 226).

Looking Ahead

We envision the end goal of metamemory research to be a system of metamemory that contains a refined account of both how self-directed human memory works and how it can work better. At present there is only a framework of that system, a growing body of experimental findings, and the beginning of a theoretical interplay between models of learning/retrieval and framework mechanisms. Nevertheless, this initial effort is overdue. Almost two decades ago, Skinner (1974) wrote: "there is therefore a useful connection between feelings and behavior. It would be foolish to rule out the knowledge a person has of his current condition or the uses to which it may be put" (p. 209). We believe that the continuation of research on metamemory will result in a scientific understanding of how metacognitive monitoring and control mechanisms are acquired and how they can be employed in naturalistic settings, although perhaps not via explanatory concepts that Skinner would have advocated.[9]

Acknowledgments

This research was partially supported by NIMH grants R01MH32205 and K05MH1075 to the first author. We thank Nancy Alvarado, Harry Bahrick, and William Talbott for comments and suggestions.

T. O. Nelson and L. Narens

Notes

1. By comparison, during the decade 1941–1950 the theoretical framework developed by Clark Hull was cited by 40% of all articles in the *Journal of Experimental Psychology* and the *Journal of Comparative and Physiological Psychology* (and by 70% of the articles on the topic of learning in those two journals).

2. Cumulative progress occurs within a given pocket of research, but the point is that there has been a notable lack of cumulative progress across pockets of research.

3. Whereas *zeitgeist* refers to the spirit of the times, *fachgeist*, which refers to the spirit of the field, seems more appropriate for describing the trends of research in psychology (e.g., see the quotation from Boneau in the text below).

4. For human learning and memory, other acceptable targets could include ones that are non-naturalistic and/or have a large biological/neuropsychological emphasis.

5. But not necessarily all of the products that those processes can produce, which may be one reason that researchers produce computerized learning algorithms.

6. Some aspects of lower level processing may be cognitively impenetrable, not unlike a computer program in which one subroutine may receive input from another subroutine without any direct connection to the internal aspects of that subroutine; other aspects may be monitored by the meta-level.

7. There is no infinite regress here anymore than in, say, the legal system, where, for instance, a trial court can be construed as an object-level court, and an appellate court can be construed as the meta-level court; moreover, the appellate court may be the object-level court for a meta-level decision by a still higher, supreme court.

8. Several points should be made about this analysis. First, "higher" here has no meaning other than as defined above in terms of control and monitoring, similar to an organization such as a business, the military, or a university where the person who is said to be "higher up" is the one who controls and monitors someone else, who in turn may be higher up than yet another person, and so on. Second, it is also possible to have two levels (e.g., L_{h_1} and L_{h_2}) in which neither of them controls or monitors the other; therefore, the aforementioned dominance relation does not apply, and neither of them is a meta-level for the other (e.g., in a university, the chairman of physics versus the chairman of psychology; in memory, rehearsal versus retrieval). In mathematical terminology, the ordering of all the components is transitive (i.e., if P dominates Q, and if Q dominates R, then P dominates R) but need not be connected (i.e., may have distinct components J and K, such that neither J dominates K nor K dominates J). Third, the system described in the text is only one simple instantiation of the

multilevel hierarchical idea; more complex versions are possible (e.g., two sequences designated L_{h_1}, L_{i_1}, and L_{h_2}, L_{i_2} for which L_j is a meta-level for L_{h_1}, L_{i_1} but not for L_{h_2}, L_{i_2}, and so on). Lefebvre (1977, 1992) has used similar ideas about multilevels of meta- and object-level processing in social cognition.

9. Skinner (1974, p. 220 f.) proposed a "consciousness$_2$" that allows people to be self-reflective, but he construed it as only a response (cf. monitoring) and did not allow it to have any causal role in affecting (cf. controlling) external behavior. We believe that such a causal role of metacognitive processing is important for a sound and coherent conception of cognition.

Frustrated Feelings of Imminent Recall:
On the Tip of the Tongue

Steven M. Smith

In the course of recalling names or words, people sometimes find themselves in a "tip-of-the-tongue" (TOT) state, a discomfiting experience in which a seemingly well-known term appears to be blocked from conscious awareness. R. Brown and McNeill (1966) described such TOT states as similar to the feeling of an impending sneeze, a description that emphasizes that TOT states are frustrating, and that resolution of such states (i.e., finally remembering the target) is a relief. Other similar states might include a variety of commonplace phenomena in which responses that typically function automatically are thwarted, such as trying to speak after dental anesthesia, or trying to read with pupils dilated by an ophthalmologist. Each of these experiences is caused by malfunctioning of a usually reliable system, and is treated as a momentary predicament that will be eventually resolved.

Like déjà vu or slips of the tongue, the TOT state is a commonly experienced oddity of everyday cognition, and is therefore an interesting phenomenon to study in and of itself, according to naturalistic or ecological approaches to the study of memory (e.g., Neisser, 1982). Methods for systematically inducing and observing TOT states are important for demystifying such phenomena, helping us understand them in terms of scientific mechanisms.

R. Brown and McNeill (1966) reported a now classic method for inducing TOT experiences in the laboratory. Subjects were given definitions of rare words, and were asked to retrieve the objects of the definitions. For example, for the definition, "An ornamental stoppered glass vessel used for serving wine," the target would be "decanter." In many cases subjects reported TOT experiences; that is, they were unable to immediately recall a target, but believed that they knew the target, and would successfully recall it at any moment. That R. Brown and McNeill's subjects could often report the first letter and the number of syllables of an unrecalled target suggests that subjective TOT reports elicited by rare word definitions are valid indicators of subjects' knowledge.

Another method for eliciting TOT states under laboratory conditions involves naming famous people from pictures or descriptions (e.g., Brennen, Baguley, Bright, & V. Bruce, 1990; Yarmey, 1973). For example, for the description, "The actor who played Captain James T. Kirk in 'Star Trek'," the target would be "William Shatner." The efficacy of this technique for inducing TOT states reflects the high frequency of naturally occurring TOTs that result from attempts to recall names (e.g., A. Brown, 1991; Burke, MacKay, Worthley, & Wade, 1991).

From the theoretical point of view, the TOT experience may be a key phenomenon for understanding memory retrieval. One reason for this is that retrieval proceeds slowly, if at all, when the subject enters a TOT state. This slowed, or even halted retrieval has been likened to "slow-motion photography" (A. Brown, 1991), because it may facilitate observations of retrieval by slowing down the process. The slow, piecemeal retrieval of target-related information that sometimes accompanies TOT states has been cited as evidence related to the nature of factual or semantic memory (R. Brown & McNeill, 1966).

Alternatively, TOT states may represent memory retrieval blocks (e.g., Jones, 1989; Jones & Langford, 1987), providing a paradigm for studying the induction and dissipation of such blocks. That is, when an initial search for a retrieval target fails, subjects sometimes recall "interlopers," incorrect items related to the target. Although R. Brown and McNeill (1966) believed that such retrievals mediated successful resolution (i.e., retrieval of the correct target) of TOT states, Jones (1989) hypothesized that these interlopers may block target recall, thus causing TOT states, rather than helping to resolve them. Some evidence has shown that if "blocker" words are presented along with definitions used to cue recall, there is an increase in the frequency of TOT states (Jones, 1989; Jones & Langford, 1987; Maylor, 1990). For example, the blocker "abnormality" might be given to accompany the definition, "Something out of keeping with the times in which it exists" (the correct target is "anachronism").

Both the slow retrieval and retrieval block explanations of TOT reports are based on the commonly held assumption that the retrieval target is truly available in memory. Is this really the case that all TOT experiences reflect retrieval difficulties rather than storage deficiencies? Many studies show clearly that at least some TOT reports are misleading, that subjects do not know some targets they believe to be "on the tip of the tongue." Categories of TOT experiences delineated by researchers acknowledge this possibility of storage deficits, distinguishing positive vs. negative TOTs and subjective vs. objective TOTs. Negative TOT states are those in which the subject indicates that an experimenter- defined retrieval target differs from the target of the subject's search, whereas a positive TOT is one in which the subject and experimenter agree on the same target (e.g., Koriat & Lieblich, 1974). For example, if a subject in a reported TOT state searches for the target "carafe" when given the definition of "decanter," the event is referred to as a negative TOT. Furthermore, a TOT is defined as objective rather than merely subjective only when there is some objective evidence that the subject knows the correct target. Objective evidence might include correctly reporting the first letter or the number of syllables of an unrecalled target. Thus, a correct target may not be known when TOTs are negative or subjective.

Given this background, the present chapter will address the following questions: (1) How can TOT states be elicited and examined under controlled laboratory conditions? (2) What causes TOT states? (3) How are TOT states resolved? (4) Are people aware of how imminent a retrieval is? and (5) What does it mean when a subject reports a TOT state? These questions will be considered in regard to a growing literature on the subject of TOTs, with the discussion focusing on recent experiments I have conducted using a new methodology for observing TOT experiences.

How Can TOT States Be Elicited and Examined under Controlled Laboratory Conditions?

Beyond anecdotal accounts of TOT experiences, there have been three basic methods for systematically studying TOTs: diary studies (e.g., Read & D.Bruce, 1982; Reason & Lucas, 1984), questionnaires (e.g., Burke et al., 1991), and experimental laboratory methods for inducing the states (e.g., R. Brown & McNeill, 1966; Yarmey, 1973). Although there are advantages to each of these methods, the present chapter will consider only laboratory methods.

As previously noted, the primary method for experimental elicitation of TOTs has been naming rare words from their definitions (e.g., R. Brown & McNeill, 1966; Burke et al., 1991; Jones & Langford, 1987; Koriat & Lieblich, 1974; Kozlowski, 1977; Yaniv & Meyer, 1987). Other methods have included naming famous people from pictures (Brennen et al., 1990; Yarmey, 1973), and answering trivia questions (Finley & Sharp, 1989). Although there are variations in the way that TOT experiences have been defined in these studies, the typical definition given to subjects is that the target cannot be currently retrieved, but it is known, and recall of the target (i.e., resolution of the TOT) seems imminent (A. Brown, 1991).

A. Brown (1991) noted a number of common findings in experimental laboratory studies of TOTs. In such experiments TOT levels have been fairly low; overall, TOTs are reported for approximately 13% of the memory cues (plus or minus 5%). Many of these are negative TOTs; positive TOT rates, when reported, are considerably lower. Subjects often recall the first letter and the number of syllables of the target when subjects report a TOT state. Names of famous people, acquaintances, and famous landmarks are especially susceptible to TOT states.

Although much has been learned with existing methods of eliciting TOT states in controlled laboratory conditions, there are a number of problems and limitations with them. One of the most basic problems concerns a fundamental issue in empirical research on memory, namely, mechanisms for controlling and/or observing acquisition and retention factors. When subjects are tested for their memories of rare words, names, or general knowledge, observations are for memories acquired preexperimentally. An experimenter cannot know such an item's learning history. The frequency and recency of encounters with targets cannot be known, nor can one know an item's level of processing, its associative or relational structure in memory, the appropriateness of processing and contextual similarity of the test question in relation to the item's acquisition context, or the way(s) in which the target has been used as a response, such as in reading, writing, or speaking. Such factors may be critical in the occurrence of TOTs, and their roles may need clarification if we are to understand the cause(s) of TOT states, the ways in which such states can be resolved, and what TOT reports tell us about the nature of memory.

A second problem in experimental studies has been that TOT levels have been fairly low, particularly for positive TOTs. Failed attempts to reduce already low TOT rates would need to be interpreted in light of floor effects, if such attempts were made.

A related problem is that of observing negative TOTs in studies that test preexperimental knowledge. If one is interested in the frequency of subjective TOT experiences, there is no real need to differentiate positive and negative TOTs. If, however, the experimental questions concern characteristics of the target, such as its spelling, frequency, or concreteness, then negative TOTs must be removed from consideration, because the subject's intended target cannot be known. To use an earlier example of a negative TOT, a subject given a definition of "decanter" who is searching for the unintended target "carafe" may be judged to have incorrect partial knowledge if "c" were given as the first letter of the unrecalled target, even though it would represent correct partial knowledge of the subject's intended target. In this case, guessing that the first letter is "d" would be counted as correct partial knowledge, even though it would be incorrect for the subject's intended target.

Another problem with most of the existing experimental methods of TOT induction is that the experimenter lacks control over the phonological and semantic information contained in the experimental targets. Choosing targets with specific characteristics is difficult or impossible in many cases because our existing language and common knowledge may not contain targets with the desired qualities. Similarly, if one wishes to present "blockers" along with recall cues, as in Jones and Langford's (1987) study, it is not possible to control the phonological or semantic similarity of blockers and targets beyond what is available in the natural language.

Experiments reported by Smith, J. Brown, and Balfour (1991) were motivated by the need for an experimental paradigm that can induce high levels of TOT states using stimuli whose acquisition and retention can be controlled, and that refer unambiguously to experimenter-designated recall targets. The occurrence of TOT states was examined for recently learned names and concepts. Conceptually realistic targets with names were created that were new for all subjects, but that could be learned in a controlled laboratory setting. Whether or not a target had ever been encountered could be experimentally controlled, as could the recency and frequency of the encounters. Each target name referred unambiguously to a specific imaginary animal, referred to as a "TOTimal." The efficacy of TOTimals for inducing TOT states was tested in two experiments reported by Smith et al. (1991).

Twelve TOTimals were created for the experiments (figure 2.1). Each consisted of a three-syllable name, a picture of the imaginary animal, a brief description of the TOTimal, its size, what it eats, and where it lives. Each TOTimal name began with a different first letter. The descriptions, habitats, and diets were unique for each TOTimal.

After studying two sets of six TOTimals, subjects were given cued recall tests, with each test cue consisting of a picture of one of the TOTimals. For each picture cue subjects were asked the name (or any part of the name) of the imaginary animal, whether they experienced a TOT state when trying to recall the name, and whether they would recognize the name if it were mixed in with other similar names. This last question was a feeling-of-knowing (FOK) judgment. A recognition test was given after all 12 cues had been tested.

In question was whether the procedure would induce TOT states when subjects attempted to recall the TOTimal names. It was expected that if an unrecalled name were in a TOT state, as compared with those not in TOT states, the subject would be more likely to recognize the name, and to recall the correct first letter of the name. FOK was a measure intended to augment the TOT judgment; it was expected that FOK would be greater for unrecalled items in TOT states than for those not in TOT states. Such results would support the idea that subjective TOTs for TOTimals relate empirically to

Boshertin

Chubby carnivore   **2.5'**
Eats mice   **Canada**

Rittlefin

Amphibian   **3"**
Eats flies   **Congo River**

Figure 2.1
Black-and-white versions of the TOTimals used by Smith et al. (1991).

measures of memory (recall and recognition) and metamemory (FOK).

Acquisition involved an initial input of the TOTimals, followed by a number of study trials. Instructions directed subjects to learn the imaginary animals as well as they could for a test to be explained later. A second list was then presented in the same way as the first, except that there were more study trials for list 2 than for list 1.

After both lists 1 and 2 had been studied, the critical cued recall test over the TOTimal names was given. For the recall test subjects were shown a picture of a TOTimal for 20 seconds, during which time they were instructed to indicate the answers to four questions: (1) What is the imaginary animal's name? (2) What is the first letter of the name? (3) Would they be able to recognize the name if it were mixed in with other similar sounding names? and (4) Are they in a TOT state? A TOT state was described as one in which the subject knew the name, felt that they might recall it at any time, but could not think of the name at that moment. All 12 TOTimals were tested, examining both list 1 and list 2.

After the recall test subjects were given a four-alternative forced-choice recognition test over the TOTimal names. One of the four words was the correct name of a TOTimal, and the other three were similar sounding names. All four choices for a recognition test item had three syllables, all began with the same letter, and all four had the middle syllable in common. For example, for the TOTimal named "BOSHERTIN," the foils on the recognition test were "BOSH-ERGEN," "BANTERTIN," and "BANTERGEN." The experimental methodology appears to have been very successful for inducing high levels of validated TOTs. The overall proportion of retrieval targets for which subjects reported TOT states was 0.25 in experiment 1 and 0.34 in experiment 2. TOTs were reported 32% of the time for list 1 items in experiment 1 and on 42% of the list 1 recall trials in experiment 2. This is considerably higher than previously reported TOT rates in published experimental studies.

Smith et al.'s evidence supported the idea that reported TOT states were genuine TOT experiences, rather than whimsical subjective reports. FOK rates were greater for unrecalled TOT items than for unrecalled non-TOT items. More compellingly, objective measures of memory (first letter recall and recognition) of unrecalled items validated the reported TOT states. Recognition rates, which were overall very high (93% hit rate), were significantly higher for unrecalled TOT names than for unrecalled non-TOT names. First letter recall was also significantly higher for unrecalled TOT names than for unrecalled non-TOT names. Therefore, these observations, which have gone farther to validate the TOT reports than have many TOT studies, indicate that TOTimal induced TOTs resemble TOTs observed in other studies.

In both of Smith et al.'s experiments, recall was significantly higher, and TOT rates were lower for the second presented list than the first. These findings indicate that within a particular range of recall rates, improvements in memory are associated with decreases in TOT reports. If the range of recall levels were somewhat lower the reverse might be observed; at too low a level of learning, too few targets may be known for any to reach even TOT levels of activation, whereas slightly better learning would increase the pool of known targets, thereby increasing the possibility of retrieval failures as well as successes. This question can be investigated with methods such as Smith et al.'s (1991), because learning of targets can be observed and manipulated.

What Causes TOT States?

Theoretical accounts of TOT experiences have centered around two different explanations: retrieval blocking and incomplete activation (e.g., A. Brown, 1991; Jones, 1989; Meyer & Bock, 1992). Retrieval blocking refers to the idea that activation of items in memory that are similar to the target compete with the target when memory is searched, suppressing target retrieval. The incomplete activation account of TOT states is that an initial memory cue may not activate a target word or name enough for retrieval of the target. Both of these explanations assume that subjective TOT reports indicate that unrecalled targets are truly known. After the blocking and incomplete activation theories have been briefly discussed, explanations will be considered that describe TOTs as failures of metacognition, rather than retrieval failures.

The blocking theory of TOT experiences states that a memory search can be diverted at some point when a related word or name, rather than the intended target, is initially retrieved. Such a related word, referred to as a "blocker" or "interloper" (Jones, 1989), becomes temporarily activated when it is mistakenly retrieved. Subsequent search attempts may then have an increased chance of finding the same interloper rather than the correct target, creating at least momentarily a retrieval "trap" that effectively blocks access to the target. This increasingly stronger retrieval block resembles output interference in free recall (e.g., Rundus, 1973), in which recalled list items are theorized to increase in accessibility once they are retrieved, thus blocking recall of other list words.

The other major explanation of TOTs is the incomplete activation theory (e.g., A. Brown, 1991; R. Brown & McNeill, 1966). This theory states that when a retrieval cue does not bring a known target immediately to mind, the subject often becomes aware of general information related to the target, activating, for example, the target's first letter, or related words that are similar to the target. R. Brown and McNeill (1966) referred to this retrieval of general information as "generic recall." According to this explanation, retrieval in these cases proceeds iteratively, initially producing generic information, and gradually narrowing in scope until the correct target is successfully retrieved.

Both the blocking and incomplete activation theories of TOTs are based on the observation that when recall is not immediate, subjects often generate related words in lieu of the target. The critical difference between the explanations is that the incomplete activation theory states that the related words facilitate eventual retrieval of the target, whereas the blocking theory states that the related words serve to block the correct target.

Evidence testing the blocking and incomplete activation theories has been somewhat equivocal. The partial recall often exhibited by subjects in TOT states was initially taken as support for generic recall and incomplete activation of the target. Jones and Langford (1987) and Jones (1989), however, pointed out that those related words could be blocking recall rather than facilitating it. As a test of the blocking theory, Jones and Langford (1987) read subjects definitions of rare words, accompanied by related "blockers," words similar to the targets. Some blockers were phonologically related to the accompanying target, some were semantically related, and some were unrelated. More TOTs were reported for definitions accompanied by phonologically related blockers than for those with unrelated or semantically related blockers. This result, which supports a phonological interpretation of the blocking hypothesis, has been replicated by Jones (1989) and Maylor (1990), whose materials were drawn from Jones and Langford's (1987).

Unfortunately, there were some problems with the materials and methods used in these three blocking studies. One of the main problems was that the type of related word/blocker that accompanied a particular definition was not counterbalanced. Consequently, the TOT levels that were reported may have been specific to items, rather than caused by the blocker conditions. Meyer and Bock (1992) used a paradigm very similar to that used by Jones (1989), but counterbalanced blocker type so that each definition could be tested with all blocker types. Contrary to Jones (1989), Meyer and Bock (1992) found no evidence of blocking. TOT rates did not differ for different blocker conditions. Furthermore, Meyer and Bock found that the so-called blockers actually facilitated correct recall of targets, rather than suppressing it. They concluded that the related words that accompanied rare word definitions supported target retrieval, consistent with the incomplete activation theory of TOTs.

An unpublished study done in my laboratory (Balfour, 1992) found some support for both blocking and incomplete activation theories. It is possible that subjects tend to code blockers phonologically, even when they are intended as semantic blockers. Controlling the type of processing given to blockers, and the input modality, Balfour found, consistent with Meyer and Bock, that phonologically related words increased recall without affecting TOT rates. Semantically related words, however, increased both recall and TOT rates. Balfour's results support the idea that semantically related interlopers can cause TOT states, but whether the increased TOTs were due to blocking or incomplete activation is not clear.

Consistent with Balfour's (1992) findings are those of Smith (July 1991), who examined TOT blocking in TOTimals. After learning TOTimals, as described earlier, subjects were tested for name recall by presenting a picture of the imaginary animal. Accompanying the picture cue was a phonologically related word, an unrelated word, or else the name of another TOTimal. Although phonologically related words decreased TOTs, inappropriate TOTimal names increased TOT rates, indicating a TOT blocking effect.

Although the blocking and incomplete activation theories have typically been posed as mutually exclusive explanations of TOTs, such is not necessarily the case. There is no reason that subjective TOT reports must all have a single common cause, any more than recall or recognition of a word can be traced to a unitary cause. Evidence is clearly available that refutes either theory as "the" only cause of TOT states. Diary studies showing that subjects often experience repeated unwanted recall of "blockers" when trying to resolve a TOT, and experimental studies that show blocking effects refute the incomplete activation theory. Studies that show a large portion of TOTs are not accompanied by unwanted recall of blockers, and those showing that related words cause facilitation of retrieval rather than blocking weaken the blocking theory. Future research on TOT states should consider the possibility that some TOTs may be caused by blocking, whereas others are caused by incomplete activation, and should search for ways of distinguishing between the two different types of TOTs.

Another theory of TOTs resembles the incomplete activation theory, but is more specific about the cause of the initial retrieval failure (Burke et al., 1991). This explanation states that associative links that typically interconnect semantic and phonological codes in word representations are weak or missing. This "missing link" explanation provides a mechanism for the possibility that a word's phonological code could be less than fully activated by the word's semantic code. Burke et al. (1991) used this theory to explain the increase in TOTs seen in older adults, conjecturing that links between semantic and phonological codes may be lost or weakened with age.

Nelson, Gerler, and Narens (1992) divided reasons for subjects' metacognitive reports into the categories of trace access mechanisms, such as priming information without fully activating it, and inferential mechanisms, such as judging one's knowledge on the basis of domain familiarity. Most theoretical explanations of TOT reports, including those just reviewed, utilize trace access mechanisms to explain TOT states. It is important to consider, however, that inferential mechanisms may be the cause of some portion of TOTs that subjects report (e.g., Metcalfe, Schwartz, & Joaquim, 1993). If subjects sometimes infer the presence of a TOT state, then there may be cases when TOTs are reported even though the subject does not actually know the target. For example, feeling that the name of a new neighbor or colleague is on the tip of one's tongue, even though the name is not truly known, could be inferred from the type of information one believes one ought to know, or from rapid retrieval of the target person's face, occupation, or other relevant information.

I propose a modification of Burke et al.'s (1991) "missing link" TOT theory, the incomplete storage theory, which states that missing associations to a target's name (i.e., the verbal label of a concept) or incomplete storage or integration of a name's components can prevent retrieval of a target. Activation of the partial information that is truly stored may lead one to infer that one is in a TOT state. Whereas complete storage might lead to successful recall, and a total storage failure would not yield TOT reports, an incomplete storage of a target's name could cause an inferentially based illusory TOT.

Smith (July 1991) reported some evidence in support of this inferentially based incomplete storage theory, testing the effects of different types and amounts of name practice, using the TOTimal methodology described earlier. This theory cannot be tested with traditional methods of TOT research, such as recalling rare words from their definitions, or naming famous people, because it is not possible to manipulate or even to observe learning of such targets. TOTimal targets are learned within the laboratory setting, and therefore provide the means for manipulating storage factors.

Manipulating the degree of name storage at input, Smith (July 1991) found that less complete storage of TOTimal names increased the rate of TOT experiences. These results are consistent with the theory that some TOTs (i.e., those for targets whose names are incompletely stored) may result from illusory inferential processes, although the findings do not clearly distinguish between incomplete storage and Burke et al.'s version of an incomplete activation theory. These results suggest that the TOTimal methodology may provide a way in which such questions can be more thoroughly investigated.

How Are TOT States Resolved?

Resolution of a TOT state refers to the eventual successful recall of an intended retrieval target. If trace access mechanisms underlie TOT reports, then one might expect that nearly all TOTs are eventually resolved. Burke et al. (1991) found exactly that; 96% of the naturally occurring TOTs reported by their subjects were resolved, according to the subjects' own diaries. This high level of resolution, however, could result in part from a recording bias; resolvable TOT experiences might have been more accessible to subjects than unresolvable TOT experiences when they made their diary entries, thus underestimating unresolved TOTs. Consistent with this possibility are results reported by Read and D. Bruce (1982), who tracked resolutions of TOTs induced in the laboratory, an induction procedure that is less likely to omit observations of TOT experiences. Read and D. Bruce found that 74% of the TOTs that were not initially resolved were resolved within 2 days. Although this figure is still high, the possibility remains that 26% of the TOTs in Read and Bruce's (1982) study could have been illusory, caused, for example, by inferential mechanisms.

Of the TOTs observed by Read and D. Bruce (1982) that were correctly resolved or recognized, many more resolutions occurred when subjects varied their search strategies, rather that sticking with a single strategy. For example, subjects in TOT states were encouraged to try to recall contextual material related to unrecalled targets, or to run through the alphabet, trying each letter as a possible cue. This appears to be consistent with the idea of a narrowing search process using generic recall (e.g., R. Brown & McNeill, 1966).

Brennen et al. (1990) examined resolutions of TOTs induced when subjects named famous people and landmarks from pictures and verbal descriptions. On retests subjects were given extra information to facilitate resolution of TOTs, either a picture of the target or the correct initials. Pictures of targets yielded no better resolution levels than did retests using the original cues; both produced resolution rates of approximately 13%. Initials of targets, however, improved resolution rates to 44–47%. These results, like those of Read and D. Bruce (1982), indicate that extra information, in this case phonological cues, helps narrow a memory search. It might also be noted that resolution rates were far from perfect. As in other studies, it is possible that some of Brennen et al.'s TOTs were illusory.

A question rarely asked in TOT studies concerns the fate of un-retrieved items for which no TOTs are reported (i.e., unrecalled non-TOT targets). Are non-TOT recall failures also resolved with extra retrieval attempts or extra retrieval cues, as are TOT recall failures? Would feeling-of-knowing judgments be as good as TOT reports for predicting subsequent recall of initially unrecalled targets? Besides knowing the absolute likelihood of subsequent recall following TOT reports, it would be useful to know whether TOT recall failures, in comparison to non- TOT recall failures, are relatively more likely to predict subsequent recall.

What Awareness of Retrieval's Imminence Exists?

Feeling-of-knowing reports are often good predictors of recognition performance following initial retrieval failures (e.g., Metcalfe, 1986a), a correlation that gives face validity to the FOK measure. Do TOT reports also have face validity? TOT experiences are often as-sociated with correct recall of a target's first letter, and the number of syllables in the target (A. Brown, 1991). In addition, TOT reports have been found to predict subsequent recognition memory of un-recalled targets (e.g., Smith et al., 1991). Although these associations between TOT reports and objective memory measures lend some validity to the measure, an important issue of face validity concerns the prediction of imminent recall. The way that the TOT state is typically defined for subjects includes the idea that an unrecalled target seems like it will be recalled at any moment. Do TOT reports predict imminent recall?

Evidence from several laboratory studies indicates that approxi-mately 40–50% of reported TOTs are resolved within a few minutes (A. Brown, 1991). Although these resolutions appear consistent with the idea of imminent recall, it is also the case that in the same studies 50–60% of the TOT items were not resolved in a brief time. A. Brown distinguished between immediate and delayed resolution of TOTs, noting a recovery plateau in Burke et al.'s (1991) cumulative fre-quency distribution of TOT resolutions at about 1 or 2 minutes after the onset of the TOT state. The TOTs that were not resolved right away (i.e., a majority of the TOTs in Burke et al.'s study) often took hours or days to resolve, a result clearly at odds with the idea that recall is imminent.

This distinction between immediate and delayed resolutions might correspond to the distinction between blocked TOTs (i.e., TOT targets that are blocked by activated competitors) and mediated ones (i.e., TOT targets whose resolutions are mediated or facilitated by related words), which was described earlier in this chapter. Persistent attempts to retrieve mediated TOT targets may succeed within a minute or two, whereas persistent retrieval of blockers in a blocked TOT may prevent immediate resolution. Resolution of blocked TOTs may require a period of incubation, which would allow blockers to decay and decrease in accessibility, therefore weakening their blocking effect.

Smith (November 1991), using the TOTimal methodology described earlier, examined incubation effects for unrecalled items in TOT and non-TOT states. After several study trials with the imaginary animals, subjects were given two 30-second recall tests for each TOTimal name. The second recall test was given either immediately after the first, or delayed by an incubation interval of 6 minutes. For items not recalled in the first 30 seconds, few were resolved if the retest was given immediately; only 9% of TOT items and 3% of non-TOT items were resolved without an incubation interval. Considerably more resolutions of initial recall failures were found when the retest followed an incubation interval, with subjects resolving 43% of TOTs and 19% of non-TOTs. This memory incubation effect was equivalent for both TOT and non-TOT items. These results show that (1) TOTs were more likely to be resolved than non-TOTs, although many non-TOTs were resolved, and (2) incubation effects were just as likely to occur for non-TOT items as for TOTs.

The TOT reports in Smith's (November 1991) study predicted target accessibility, but not the imminence of target access, because patterns of immediate vs. delayed resolutions were the same for both TOTs and non-TOTs. Although it is speculative, it may be that TOT reports consist of two components combined into a single judgment. One component, analogous to a feeling-of-knowing judgment, may predict an estimate of one's own knowledge. Whether based on trace access or inferential mechanisms, this putative metamemory component is predictive of recall, just as FOK judgments predict recognition. A second component of a TOT report may be analogous to a "warmth" judgment (e.g., Metcalfe, 1986b; Metcalfe & Wiebe, 1987), a prediction of imminence. Metcalfe found that warmth ratings predicted the imminence of solutions only for noninsight problems, which are solved in incremental steps. Warmth ratings did not predict the imminence of solutions to insight problems in her studies. In this analogy, mediated TOTs correspond to noninsight problems, because both are resolved incrementally, and the imminence of both may be predicted by TOT judgments and warmth ratings. Blocked TOTs correspond to insight problems, because the imminence of neither can be predicted by TOT or warmth judgments, and incubation may promote successful resolutions in both cases. This explanation implies that solutions to insight problems often get initially blocked, perhaps by inappropriate approaches, and further, that predictions of imminence guided by inappropriate approaches are inaccurate (Smith, 1993).

What Does It Mean When a Subject Reports a TOT State?

The subjectivity of metacognitive monitoring reports makes them suspect if they are used as observational data. Nonetheless, the reports are often found to be reliable predictors of certain performance measures, indicating that they can be useful under some circumstances. To state that an unrecalled target is on the tip of one's tongue implies at the very least that the target is known, and that recall will occur very soon. Do TOT experiences reported by subjects accurately predict knowing and imminent recall? When such predictions are not correct, what do TOT reports mean?

Koriat and Lieblich (1974) were among the first to point out the multiplicity of TOT reports, noting several different categories of TOTs based on whether (1) the TOT is quickly resolved (2) the subject's stated target is the same as that intended by the experimenter, and (3) the target was eventually supplied by the subject or the experimenter. This analysis marks an important beginning in the interpretation of TOT reports.

As previously noted, TOTs may not always reflect actual knowledge of targets. However, researchers have not typically acknowledged this possibility. Even "negative" TOTs (Brown & McNeill, 1966), that is, cases in which the experimenter's intended target is not the same as the subject's, have generally been regarded as retrieval confusions rather than knowledge deficits. The clear indication in the feeling-of-knowing research literature, however, is that inferential mechanisms (such as cue familiarity; Schwartz & Metcalfe, 1992) rather than trace access may often be responsible for metamemory judgments. Therefore, we must consider the possibility that although TOT feelings are thought of as stronger and more compelling metamemory predictors than FOK judgments, they may nonetheless be illusory, at least in some cases.

Examples of inferential mechanisms that could lead to TOT reports are cue familiarity, retrieval of related information, or domain familiarity. Furthermore, the demand characteristics of an experiment may evoke illusory TOTs. Most TOT studies have presented subjects with long lists of definitions of rare words or trivia questions (e.g., R. Brown & McNeill, 1966; Jones & Langford, 1987; Read & D. Bruce, 1982). Recall levels are often not reported, but it is clear that the test questions are chosen to be difficult. Subjects who are embarrassed when they repeatedly fail to answer questions may occasionally opt to report a TOT because of such demand characteristics.[1] Many studies of TOT states have been careful to eliminate negative TOTs from data analyses so that their conclusions are not contaminated by such cases. Nonetheless, when considering the meaning of a subjective TOT report, in the absence of objective memory performance measures, one must take into account that TOTs do not necessarily signal either knowledge or imminent recall.

Conclusions and Directions for Future Research

Although a great deal of research has taught us much about TOT states, many studies have had low TOT levels, and exercise minimal control over the learning history, phonological components, and semantic components of targets and blockers. The TOTimal method (Smith et al., 1991) has been successful enough in preliminary studies to warrant further research because it provides a means of controlling target storage factors as well as blockers.

On the Tip of the Tongue

Tip-of-the-tongue states have typically been treated as unitary phenomena, deriving from a single cause, characterized by common features, and resolved by similar means. These assumptions, on inspection, seem tenuous, yet they are rarely challenged, either on logical or empirical grounds. Although TOT reports often predict partial recall, subsequent resolution, and recognition of unrecalled targets, they often do not.

Positive TOT states may result from initially incomplete activation, in which retrieval is slower because target resolution is mediated by iterations of a retrieval process. Alternatively, or additionally, positive TOTs may indicate that retrieval is blocked by activation of competitors, similar words or names in memory that are not correct targets. Future research should explore methods of distinguishing mediated TOTs from blocked TOTs, rather than treating all positive TOTs as having a single cause.

Negative TOT states, which are often not distinguished (or distinguishable) from positive ones, occur frequently. The role of inferential mechanisms, such as cue familiarity, or retrieved related information, should be tested in regard to TOT states, as should the role of demand characteristics.

There may be two components to TOT judgments: a feeling-of-knowing and a sense of warmth or imminence of recall. Whereas feelings-of-knowing may be somewhat accurate, predictions of imminence may be accurate only for mediated TOTs, not for blocked TOTs.

Acknowledgment

This work was supported by NIMH grant R01 MH4473001 awarded to Steven Smith.

Note

1. The possible effects of demand characteristics was suggested by Robert Widner, who is currently testing the hypothesis.

FOK is strictly human.
I take it back pre-retrieval FOK may apply
to machines.

A New Look at Feeling of Knowing:
Its Metacognitive Role in Regulating
Question Answering

Ann C. Miner and Lynne M. Reder

This book has approached metacognition, control strategies and knowledge about the process of knowing, from various perspectives ranging from neurological to developmental. This chapter is going to focus on one particular metacognitive process in adults, the "feeling of knowing" process. The discussion of feeling of knowing will begin by examining the phenomenon itself, beginning with early explorations leading to present research, then will explore underlying mechanisms, and, finally, will consider the functional utility of this process. Our argument will be that feeling of knowing should be reconceptualized as a rapid, pervasive process beginning prior to actual memory retrieval. Such a reconceptualization should clarify the metacognitive role of feeling of knowing and emphasize its importance as a central rather than an incidental process in cognition.

What Is Feeling of Knowing?

Early Interest in Feeling of Knowing

The classic definition of feeling of knowing is that it is the state of believing that a piece of information can be retrieved from memory even though that information currently cannot be recalled. It is this insistent impression that intrigued William James more than a century ago (James, 1890/1950). He deliberated at length concerning the *tip-of-the-tongue* phenomenon, which is defined as the frustrating experience of being aware of having knowledge but not being able to retrieve that knowledge on demand. In his words,

Suppose we try to recall a forgotten name. The state of our consciousness is peculiar. There is a gap therein; but no mere gap. It is a gap that is intensely active. A sort of wraith of the name is in it, beckoning us in a given direction, making us at moments tingle with the sense of our closeness, and then letting us sink back without the longed-for term. If wrong names are proposed to use, this singularly definite gap acts immediately so as to negate them. They do not fit into its mould. (p. 251, James, 1890).

The process that James described as coming from "consciousness" and as being "intensely active" piqued the interest of a few subsequent psychologists, but it was Harts' doctoral dissertation in 1965 from which modern research on feeling of knowing traces its roots. He changed the focus of interest beyond the intense impressions following retrieval failure to instead inquire about the degree of predictive validity of these impressions. That is, he did not examine how subjects searched for information they could not retrieve, but instead scrutinized the actual accuracy of the feeling-of-knowing impression. Hart perceived that earlier psychologists had treated feeling-of-knowing judgments and actual knowing as almost redundant concepts (see Woodworth & Schlosberg, 1954, for a summary of early work) and he decided to examine that assumption (Hart, 1965a, 1965b).

His paradigm involved three steps. First, he administered a recall test. Second, for those items that were not correctly recalled, subjects were required to give a feeling-of-knowing rating. Third, these ratings were followed by a recognition test to measure the accuracy of the feeling-of-knowing assessment. This design has typically been labeled the RJR (recall–judgment–recognition) paradigm. His experiments demonstrated that subjects who could not recall answers were able to successfully predict correct recognition and recognition failure of those answers on a subsequent multiple-choice recognition test. His results also suggested that the feeling-of-knowing experience operates at various graded strengths ranging from strong affirmative to strong negative judgments. When subjects felt that they did not know an answer, their scores on such items were at chance, but when they felt that they did know the answer, their scores were roughly three times the level of chance.

Recent Investigations on Feeling of Knowing

Since Hart's seminal work, other researchers, most notably Nelson (e.g., Nelson & Narens, 1980b; Nelson, Gerler, & Narens, 1984), have extended his findings. Given that the focus has remained on the accuracy of the feeling-of-knowing state, researchers have shown that feeling of knowing ratings can be used to reliably predict more types of behavior than just recognition performance. For example, feeling of knowing ratings were highly related to performance on cued-recall tests (e.g., Gruneberg & Monks, 1974), relearning rates (Nelson et al., 1984), and feature identification (Schachter & Worling, 1985).

It has also been demonstrated that as feeling-of-knowing ratings increased, perceptual identification latencies for tachistoscopically presented answers to previously unrecalled general information questions decreased (Nelson et al., 1984). The conclusion that this metacognitive system is more sensitive to perceptual information than a high-threshold task such as recall is qualified by a later study, however. Jameson, Narens, Goldfarb, and Nelson (1990) found that feeling of knowing ratings were not influenced by the perceptual input from a near-threshold prime, while that same perceptual input increased recall for previous recall failures, if the information had been recently learned. The caveat of this finding is consistent with an earlier study from the same laboratory; Nelson et al. (1982) reported that feeling-of-knowing ratings were not accurate for word pairs learned only to a criterion of one successful recall, while accuracy increased significantly beyond chance for overlearned word pairs. It is an interesting question why feeling of knowing was not a good predictor of performance in a verbal learning paradigm where word pairs were only learned to criterion. An important overall conclusion from this entire line of research is that the accuracy of feeling-of-knowing judgments is well above chance yet "far from perfect" (Leonesio & Nelson, 1990).

Distinguishing between Feeling of Knowing and Confidence

The broad definition of feeling of knowing as the state of believing that a particular piece of information can be retrieved from memory shares aspects with the definition of confidence, the state of believing that a particular piece of information has been correctly retrieved from memory. Similarly, subjects are reasonably accurate in predicting recognition performance as well as in judging the correctness of their complete or partial reports (see Schacter & Worling, 1985). One distinction is that feeling of knowing is a prospective judgment, a rating that reflects an opinion about an event yet to occur, while confidence is a retrospective judgment, a rating regarding an event that has already occurred. A second distinction is that memory accuracy is an implicit issue in research on feeling of knowing (see Koriat, 1993), while it is explicitly addressed with confidence ratings.

A third distinction is empirical; dissociations between these two phenomena have been reported. In a study with climbers on Mount Everest (Nelson, Dunlosky, White, Steinberg, Townes, & Anderson, 1990), altitude had no effect on recall or recognition accuracy or latency, nor was self-confidence about retrieval affected by altitude. Feeling-of-knowing judgments, on the other hand, declined at extreme altitudes and remained lower even after returning to Kathmandu. Another dissociation was reported earlier by Nelson et al. (1984), who found a positive relationship between feeling-of-knowing ratings and search duration for retrieval failures, while no relationship was found between search duration and confidence ratings for incorrect responses (retrieved answers that were wrong). Costerman, Lories, and Ansay (1992) demonstrated two additional dissociations between feeling of knowing and confidence. First, they found that feeling-of-knowing judgments were more highly correlated with a set of inferential questions (i.e. is this question familiar, has it been seen recently, under what circumstances was it seen, and can other people answer this question) than were confidence judgments. Second, they reported that feeling of knowing is positively related to search duration, while confidence level was negatively correlated with the amount of time allocated for searching memory. This last distinction foreshadows the final section of this chapter regarding the functions of the feeling-of-knowing process.

A Revised Definition of Feeling of Knowing

Several researchers have recently suggested expanding the original definition of feeling of knowing as a phenomenon that operates only after retrieval failure. This modified perspective instead suggests that feeling of knowing is a rapid, preretrieval stage during which individuals judge the expected retrievability of a queried piece of information (Reder, 1987, 1988; Reder & Ritter, 1992; Schreiber & D. Nelson, 1993), a stage that occurs frequently but becomes salient only in those instances when successful retrieval does not occur.

This definition also clarifies the distinction between feeling of knowing and tip of the tongue. The intense and frustrating experience that an answer is known but not currently retrievable, the tip-of-the-tongue experience, is one example of a situation in which an early judgment of retrievability is discordant with the results of the subsequent retrieval attempt. In most instances, however, processes proceed more smoothly and more quickly and such a mismatch does not occur.

Empirical Support for This Revision

A line of research by Reder (Reder, 1987, 1988; Reder & Ritter, 1992) motivated this conceptualization of feeling of knowing as a rapid, preretrieval process. For example, Reder (1987) devised a game-show paradigm in which subjects were given questions of varying difficulty and, depending on condition, either answered the question immediately or estimated whether or not they could answer it. As with typical game shows, response speed was stressed in the instructions. If subjects judged that they knew the answer in the estimate condition, then they were expected to demonstrate that knowledge, a determination of how accurate their initial feeling of knowing had been. This paradigm differs from the RJR design used by Hart (1965a) since subjects estimate answer retrievability *before* attempting to recall the answer.

Subjects in the estimate condition were more than 25% faster to respond than those in the answering condition, a mean difference of over 700 milliseconds. This difference existed regardless of whether subjects were responding affirmatively or negatively. Because subjects in the estimate condition attempted fewer questions than those in the answering condition yet answered the same number of questions correctly, they were 10% more accurate in their judgments. Thus, the greater response speed of subjects in the decision condition was not the result of a speed accuracy trade-off.

Another piece of data from the same experiment further supports the notion that feeling of knowing may be a general process preceding retrieval attempts. The total time in the decision condition, the time to estimate that one can answer the question plus the time to then come up with the answer, was equal to the total time in the straightforward answering condition. This finding suggests that the feeling of knowing stage occurred automatically in the answer condition and took the same amount of time as in the forced judgment condition.

In the experiments by Reder and Ritter (1992), subjects were not assigned to answer or estimate conditions. Instead, subjects had a 850-millisecond deadline for *choosing* a strategy after seeing an arithmetic problem. If they believed that they had learned the answer to this problem from previous exposures to it during the experiment, they could chose direct retrieval, in which case they had about one second to recall the correct answer. If the problem seemed unfamiliar, they could choose to calculate the answer, in which case they were given ample time to compute it (more time than anyone required to finish calculating).

Quick strategy selection was accomplished by all subjects with a little practice at the task. The appropriateness of the chosen strategies, as measured by d' and gamma scores, was quite high even at the beginning of the experiment. The finding that subjects can judge quickly and accurately was taken as evidence for the conceptualization of feeling of knowing as a rapid, metacognitive process beginning prior to the stage during which retrieval occurs (or might occur). Other data described later in this chapter nail down this interpretation.

Schreiber, Nelson, and Narens (unpublished data cited in Nelson & Narens, 1990) also investigated the preliminary feeling-of-knowing judgment as a metacognitive monitoring process that begins prior to memory search. Subjects in their experiment were presented with general-information questions and were required to quickly indicate their degree of feeling of knowing for each item using a six-point Likert scale. By examining response latencies, they discovered a nonmonotonic function: extreme feeling-of-knowing judgments had the shortest latencies. In other words, subjects could respond very quickly when they strongly felt that they did or did not know an item. Schreiber et al. concluded that there exists (1) an affirmative feeling-of-knowing process that determines the presence of information in memory and (2) a negative feeling-of-knowing process determining the absence of information in memory, a process analogous to Kolers and Palef's (1976) concept of "knowing not." These findings are reminiscent of Hart's (1965b) report that feeling of knowing predicted recognition failure as well as recognition success.

Thus, this definition of feeling of knowing as a rapid, preliminary process is consistent with a metacognitive function where this early stage controls actions as duration of retrieval efforts (e.g., Reder, 1987, 1988) and, as will be discussed later, retrieval strategy selection (e.g., Reder, 1987).

What Mechanisms Underlie Feeling of Knowing?
Diverse Speculations

Several researchers exploring the feeling-of-knowing phenomenon have speculated on which underlying mechanisms are involved in this process. One viewpoint that has received a great deal of attention is the *trace access hypothesis,* which presumes that subjects have partial access to, and are able to monitor some aspects of, the target item during feeling-of-knowing judgments (Nelson et al., 1984; Schreiber & D. Nelson, 1992). Several studies have shown that even when subjects cannot recall a target item such as a word, they can still identify information such as the beginning letter or the number of syllables it contains (e.g., Blake, 1973; Koriat & Lieblich, 1974). However, different researchers have interpreted trace access somewhat differently (for example, see Koriat, 1993), and a considerable number of other mechanisms have been proposed.

Nelson et al. (1984) brought order to this proliferation by subsuming the dozen mechanisms advocated up to that time under two main categories, *trace access* mechanisms and *inferential* mechanisms. What Nelson was summarizing can be described as the classical feeling-of-knowing research with accuracy as the typical dependent variable. Because Reder (1987, 1988; Reder & Ritter, 1992) employs a revised definition of feeling of knowing, she has suggested a different dichotomy. She distinguishes between partial retrieval of the answer to a question, a mechanism that most researchers refer to as trace *access,* and a feeling of familiarity with the question itself, which we refer to as the cue *familiarity* mechanism. Reder's viewpoint (see Reder & Ritter, 1992) pays particular attention to the functional utility of the feeling-of-knowing process and is less concerned with the accuracy of feeling of knowing in predicting recognition after recall failure. Both perspectives will be articulated in this section.

Trace Access versus Inferential Mechanisms

Nelson et al. (1984) have identified six frequently overlapping types of explanations that can all be subsumed within the *trace access* category. Two explanations use the mechanism of association between the question and the answer. The *subthreshold strength explanation* specifies that when there is a high strength of association between the question and the answer, the subject recalls the answer. With an intermediate strength of association, the subject cannot immediately retrieve the answer but believes that he/she knows the answer. With a minimal degree of association, the subject neither recalls the answer nor believes than the answer can be retrieved at a later point. The *forward-backward associations explanation* suggests that the degree of forward association from the question to the answer may be different than the backward association between the answer and the question. The feeling of knowing judgment might be based just on the forward association, while memory performance such as recognition might be based on both associations.

Three additional trace access explanations suggest that retrieval failure along with positive feeling-of-knowing judgments occur when (1) the subjects has only partial recall of the label for the target item, (2) the subject has access to other information relevant to the target but not access to the label itself, or (3) the subject retrieves the wrong semantic referent. The sixth and final explanation in this category assumes that the target is a multidimensional item and, even if the subject cannot retrieve information from enough dimensions for the correct recall of an answer to occur, the subject will still experience a strong feeling of knowing.

Nelson et al. (1984) give the label of *inferential mechanisms* to the major group of mechanisms assumed to oppose the trace access category in accounting for the feeling of knowing process. Here too, six subcategories are identified. Subjects might base a feeling of knowing judgment on related episodic information in their personal memories or on perceptions of those episodes. It was also suggested that feeling-of-knowing judgments might be based on impressions of the normative difficulty of an item (although a later study by Nelson, Leonesio, Landwehr, & Narens, 1986, casts doubt on the adequacy of this explanation). Social desirability, the urge to claim to know what one believes should be known, is another factor that could account for feeling-of-knowing ratings.

The final two types of feeling-of-knowing mechanisms outlined by Nelson et al. (1984) in the inferential category seem to be driven by the content of the questions posed in the experimental session. First, subjects may base a feeling-of-knowing judgment on their presumed expertise on the topic of the question, whether this expertise was induced in the experiment (Koriat & Lieblich, 1974, 1977) or existed prior to the experiment (Bradley, 1981). Second, feeling of knowing for an unrecalled item may be based on the subjects' degree of recognition of the cue. If the cue seems familiar then the subject may infer that the unrecalled item is known. A study by Koriat and Lieblich (1977), which demonstrated that cue redundancy (repeating questions verbatim or with altered wording) increased feeling-of-knowing ratings without increasing ability to actually answer the questions, lends credence to this position.

Trace Access versus Cue Familiarity Mechanisms

Reder and Ritter's (1992) consideration of whether feeling of knowing is determined by partial retrieval of the answer matches Nelson et al.'s (1984) use of the term trace *access* in assuming that subjects have partial access to the target and, therefore, are able to monitor some aspects of the target item during feeling-of-knowing judgments. In a 1990 publication, Nelson and Narens presented a "No magic" hypothesis in which they asserted that feeling-of-knowing judgments were driven by retrieved information. Despite failure to retrieve the actual target, subjects are often still able to access other information concerning the target item. Koriat (1993) makes a similar proposal, that an accessibility heuristic tapping retrieved target-relevant information is the basis of feeling of knowing.

The opposing argument that feeling-of-knowing judgments rely on the familiarity of cues in the questions themselves (e.g., Reder, 1987, 1988; Reder & Ritter, 1992; Schreiber and D. Nelson, 1993; Schwartz & Metcalfe, 1992) would seem to include both the expertise and cueing mechanisms mentioned by Nelson et al. (1984). (Other mechanisms identified by Nelson et al., 1984, such as social desirability, seem pertinent only with the classic feeling-of-knowing research where subjects have longer to respond than with the revised feeling-of-knowing paradigm.) Reder (1987, 1988) has suggested that individuals make feeling-of-knowing judgments using cue familiarity, a heuristic that employs information provided by or associated with the question / cues presented. As cue familiarity increases, so should feeling of knowing. For instance, Reder (1987) reported the following dissociation between feeling of knowing and accuracy: subjects believed they could answer questions after the terms in those questions had been primed, yet such beliefs were not supported by increases in recall rates. Conversely, another study has reported that when answers were primed, the availability of the answers increased but feeling-of-knowing ratings were not influenced (Jameson, et al. 1990).

This realignment of the issues fits well with the redefinition of feeling of knowing as a general process in which a rapid, preliminary judgment to guide retrieval actions is made (e.g., Reder, 1987, 1988; Reder & Ritter, 1992; Schreiber & D. Nelson, 1993). This faculty is assumed to operate automatically as soon as a question is seen and before retrieval is actually attempted. Refining the feeling-of-knowing concept in this way should make identifying the underlying mechanisms easier, since classic feeling-of-knowing paradigms such as the RJR or tip-of-the-tongue experiences extend over a relatively long period of time and may therefore incorporate additional mechanisms, such as the inferential ones postulated by Nelson et al. (1984).

An early study conducted by Koriat and Lieblich (1977) seems pertinent to the trace access versus cue familiarity discussion. Subjects were presented with word definitions and asked to judge whether or not they knew the word being defined. Definitions containing more redundant information triggered higher feeling-of-knowing ratings, while ability to provide the target words was not increased. This research team interpreted their findings as support for the trace access position because redundancy of cue information allowed for more partial target information to be retrieved. These redundant cues, however, probably increased cue familiarity and therefore also increased feeling-of-knowing ratings. Several recent studies (e.g., Reder & Ritter, 1992; Schreiber & D. Nelson, 1992; Schwartz & Metcalfe, 1992) that have deliberately pitted the trace access hypothesis against the cue familiarity heuristic are discussed in the following section.

Empirical Evidence on Trace Assess versus Cue Familiarity

Two experiments by Reder and Ritter (1992) examined whether feeling of knowing is due to partial retrieval of an answer or to a feeling of familiarity with a question. They used unfamiliar arithmetic problems such as "29 × 32" as stimuli in order to control the associative strength between problem questions and answers. They varied how often subjects were exposed to one of these previously unlearned math facts. They also chose math problems because they could independently vary familiarity with the terms in the questions. First, subjects were trained on novel 2-digit by 2-digit arithmetic problems. Over the course of the experiment, the level of exposure to problems varied from once to 20 times. Problems were individually displayed on a computer screen and subjects had to quickly choose whether (1) to directly retrieve the answer or (2) to calculate the answer. The payoffs were adjusted to encourage selection of direct retrieval when the answer was known. After deciding, subjects then had to perform the chosen action.

During the last fourth of the test trials, new problems began to appear that might seem old in the sense that they consisted of old operands and operators rearranged into new combinations. For example, a subject might have been tested on "18 + 23" 20 times, and now be asked to rapidly judge "18 × 23." If feeling of knowing is based on a partial retrieval of the answer, then feeling of knowing should be no stronger for these posttraining problems than for genuinely new problems; subjects could not retrieve an answer not already in memory. On the other hand, if feeling of knowing is instead based on familiarity with the terms of a question, then the posttraining problems should entice subjects into higher feeling of knowing ratings. Because frequency of exposure to problems and parts of problems was varied independently, they could examine which contributed more to rapid feeling-of-knowing judgments.

As the number of previous exposures to entire problems increased, subjects increasingly chose to retrieve rather than calculate answers. In this condition, however, exposure to the problems was confounded with exposure to the answers. For the posttraining problems, frequency of exposure to *parts* of problems also had a positive correlation with choice of the retrieval strategy. In other words, subjects were indeed misled by the posttraining problems, thereby supporting the cue familiarity explanation, not the hypothesis that feeling of knowing is based on partial retrieval of the answer.

The two contrasting explanations discussed by Reder and Ritter (1992) have also been the focus of recent research by Metcalfe and associates (Schwartz & Metcalfe, 1992; Metcalfe, Schwartz, & Joaquim, 1993). To test the trace access hypothesis, that feeling of knowing results from partial access to the answer or target, a manipulation that has been shown to affect target memorability was employed by Schwartz and Metcalfe (1992). Target words were always the second word in a pair of rhyming associates; in the read condition the target was complete, while the target was missing letters in the generate condition. (Studies have shown that generated words are recalled better than read words, e.g., Slamecka & Graf, 1978.) To test the cue familiarity hypothesis that feeling of knowing is triggered by the cues/questions presented to the subjects, a cue priming technique (from Reder, 1987) was used. In an ostensibly unrelated task, subjects made a pleasantness rating on half of the cues prior to learning. Cue familiarity was therefore enhanced without rehearsal of the cue-target pair.

Schwartz and Metcalfe's (1992) findings were quite consistent with the cue familiarity hypothesis: the generation manipulation significantly improved recall but had no impact on feeling-of-knowing judgments. The cue priming manipulation, on the other hand, had no effect on recall but did affect feeling-of-knowing ratings. They concluded that increasing the familiarity of a cue by priming it resulted in enhanced feeling of knowing.

Metcalfe et al. (1993) applied a classic interference theory paradigm to contrast the trace access and cue familiarity accounts of feeling of knowing. Stimulus materials were paired associates for which subjects were then given a cued-recall test. At encoding, the cue word "A" was initially presented with the target word "B." Later in the same list, the word A would then be paired with either (1) the original B, (2) a similar B', or (3) an unrelated word D. A fourth of the time, the cue A would not be given again and a new cue–target pair, C and D, would be presented instead. The word "A" was then presented during the cued recall test and subjects typed in the targets.

The expected pattern of findings with this paradigm is that memory is superior for the identical condition (A presented both times with B), almost as good for the similar condition (A-B then A-B'), moderate for the new pair (A-B and C-D), and very poor for the unrelated word condition (A-B and A-D). If feeling of knowing is primarily based on access to the target/answer, then the rank ordering of feeling-of-knowing judgments should be identical to this list of recall/recognition ordering. Cue familiarity makes a different prediction, however. Since the cue is presented twice in the A later paired with D condition, feeling of knowing judgments should not be as low there as in the C with D condition, where the cue (A) was seen only once. Specifically, cue familiarity predicts that feeling of knowing in all three of the conditions in which the cue A was presented twice should be roughly equivalent and should be significantly greater than feeling of knowing when the cue is only seen once. This is precisely what they found.

Although Schreiber and D. Nelson (1993) did not vary the strength of the relationship between cues and targets as did Metcalfe et al. (1993), they did manipulate the strength of the cue and of the target separately. To test the trace access hypothesis, they examined whether feelings of knowing were sensitive to the encoding strengths of targets. Those targets that had been studied during one trial were considered to have a low strength of encoding, while targets that had been studied twice were considered high in strength. To test the cue familiarity hypothesis, they examined whether feelings of knowing were affected by the amount of competing information linked to test cues. Competing information was operationalized as *cue set size*, the number of associates preexperimentally linked to test cues as determined by earlier normative studies (D. Nelson & McEvoy, 1979). Recall has been shown to be higher when cues and targets are linked to fewer associates, while recognition does not seem to be reliably affected by cue set size.

Schreiber and D. Nelson's manipulation of target strength did not reliably affect feeling-of-knowing judgments, but did affect the probability of both correct recall and recognition. On the other hand, each of their three experiments demonstrated a robust effect of cue set size on feeling of knowing. Feeling-of-knowing ratings were lower for cues from large sets (i.e., that could cue many words besides the target) than for small sets, regardless of whether these sets were operationalized as category names or word endings. In other words, a characteristic of the cue (test question) repeatedly influenced feeling-of-knowing ratings while a characteristic of the target (answer) rarely did. From these findings, they concluded that their work provided no support for the trace access hypothesis but instead lent credence to the cue familiarity explanation.

More Empirical Evidence

Research by Yaniv and Meyer (1987) could be interpreted as support for the trace access hypothesis rather than the cue familiarity explanation of feeling-of-knowing judgments. Subjects were presented with the definitions of rare words and were asked to generate the defined words. When retrieval failure occurred, subjects were asked to rate their tip-of-the-tongue and feeling-of-knowing states. These ratings were categorized into three accessibility categories: high, medium, and low. After each set of four rare word definitions, subjects were given a lexical decision task that contained target words from the set they could not generate and control words and nonwords. Unrecalled words given high accessibility ratings produced faster reaction times in the lexical decision task than unrecalled words with low accessibility ratings.

When a definition (cue) was presented it was assumed to activate the target word. If activation was above threshold, the target was successfully recalled. If the activation was below threshold, recall did not occur. Activation lingered in both cases, but was evaluated with accessibility ratings only when recall had failed. Each accessibility rating was considered by to be an indicator of the potential retrievability of an item in the semantic network. An item that is highly retrievable is assumed to be more activated than an item that is not as retrievable. Yaniv and Meyer concluded that the increased activation of the traces of the unsuccessfully retrieved answers was triggering the fast reaction times on the lexical decision task.

Connor, Balota, and Neeley (1992) turned this activation explanation on its head. First, they conceptually replicated the finding that rare words at higher accessibility levels (a hybrid of feeling-of-knowing and tip-of-the-tongue ratings) had faster lexical decision times than words at lower levels of accessibility. Next, they found the same empirical relations held even when the lexical decision task preceded exposure to definitions and accessibility estimates by a full week. The trace access hypothesis, that subthreshold activation of answers to questions determines feeling-of-knowing ratings, simply cannot account for these data: the lexical decisions in this paradigm preceded the definition task. Based on their findings, they advocated a topic familiarity account. They argued that both accessibility estimates and lexical decision performance are influenced by the familiarity that a subject has with a particular topic. The subject recognizes that the topic seems familiar due to words in the question meshing or not meshing with well-learned information. The metacognitive judgment of accessibility reflects the subject's assessment of the level of expertise he/she has in a given area; response time in the lexical decision task is affected by whether an item comes from a category with which the subject is familiar (Balota & Chumbly, 1984). The presentation order of the feeling-of-knowing judgment and the lexical decision task is not critical for the relation to occur, because the correlation between these two tasks is caused by a third factor, level of expertise/familiarity with a topic.

The relationship between feeling of knowing and topic familiarity was also the focus of a study by Reder and Fabri (reported in Reder, 1988). Subjects rank-ordered their own level of expertise in four domains: movies, sports, geography, and U.S. history. Questions were varied in terms of how many words in the question were associated with the topic. Of interest was whether the extent of sentence terms associated with a topic would influence feeling of knowing and speed of judgment, and whether this would interact with self-rated expertise. Half of the subjects were assigned to the answer condition, i.e., immediately answered the questions or stated that they did not know the answer; the other half were asked to estimate their ability to answer the questions. If the subjects in the latter condition judged that they could answer a question, they were then given the opportunity to answer that question.

Reder and Fabri found, not surprisingly, that subjects attempted to answer more questions on those topics in which they felt they had the most expertise. More interesting was the finding that subjects' self-classification of expertise had a greater impact when they were making feeling-of-knowing ratings (the estimate condition) than when they were simply answering questions. That is, tendency to attempt to answer a question was more influenced by topic category and expertise in the estimate condition. These data suggest that the assessment of self-knowledge is an example of an inferential metacognitive strategy that may play an important role in making feeling-of-knowing judgments. A similar conclusion was reached by Nelson and Narens (1990) who found that a person's feeling of knowing was more strongly related to his/her claimed frequency of previous exposure than to the actual frequency of previous exposure. Although both Nelson and Narens (1990) and Connor et al. (1992) used the classical feeling-of-knowing paradigm defined in terms of retrieval failure while Reder and Fabri employed the revised paradigm in which rapid, feeling-of-knowing judgments are obtained irrespective of retrieval success or failure, their results are all consistent with the perspective that the metaknowledge of expertise operates at both speeds.

A complementary finding of Reder and Fabri was the markedly different influence of expertise on the time to say "don't know" in the estimate and answer conditions: Self-assessed expertise had more impact on the time to respond "don't know" in the answer condition than in the feeling-of-knowing condition. In other words, subjects searched longer in the answer condition before saying they did not know a fact if they rated themselves as being familiar with the topic. This type of pattern, that feeling-of-knowing judgments manifest themselves in longer "don't know" response times for the answer condition than for the estimate condition has been reported elsewhere by Reder (1987). This dissociation is consistent with the other dissociations between feeling-of-knowing measures and trace retrieval measures already discussed in this section, such as the dissociation between feeling-of-knowing and recall accuracy when cue priming is manipulated (Reder, 1987; Schwartz & Metcalfe, 1992). By eroding the empirical evidence beneath the trace access hypothesis, such dissociations lend credence to the cue familiarity explanation of feeling of knowing.

Distinctions between Classic and Revised Feeling-of-Knowing Research

Nelson and Narens (1990) have suggested using different terminology depending on when a feeling-of-knowing rating is made. For a rating that is made before retrieval is attempted, such as in the estimate condition used in Reder's research (Reder, 1987, 1988; Reder & Ritter, 1992), Nelson and Narens (1990) prefer the term "preliminary feeling of knowing." Similarly, Schreiber and D. Nelson (1993) suggest the term "prediction of knowing." Both groups reserve the traditional "feeling-of-knowing" term for ratings made after retrieval failures, such as in Hart's (1965a) RJR paradigm.

When both the classic (predicting recognition after failing at a recall attempt) and the revised feeling-of-knowing ratings (simply predicting recall) were used in the same experiment, the same pattern of results obtained (Schreiber and D. Nelson, 1993). The only reliable difference between the two types of ratings in that study was that response latencies were shorter for the prediction-of-knowing ratings, presumably because the instructions emphasized speed of processing (consistent with Reder, 1987, 1988; Reder & Ritter, 1992).[1]

Despite this failure to find differences between prediction-of-knowing and traditional feeling-of-knowing ratings, it seems probable that some differences exist. Classic feeling-of-knowing rating tasks, those that occur after a failed recall attempt, may be influenced by a partial retrieval of the answer in a way that the prediction-of-knowing ratings are not. The tip-of-the-tongue phenomenon is an example of a feeling-of-knowing process that is unrelated to the prediction-of-knowing. A considerable body of research attests to the partial availability of information about the answer to a question when subjects are in the tip-of-the-tongue state. For instance, subjects correctly guess the first letter of the target word about 50% of the time, can identify the number of syllables in the word 38% of the time (after guessing probabilities are removed), and spontaneously produce semantically related words between 40 and 70% of the time (see review in Brown, 1991).

An example of a conventional feeling-of-knowing study in which partial retrieval of the answer is the only logical explanation of the results is provided by Blake (1973). Subjects were shown three-letter trigrams, given a filler task, and then asked to recall the trigrams. When correct recall failed, subjects made feeling-of-knowing ratings and then completed a recognition test. Blake found that feelings of knowing systematically increased with the number of letters recalled. For instance, he reported in his first experiment that feeling-of-knowing ratings jumped from 32% when no letters had been recalled to 73% when two letters had been recalled. The cue familiarity hypothesis may not be irrelevant since these are slower judgments; however, the letters in a to be recalled trigram may serve both as part of the answer and as part of the retrieval cues (question).

What Is the Function of This Process?

As discussed in the initial section of this chapter, the research emphasis triggered by Hart's (1965a) doctoral dissertation has been on the accuracy of feeling-of-knowing ratings in predicting subsequent recognition. Three decades of research have firmly established feeling of knowing as a viable area of interest and have delineated many of the characteristics of this phenomenon. Current work, however, has begun to broaden the research focus beyond the overlap between feeling-of-knowing ratings and recognition to address this fundamental question: *why* do we have the feeling-of-knowing process?

Given the original definition of feeling of knowing as the state of believing that currently unrecallable information will be available at some later point, the usefulness of feeling of knowing as a metacognitive process is unclear. As a purely post hoc judgment following retrieval failure it seems incidental in directing future behavior. Possibly feeling of knowing could serve a self-protective function along the same lines as other self-serving biases identified in social psychology. Or it could serve a corrective, after-the-fact function of eventually allowing individuals to correct lapses in memory. Both of these notions seem rather peripheral, however.

Monitoring and Controlling Functions

Such speculation on the usefulness of feeling of knowing becomes much less strained when feeling of knowing is redefined as a rapid, metacognitive stage that precedes retrieval attempts and becomes particularly salient only when retrieval fails. Since the two functions of a metamemory system are to *monitor* and to *control* cognition (see Nelson & Narens, 1990), a preliminary feeling-of-knowing judgment could logically perform both functions. When a person is presented with a question, we believe that person uses a heuristic based on cues in the question to quickly determine whether a memory search is warranted. Feeling of knowing proceeds rapidly with minimal effort, since it does not require careful inspection of the memory traces (e.g., consistent with research reported by Reder & Ritter, 1992). In other words, this initial evaluation is an automated process (Reder, 1987, 1988). Feeling of knowing could therefore be categorized as a *monitoring* process, a label also given to feeling of knowing by Nelson and Narens (1990).

The next point to consider is whether feeling of knowing also serves a *control* function. Assuming that the individual's feeling of knowing surpasses a certain threshold so that the affirmative decision to search memory is made, the issue centers on *how* memory should be searched. Feeling of knowing has been demonstrated to impact memory search in two ways: first, as a rapid, preliminary stage, feeling of knowing affects strategy choice (e.g., Reder, 1988), and second, feeling of knowing affects search duration (Gruneberg, Monks, & Sykes, 1977; Lachman & Lachman, 1980; Nelson et al., 1984; Reder, 1987, 1988; Ryan, Petty, & Wenzlaff, 1982; Schreiber & D. Nelson, 1993). On this issue of search duration, both the classic research on feeling of knowing and the research using the modified paradigms regarding feeling of knowing converge, since retrieval activities extend over time.

Support for the Existence of Strategy Choice

Reder (1987, 1988) empirically demonstrated that subjects do select among question answering strategies. In her research paradigm subjects choose between two strategies, direct retrieval and plausible reasoning. The direct retrieval strategy means searching memory for a close match to the query, or searching for a targeted fact that has been explicitly stored in memory. The plausibility strategy is defined as computing a plausible answer to a question given a set of facts stored in memory. A considerable body of research assumes that direct retrieval is preferred to an inferential or constructive strategy since retrieval is presumably more efficient than plausible reasoning (see Reder, 1982, for a more general discussion). On the other hand, a growing body of evidence attests to the fact that searching memory for a verbatim match is not necessarily done even in tasks that seem to mandate direct retrieval (e.g., Reder, 1982, 1988; Reder & Anderson, 1980; Reder & Ritter, 1992; Reder & Ross, 1983; Reder & Wible, 1984).

In the experiments of Reder (1979, 1982, 1987, 1988), subjects read stories and then were asked to make judgments about statements based on these stories. Subjects were asked to make either a verbatim recognition judgment ("Did you see this sentence when you read the story?") or a plausibility judgment ("Is this sentence plausible given the story you read?"). There were two plausibility categories, highly plausible or moderately plausible. Determination of subjects' propensity to use the plausibility strategy was operationalized as the difference in reaction time between the moderately plausible and highly plausible statements. Likewise, determination of subjects' use of the direct retrieval strategy was operationalized as the difference in reaction time between statements that had not previously been stated and those that had. When the difference between stated and notstated reaction times was large and the difference between moderate and highly plausible was small, that was taken as evidence for the direct retrieval strategy. When the opposite was true, namely the difference between stated and notstated reaction times was small and the difference between moderate and highly plausible was large, this was taken as evidence for the plausibility strategy. In addition, error rates served as converging measures. For example, when subjects tended to use predominantly the plausibility strategy for a recognition task, there were many erroneous acceptances of highly plausible, notstated items.

Reder's line of research has shown that subjects are more likely to switch their strategy preference from direct retrieval to plausibility as the delays between study and test lengthen (Reder, 1982; Reder & Ross, 1983; Reder & Wible, 1984). Other studies demonstrated that people are sensitive to the requirements of the situation in which they find themselves; they can alter their strategy preference within the same testing session as the probability of success of each strategy is manipulated (Reder, 1987) and can deliberately choose one of the two strategies as advised before each question (Reder, 1987).

These and other related data led Reder (1988) to theorize that the strategy selection process involves two mechanisms, one sensitive to extrinsic factors and one sensitive to intrinsic factors. The mechanism sensitive to extrinsic factors does not respond to cues in the question itself, but to situational factors. For example, Reder (1988) found that official task instructions, an extrinsic factor, influence strategy choice even when either strategy would produce the correct response. The mechanism sensitive to intrinsic factors responds to cues within the question itself, such as the familiarity with the terms in the question, giving a quick feeling-of-knowing judgment. In other words, feeling of knowing is categorized as an intrinsic mechanism.

Empirical Support for the Role of Feeling of Knowing in Strategy Choice

There are three studies that support feeling of knowing as a rapid, preretrieval process involved in the selection of retrieval strategies. The first piece of evidence comes from the arithmetic study of Reder and Ritter (1992) discussed earlier. Carefully constructed new arithmetic problems containing parts from old problems gave subjects spurious feelings of familiarity at test. Although feeling-of-knowing ratings were not collected in this experiment per se, it has already been established that priming terms from questions increases feelings of knowing without improving retrieval (e.g., Reder, 1987). Reder and Ritter found that degree of familiarity with the problem significantly influenced whether subjects chose to calculate or retrieve answers to the problems. There were many instances where subjects mistakenly believed they knew a problem because of the familiarity of the parts of the problem and chose to retrieve the answer. Of course, these impressions proved to be wrong.

It is not problematic that subjects' judgments are off the mark in these cases. This study was intended to illustrate the fallibility of a rapid, heuristic-based process as imperfect monitor, sensitive to some types of information and insensitive to other information. Our thesis is that this cue-driven heuristic is efficient in most situations.

The second piece of evidence comes from a conceptual replication of Reder and Ritter (1992). Reder and Richards (1993) also manipulated the frequency of exposure to arithmetic problems, but sometimes did not allow subjects to answer the problems after selecting a strategy. In this way, exposure to the answer was manipulated separately from exposure to the problem. Data showed that frequency of exposure to the problem, rather than frequency of exposure to the answer predicted explicit strategy choices by subjects, supporting the contention that feeling of knowing is a rapid, preretrieval stage involved in the selection of retrieval strategy.

The final and perhaps most compelling piece of evidence for the implication of feeling of knowing in strategy selection comes from a modification of the typical Reder paradigm in which subjects read some stories 2 days prior to testing and other stories on the same day as testing. Previous research (Reder, 1982) showed that subjects prefer the direct retrieval strategy for questions about stories just read and the plausibility strategy for questions pertinent to the older stories. In those experiments subjects knew the age of the to be queried information prior to seeing the question since subjects answered all questions on the same day or came back 2 days later to answer all of them. Thus, in the prior research, the decision to use one strategy or another could be based on extrinsic factors, namely explicit knowledge of how long ago the story had been read, as opposed to the apparent familiarity of the terms in the question (an intrinsic factor). The critical design change in Reder (1988) was that subjects did not know before seeing a question in the testing phase whether it referred to a story that had just been read or to a story from 2 days earlier. In this manner it was possible to determine if a rapid inspection of the question affected response strategy selection.

In fact, subjects did use different strategies depending on the age of the story to which the questions referred. The results included some intriguing interactions. Subjects who were asked to make plausibility judgments did use inferences when the questions referred to old stories, but were instead using a direct retrieval strategy for questions concerning new stories. When recognition was the dependent variable, error rates indicated that subjects tended to use the plausibility strategy for questions regarding older stories and only used direct retrieval for the new stories. Generally speaking, this study found evidence that subjects frequently employed strategies which did not match stated task requirements. In other words, immediate cue familiarity was often a stronger determinant of strategy selection than explicit task instructions.

Search Duration

The second control function that feeling of knowing has been assumed to perform is determining the length of time an individual is willing to spend in finding the answer to a question. A large body of literature attests that feeling of knowing has a positive correlation with search duration (Gruneberg et al., 1977; Lachman & Lachman, 1980; Nelson et al., 1984; Ryan et al., 1982). It is interesting to speculate, in light of the proposed two strategies, whether feeling of knowing would be related to the length of time subjects were willing to spend inferring an answer. To date, there is no research addressing this issue.

A study by Nelson et al. (1984) using a variation of the classic RJR paradigm illustrates the robust relationship between feeling of knowing and search duration. Subjects were given general-information questions, then made feeling-of-knowing judgments for the first 21 questions whose answers they could not recall. The two measures of subsequent retrieval were perceptual-identification and a multiple-choice recognition test. Half of each subject's retrieval failures were tested via perception and half via recognition. Nelson et al. (1984) found that the latency of incorrect recall, an error of comission, was not correlated with either recognition or perceptual identification. On the other hand, latency to say "don't know" was significantly correlated with feelings of knowing. In other words, when subjects experienced stronger feelings of knowing, they searched longer.

Conclusion

The contention of this chapter has been that feeling of knowing is a rapid metacognitive process that generally precedes the point at which individuals either retrieve or otherwise determine an answer to a question. This process becomes more salient to subjects and researchers alike when a question cannot be answered. This feeling-of-knowing process initially uses a heuristic based on the characteristics of a question, such as superficial familiarity of test cues, instead of partial retrieval of the actual answer itself. In addition, this feeling of knowing process has been shown to guide such metacognitive control actions as search duration and the selection of question-answering strategies.

Acknowledgments

The research reported here was supported by grant BNS-8908030 from the National Science Foundation to Lynne M. Reder. Preparation of the chapter also was supported in part by Training Grant MH 19102-04 from the National Institute of Mental Health. Authorship is alphabetic and does not represent level of contribution. An earlier version of this paper was presented by L. Reder as part of an invited symposium on Metacognition at the 1992 meetings of the American Psychological Society, in San Diego.

Note

1. Note that both latencies were still significantly shorter than the mean latency to produce an incorrect recall response.

4

Subthreshold Priming and Memory Monitoring

Louis Narens, Kimberly A. Jameson, and V. A. Lee

Priming is thought to produce a nonconscious form of human memory. This form of memory has been intensively studied over the past 15 years, and recently Tulving and Schacter (1990) proposed it as a subsystem of human memory on a par with procedural, semantic, and episodic memory. The relation between this nonconscious form of memory and metacognitive judgments derived from conscious introspection has also been an issue of recent study. This chapter describes research concerning the influence of subthreshold as well as conscious priming on (1) recall, (2) subjective evaluation of knowing answers to questions, and (3) subjective evaluation of learning. The empirical findings show different patterns of results for evaluations of knowing and evaluations of learning. A theory is presented that explains these patterns in terms of differences in putative strategies used to relate the evaluations of knowing and learning to later performance tests.

Subthreshold Priming

In the subthreshold priming and other priming paradigms described below, the subject is presented with information, called a *prime*, prior to taking a recall test on the item and/or prior to making metacognitive judgments about the item. The primes are of three types: (1) a *cue prime* (i.e., information about the question in a general information test or the stimulus in a paired-associate test), (2) a *target prime* (i.e., information about the answer in a general information test or the response in a paired-associate test), and (3) a *neutral prime* (i.e., no information or neutral information provided by a nonsense word with phonological characteristics typical of English words). The effect of cue or target priming on a metacognitive judgment is determined by comparing the mean (or median) of the judgment's ratings for the cue or target primed items with the mean (or median) of its ratings for the neutrally primed (control) items. Primes may be presented to subjects in a variety of manners. Sometimes they are presented prior to the recall task in a supposedly unrelated phase of the experiment. But sometimes, and these cases will be of particular interest here, they may be presented below a perceptual threshold by using a variant of a technique developed by Marcel (1983).

Marcel (1983) presented words to subjects using tachistoscopic flashes of such brief durations that they reported complete unawareness of the information being flashed. He showed that despite their inability to know whether a word had been presented, subjects' subsequent cognitive behaviors were altered in a variety of ways by the presentation. It is plausible that although subjects in these kinds of experiments report being unaware of the presented information, they nevertheless may be capable of being aware of various effects due to the presented information. It is of considerable importance for metacognitive theory to determine which kinds of effects can be monitored and which kinds cannot. This chapter presents empirical findings and a theory about the metacognitive monitoring of such effects on learning and memory.

In the experiments discussed below, two different methods of subthreshold priming are used. The aim of the first subthreshold priming method is to ensure that subjects cannot consciously read information presented. Since each individual differs in terms of the amount of time needed for conscious detection of visually displayed information, each subject's visual threshold must be individually determined. To do this numerous presentations are visually flashed. Each presentation consists of a word followed by a pattern mask and the subject is asked to name the presented word. The duration of the pattern mask is fixed throughout. For each subject the initial word presentation is at a fixed brief duration. If the subject correctly identifies the word, the duration of the next word is shortened. This continues until a duration is found for which the subject is not able to identify a word flashed at that duration. Once this duration is found, the next durations are gradually lengthened until the subject correctly identifies another flashed word. Then the durations are again slightly shortened every time the subject correctly identifies a flashed word, until a duration is found such that the subject is unable to identify a specific number of consecutive words, e.g., eight words. This last duration is called the subject's *threshold time*. The subject's *subthreshold presentation time* is the duration that items are presented to the subject for the remainder of the experiment. This is defined as a certain percentage (e.g., 90%) of the threshold time. Individual subthreshold presentation times are determined for each subject. In pilot experiments and experimental debriefing, subjects reported being unaware of the content of the information being flashed at subthreshold presentation times.

One question addressed in this chapter is whether and in what manner subthreshold (and, in some cases, superthreshold) priming influences metacognitive assessments. However, before this issue can be properly addressed, it is necessary to be more specific about the nature of the judgments themselves. As will be discussed later, different kinds of metacognitive judgments may be differentially susceptible to the influence of cue and target priming manipulations. To disentangle and analyze these effects it is important to distinguish among the several kinds of metacognitive judgments.

Metacognitive Judgments

In the experimental study of the monitoring and control of memory processes, three kinds of related judgments have played a prominent role: feeling-of-knowing (FOK) judgments, confidence judgments, and judgments of learning (JOLs). In the Nelson–Narens theoretical framework for metamemory (Nelson & Narens, 1990), each of these judgments corresponds to a specific theoretical metamemory decision process. FOK judgments correspond to decisions to continue searching during retrieval, confidence judgments correspond to decisions to output answers during retrieval, and judgments of learning correspond to decisions to control the amount of study during learning.

In experimental settings, FOK and Confidence judgments are made after a recall test. *FOK judgments* are about incorrectly recalled items. Incorrect items arise either through omission errors where the subject gives a "don't know" response, or through commission errors where the subject gives an incorrect answer. *Confidence judgments* are made about correctly recalled items and commission errors. In the case of omission errors, the subject has only metacognitive information about the question and the retrieval process (including the fact that no answer was produced) on which to base his or her FOK judgment. In the cases of correct responses and commission errors, the subject can use information about the produced "answer" as well as information about the question and the retrieval of this answer in making a confidence or FOK judgment.

Confidence judgments are usually framed and formulated as judgments about some recent action *in the past* (e.g., how confident the subject is that he or she gave the correct answer), whereas FOK judgments are usually formulated as judgments about some *future* action (e.g., how well the subject will do on the item in a future test).

These differences between FOK and confidence judgments prompted metamemory researchers to analyze them separately, and some researchers (e.g., Krinsky & Nelson, 1985) further distinguish FOK judgments by whether they are based on commission or omission errors. However, for the kind of priming experiments considered in this article, such separate analyses of the data often produce difficulties, and the *combination* of FOK and confidence judgments are often the appropriate metacognitive judgments to consider. This combination is designated *FOK/C* (figure 4.1). In obtaining FOK/C judgments, the same question is asked of the subject regarding both incorrect and correct answers (e.g., "Rate how likely you are to recognize the answer on a multiple-choice test") so that the FOK and confidence judgments can be compared.

JOLs are based on information about the learning of the item as well as information about the retrieval/nonretrieval of the answer. JOLs are made about some future action, and unlike FOK and Confidence judgments, JOLs are often made without a prior recall test.

Most FOK studies have been conducted using general information questions. Presumably the vast majority of these items were learned long before testing (usually years before testing). Thus for most of

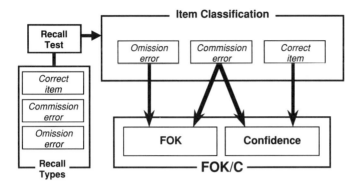

Figure 4.1
Definition of FOK/C judgments.

these items substantial time has passed between learning and the FOK judgment. In contrast, most JOL studies have been conducted using recently learned paired-associates of familiar words with lapses between learning and JOL ranging from less than 1 second to a few minutes.

A Methodological Consideration

A potential methodological pitfall in determining the effect of cue or target priming on FOK arises because priming can affect the recallability of items, and FOK judgments are made on only a portion of the items, those items that are nonrecalled. The following thought experiment illustrates the difficulty (see also Lee, Narens, & Nelson, 1993).

Suppose that a particular form of target priming does not affect an item's FOK rating, that is, if the item were nonrecalled then it would receive the same FOK rating under target priming as under neutral priming. Call an item a *potentially high FOK item* if and only if it would have a high FOK rating when neutrally primed. Now, also suppose that target priming causes potentially high FOK items to be recalled while having no effect on the recallability of other items (figure 4.2). Then given enough items and the random assignment of items to the target and neutral priming conditions, one would expect to observe the mean (or median) of FOK ratings for target

L. Narens, K. A. Jameson, and V. A. Lee

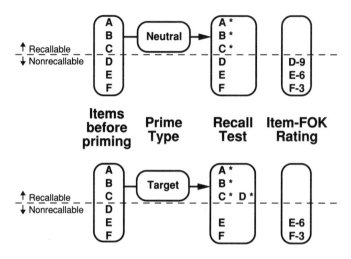

Figure 4.2
A possible influence of priming on FOK judgments and recall. Letters represent items. Items with asterisks represent correctly recalled items. Numbers represent FOK ratings on a scale of 1 to 9, with 9 the highest rating. **D** is a potentially high FOK item.

primed items to be *less than* the mean (or median) for neutrally primed items. But by construction, *target priming is not affecting the FOK of any given item. It is affecting only which items are nonrecalled.*

The potential for this methodological pitfall exists whenever the relevant priming conditions produce different effects on recall. One way to avoid this methodological pitfall is to measure the effect of priming on FOK/C instead of FOK. When FOK/C is used for this purpose, it is important that the subject is asked to make the same kind of judgment for both correctly and incorrectly recalled items in order that the judgments for correctly and incorrectly recalled items can be compared. Thus a subject could be asked to "rate how well you think you will do on this item in a six-alternative multiple-choice test," or to "rate how much you feel you know the answer to this question," etc. The important consideration is that the subject is asked the same question about each item.

Some studies in the literature on priming and FOK do not take this pitfall into account. For these studies we report only findings for which the priming did not produce a significant effect on recall. Even with this restriction, the potential for the above methodological pitfall remains if the magnitude of the effect of the cue or target prime is not large (see Lee et al., 1993, for a discussion).

Subthreshold Priming Research and Judgments of Knowing

FOK and Perceptual Identification

Nelson, Gerler, and Narens (1984) investigated (1) the effect of subthreshold target priming on the perceptual identification of non-recalled answers to general information questions, and (2) the relationship between priming and the FOK. In the first phase of the experiment, each subject was presented with a series of general information questions and asked to search their memory "hard in an attempt to find the answer," until a specific number of questions were answered incorrectly. Each subject then made an FOK judgment for each incorrectly answered question. In the next phase of the experiment the subject was presented with two screens. On the first screen, an incorrectly answered question was displayed. The subject was told that on the second screen the answer to the question would be flashed, and he or she should try to identify the flashed answer. Initially the answer, followed by a fixed-duration pattern mask, was flashed at a far too brief of an interval for the subject to identify. However, in subsequent presentations the answer duration was incremented by a small fixed amount until the subject was able to give the correct answer. The number of flashes to correct identification was one dependent variable of interest.

The main finding of interest was that items with high FOK ranks were correctly identified in fewer flashes than those with low FOK ranks. This result was found even when the effect of reminiscence was taken into account.[1] Thus, the Nelson et al.'s (1984) findings indicated that whatever FOK was monitoring influenced the power of the subthreshold primes to make the answers available to the subject. This raised an interesting question about the converse — namely, does subthreshold priming influence FOK?

FOK/C and Recall

Jameson, Narens, Goldfarb, and Nelson (1990) designed experiments to address the question of whether subthreshold primes might influence FOK judgments. They thought that Nelson et al.'s (1984) perceptual identification results might have been due to the incremental subthreshold flashes having a priming effect on memory retrieval: "whatever produced the high FOK also caused the prime to have a greater effect on memory performance" as measured by perceptual identification (p. 56). Jameson et al. (1990) also noted that this explanation was in accord with a model of metamemory proposed by Hart (1965a, 1967b), which implies that FOK is a more sensitive indicator of memory content than recall.

This suggests that in the Nelson et al. (1984) perceptual identification task FOK monitored memory strength, and items with greater memory strength were given a greater FOK ranking. If high FOK items were the (nonrecallable) items with strengths near threshold, and subthreshold priming (from the degraded presentation) only added small increments to memory strength, then it explains why the items that became identifiable through small amounts of subthreshold priming were those with high FOKs. Taking into account Hart's suggestion that FOK is a more sensitive indicator of memory strength than recall, Jameson et al. (1990) hypothesized that FOK may be able to monitor small increments in memory strength below the threshold for retrievability. They decided to directly test this.[2]

Jameson et al.'s (1990) experimental paradigm consisted of two sessions. In the first session, the subject participated in a recall test using general information questions. Incorrectly recalled items from this session were used in the second session, 1 week later. At the beginning of the second session, each subject's threshold time was determined (using the procedure discussed earlier) and the subthreshold[3] presentation time was established at 90% of the threshold time. Then each subject was presented with the sequence of events depicted in figure 4.3 for each question incorrectly recalled during the first session.

Jameson et al. (1990) found that subthreshold target priming increased recall 18% while having no effect on FOK/C judgments. In

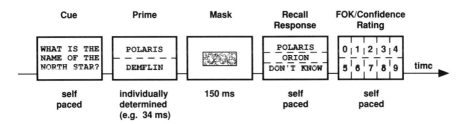

Figure 4.3
A typical sequence for session 2 of Jameson et al. Cue = "WHAT IS THE NAME OF THE NORTH STAR?" Prime = either the target, "POLARIS," or a nonsense word, "DEMFLIN." Recall response = either the correct answer, "POLARIS," an incorrect answer, e.g., "ORION," or a "DON'T KNOW" response.

a second experiment, identical to the first except that the recall stage of the second session was omitted and the FOK/C judgment was made immediately after priming, priming again produced no effect on FOK/C judgments. These results demonstrated that an increase in recall performance occurred following a subthreshold answer prime as compared to a neutral prime (in experiment 1), but no effect of prime type on FOK/C was found (in experiments 1 and 2). Jameson et al. (1990) concluded that these results contradicted the then generally accepted hypothesis of Hart (1967b) and many others that FOK/C is more sensitive than recall at detecting information in memory. Their results demonstrated that the opposite can occur — in particular, that recall is better than FOK at detecting the perceptual input from a subthreshold prime.

Jameson et al. (1990) suggested that their findings also imply that there are at least two distinct memory processes involved in facilitating recall. They theorized that

An item in memory that is below the retrieval threshold may have a subthreshold amount of information in memory that is accessed by the FOK. Then if useful information (e.g., semantically related prime, contextual information, etc.) about the item is contributed to the system by way of the perceptual input that is not monitored by the metamemory system, then these two kinds of information — one detected by the metamemory system and the other not — can combine to raise the item above the retrieval threshold so that it becomes recalled. (pp. 63–64).

They then used this theory to provide the following explanation for the Nelson et al.'s (1984) subthreshold priming perceptual identification result:

The Nelson et al. (1984) finding that high FOK predicted better performance on a subsequent perceptual identification task can be interpreted as follows: Suppose a subject reports a high FOK for the subsequent recognition of a nonrecalled item, which in theory indicates an awareness of relevant information in memory that does not exceed the retrieval threshold. Further suppose that the perceptual input from a prime contributes some amount of information, which in itself is not sufficient to produce identification. Then, according to the 'combining notion', it is possible for these two amounts of information to combine to surpass the identification threshold (perhaps by surpassing the retrieval threshold), and as a result, perceptual identification is facilitated for items previously given a high FOK. An analogous explanation can be made for the failure of items given low FOK ratings to be identified. (p. 65)

In summary, Jameson et al. (1990) provided (1) a theoretical context in which to interpret the above findings of Nelson et al. (1984), and (2) an important empirical demonstration of a situation in which subthreshold priming influenced memory performance but not FOK/C.

Related Superthreshold Priming Research

It has been known for some time that recognition for cues can influence a subject's feeling of knowing for nonrecalled targets. For example, Wellman (1977) showed that kindergartners used information about having seen the cue in making FOK judgments about nonrecalled targets, and Koriat and Lieblich (1977) showed that the addition of redundancy to the cue through repetition or adding alternative wording increased subjects' ratings for nonrecalled targets. Additional findings discussed here are the results of Reder, Metcalfe, Schwartz, and Schwartz and Metcalfe.

Cue Priming Effects on Rapid Judgments of Knowing and Rapid Recall
Reder (1987, 1988) investigated the effects of cue priming on metacognitive judgments that are similar to FOK judgments. In the first stage of her experiment, subjects made frequency-of-occurrence es-

timations for words that would be later used in some question parts of a series of general information questions. The words chosen were central to the question later presented in the general information test. For example, in a question like "What is the term in golf for scoring one under par?" the words "golf" and "par" would be selected. After the word frequency estimation task, the subjects participated in either an "estimate condition" or an "answer condition" of a *game show paradigm*. This paradigm requires subjects to make fast estimates about their ability to answer general information questions before they are able to retrieve the answer. It is modeled on television game shows where the first contestant to press a buzzer gets first chance at answering the question, and where the most successful contestants often press the buzzer before hearing the entire question. Subjects in the *estimate condition* were asked to give rapid first impressions about whether they could subsequently answer general information questions. By pressing a "Yes" button they indicated they thought they could answer the given question, and by pressing a "No" button they indicated they thought that they could not. Subjects in the *answer condition* were asked to immediately answer the question.

In both conditions priming produced an elevated propensity to attempt answers to questions. In the estimate condition, subjects pressed the "Yes" button more often to primed questions than to unprimed ones, indicating they thought they could correctly answer more primed questions than unprimed questions. In the answer condition, subjects searched longer for answers to primed than unprimed questions before saying "Don't know," indicating that during retrieval they thought they knew the answers to primed questions better than to unprimed questions. Reder (1987, 1988) describes both kinds of priming effects as "spurious Feelings of Knowing."

Reder also found the unexpected result that priming influenced the probability of subjects correctly answering questions:

There seemed to be a tendency for subjects to respond more accurately in the answer condition when the question had been primed than when it had not been primed. Conceivably, priming the terms of a question not only gives one a feeling of knowing but actually raises the level of activation for relevant information such that the answer is more likely to pass over some kind of threshold necessary to elicit an answer. (Reder, 1988, pp. 253–254)

In an intricate series of experiments, Reder and Ritter (1992) investigated the kinds of information that subjects use in making rapid strategy selections. Their research produced a number of interesting and important findings, including ones that demonstrate that cue priming but not target priming influences strategy selections. They use this result to theorize that cue priming but not target priming influences the FOK.

Cue and Target Priming Effects on FOK for Learned Paired Associates
Metcalfe (1993) and Schwartz and Metcalfe (1992) interpret the above results of the Jameson et al. (1990) and Reder (1987) experiments as evidence against the *target retrievability hypothesis* for FOK, which states that FOK is based on the retrieval of information about the target. Instead, they interpret these findings as evidence for the *cue familiarity hypothesis* for FOK, which states that FOK is based on the familiarity or recognizability of the cue. Schwartz and Metcalfe (1992) and Schwartz (1992) designed a series of experiments to test these alternative hypotheses in a priming context.

Their experimental paradigm contained the following stages: First, there was a *priming phase* in which subjects were asked to rate words in terms of pleasantness. Some of these words were used later in the experiment. Second, there was an *encoding phase* in which subjects learned pairs of words for cued recall. These pairs consisted of words that the subject rated in the priming phase — *primed* words — and new words not previously rated by the subject — *unprimed* words. In two experiments, Schwartz and Metcalfe (1992) used primed and unprimed words as cues and unprimed words as targets; in another experiment by Schwartz and Metcalfe (1992) and an experiment by Schwartz (1992), primed and unprimed words appeared as either cues or targets, and each pair included at least one unprimed element. Third, a *cued recall* test was given in which the subject was presented with a cue part of an encoded pair and was asked to recall the target part of the pair. And finally, an *FOK judgment phase* was presented in which subjects were asked to make FOK judgments estimating how well they would recognize the answer when shown the cue word of an unrecalled pair.

The essential findings of these studies (Schwartz & Metcalfe, 1992; Schwartz, 1992) for the issues of this chapter can be summarized as follows:

• In the four experiments using unprimed targets, the FOK ratings for items with primed cues were higher than for items with unprimed cues. In three of these experiments, the recall of items with primed cues was the same as the recall of items with unprimed cues.

• In the two experiments using primed and unprimed targets, the FOK ratings for items with unprimed cues and primed targets were the same as for items with unprimed cues with unprimed targets. In one of these experiments, the recall of items with primed targets was the same as the recall of items with unprimed targets. In the other experiment, recall was greater for items with primed targets.

Although they argued against the target retrievability hypothesis, Schwartz and Metcalfe (1992) and Schwartz (1992) did not take into account in the interpretation of their findings the methodological difficulties discussed earlier concerning measuring the effect of priming on FOK when recall is affected by the priming. The above summary of their results contains only results in which priming had no effect on recall. This limited portion of their research indicates that (1) cue priming can have a significant effect on FOK without having a significant effect on recall; and (2) cue priming can have a significant effect on FOK without target priming having a significant effect on FOK. However, this limited portion does not contain direct evidence against the target retrievability hypothesis. Their evidence against the target retrievability hypothesis is greatly weakened by not taking into account methodological considerations discussed earlier.

For nonrecalled items, increasing or decreasing the information used in retrieval without correspondingly increasing or decreasing FOK ratings would provide *direct* evidence against the target retrievability hypothesis. However, we would generally expect an increase or decrease in information used in retrieval to produce a corresponding increase or decrease in recall. But as discussed earlier, a change in recall performance due to priming makes it difficult to compare the influence of priming on retrievability of unrecalled items with the influence of priming on FOK ratings. If no change in recall is

observed, we can still test for a change in the retrievability of unrecalled items by using more sensitive tests, e.g., using recognition or
relearning. This was done by Schwartz and Metcalfe (1992). They
observed that cue priming increased FOK ratings, target priming left
FOK ratings unchanged, and both cue and target priming left recall
performance unchanged. In this experiment, a recognition test was
given after each subject made FOK ratings. In the recognition test,
the subject was presented with cues for unrecalled items. For each
cue the subject was asked to choose the word associated with that
cue from a list of words . They found that primed targets were more
likely to be recognized on this test than unprimed targets.

Unfortunately, due to the nature of the recognition test employed,
we believe that this result does not demonstrate increased use of
primed information in the retrievability of items. The choices in the
recognition test consisted of the target, six new words (not used in
the priming phase or the encoding phase), and one word (a *lure*)
used in the priming phase but not in the encoding phase. Thus the
increased recognition performance is entirely explainable by the
number of times a subject was exposed to the stimuli. In the experiment the subjects encountered the primed target twice before the
recognition test, the lure once before the test, and the new items
not at all before the test. To establish unambiguously that target
priming increases retrievability, other primed targets should have
been presented as the distractors.

Subthreshold Priming Research and JOL

First Study: Subthreshold Target Priming

Lee, Narens, and Nelson (1993) applied the Jameson et al. (1990)
subthreshold priming paradigm to the judgment of learning. The
modified paradigm is shown in figure 4.4. After the determination
of a subject's threshold time, the subject was presented with word
pairs for study. Approximately 3–5 minutes after studying a word
pair, the subject was presented a subthreshold prime for the pair,
containing either the target word of the pair or a nonsense word,
followed by a pattern mask. The subthreshold presentation time for
the prime was 94% of that subject's established threshold time. Im-

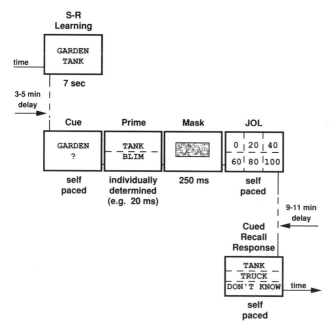

Figure 4.4
A typical sequence for a target priming and JOL experiment. S–R learning = "GARDEN–TANK." Prime = either target, "TANK," or a nonsense word, "BLIM." Response to the cue, "GARDEN," = either the correct answer, "TANK," an incorrect answer, e.g., "TRUCK," or a "DON'T KNOW" response. The 3–5 minute and the 9–11 minute intervals are filled by parts of other sequences.

mediately after the mask, each subject was presented the cue word of the pair and asked to make a prediction about the likelihood of correctly recalling the target word 10 minutes later on a final recall test. The prediction was recorded as the subject's JOL for the item. Nine to 11 minutes after making the prediction for the item a Final (Recall) Test for the item was administered to the subject in which the cue word of the item was presented, and the subject was asked to respond with the corresponding target word.

The 3–5 minute delay time between learning and JOL was selected because of theoretical considerations. Nelson and Dunlosky (1991) showed that subjects' JOL estimations at this time are extremely accurate predictors of final cued-recall performance (Goodman–

Kruskal gamma correlation = .9 or better). They called this highly accurate performance the *delayed JOL effect* to contrast it with the less accurate performance that results when the JOL estimations are made immediately after learning. We interpret part of their explanation for the delayed JOL effect as follows. The items that are cue-recallable at this delay time (i.e., items that would be recalled at this delay time if a cued recall test instead of a JOL were administered) are, except for very few items, the same items that are recalled on the final test. The high JOL accuracy results because of this and because the subject rates cue-recallable items higher than cue-nonrecallable items. (See Nelson & Dunlosky, 1992 for additional mechanisms and data for the delayed JOL effect. See also Spellman & Bjork, 1992.)

Lee et al. (1993) conjectured that with a 3–5 minute delay between learning and the time of JOL estimation, that subthreshold target priming could produce a transitory effect on recallability by changing some cue-nonrecallable items into cue-recallable items. They hypothesized that such changes of state of recallability could influence the JOL made just after priming. Because of the transitory nature of this kind of priming effect, the changed states would return to their original state of cue-nonrecallability before the later, final recall test. This suggests that subthreshold target priming could increase JOL ratings without increasing recall on the final test. Lee et al.'s (1993) experimental findings supported this hypothesis.

Lee et al. (1993) noted that JOLs for items nonrecalled on the final test had similarities to FOK judgments. FOK judgments are made for *nonrecalled* items from a prior recall test. Because of the Delayed JOL Effect, the *nonrecalled* items on the final test were, with very few exceptions, items that were *nonrecallable* when the JOLs for them were made. The JOLs for items recalled on the final test have a similar relationship to Confidence judgments.

Lee et al. (1993) found that the final recall for neutrally primed items was the same as for target primed items [$N = 46$; M(neutral) = .450, $SEM = .04$; M(target) = .431, $SEM = .04$; $t(45) = 0.922$, $p = .36$]. They also found that target priming increased JOL ratings for nonrecalled items on the final test,[4] but did not increase JOL ratings for recalled items on the final test [Wilcoxon tests: $Z = 2.346$, $p = .01$; $Z = 1.008$, $p = .16$; respectively]. Target priming did not increase

JOL ratings, although the trend was in that direction [Wilcoxon test: $Z = 1.219$, $p = .11$].

This result, that target priming increases JOL for nonrecallable final test items while producing no increase for recall on the final test, appears to contradict Jameson et al. (1990). However, Lee et al. (1993) provide a theory that explains both findings. The theory combines features of explanations offered by Nelson and Dunlosky for the delayed JOL Effect with those offered by Jameson et al. for increased recall due to subthreshold target priming.

To make the Lee et al. results more parallel with those of Jameson et al., call the JOLs for nonrecalled items on the final test *LFOK judgments* and JOLs for recalled items on the final test *LConfidence judgments* (figure 4.5). The empirical finding of the delayed JOL

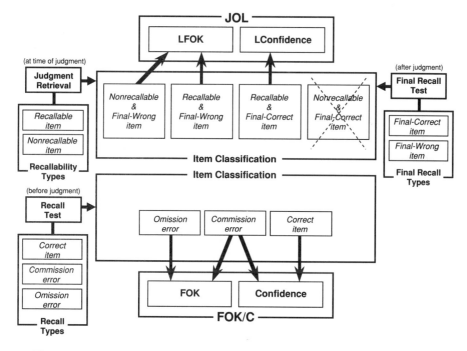

Figure 4.5
Similarities and differences between JOL and FOK/C judgments. For JOL, "Final-Wrong" items = commission and omission errors. "Nonrecallable & Final-Correct" items are ruled out by theoretical assumptions.

effect shows that almost all LConfidence judgments have higher ratings than almost all LFOK judgments. Application of the above explanation of delayed JOL effect to this situation then yields the following: Subjects, in making judgments of learning, rate recallable items (which with very few exceptions become recalled items on the final test) higher than nonrecallable items (which become nonrecalled items on the final test). In the Jameson et al. (1990) experiments, after recall all items were rated on a FOK/C scale according to their likelihood of being correctly answered on a multiple-choice test. On this common FOK/C scale, confidence judgments did not completely dominate FOK judgments, that is, many omission errors were rated higher than commission errors or correct items. (Otherwise, the increased recall due to target priming would have yielded a positive effect of target priming on the FOK/C ratings.)

The empirical evidence that LFOK has a different kind of ranking relationship to LConfidence than FOK has to confidence reflects, in our view, a difference inherent in the tasks presented to the subject. In accordance with the theoretical explanation of Jameson et al. (1990), this difference may not result from an increase in LFOK ratings due to monitoring of the information presented by the subthreshold target prime. As Lee et al. (1993) suggest, the effect of subthreshold target priming may be due entirely to the effect on memory retrieval strength, changing some LFOK items into LConfidence items. Then the difference in results of Lee et al. (1993) and Jameson et al. (1990) is more readily explainable. In the JOL task presented by Lee et al., the subject is predicting subsequent performance on a *cued-recall* test given several minutes later. In this situation, a rational strategy for the subject in estimating JOLs for items for which he or she has no response is to rate them below those for which he or she has a response, even if the correctness of that response is greatly in doubt — the "if it can't be recalled now, it is not going to be recalled in 10 minutes" strategy. This strategy leads to LConfidence items being rated higher than LFOK items. If the study by Jameson et al. (1990) were altered so that the FOK/Confidence ratings were for a recall test to be given 1 minute later, then a similar rating strategy might be rational in that situation. However, for a subsequent *recognition test* it is not. For a subsequent recognition test, it is rational for subjects to rate items with strong FOK higher than items with low confidence, that is, to rate items for which they do not have an answer but have a strong FOK higher than items for which they have answers but great doubt about the answers' correctness. In this way the findings of Lee et al. are consistent with those obtained by Jameson et al. (1990).

Second Study: Subthreshold Cue and Target Priming

In a second study, Lee et al. (1993) compared the different effects on JOL of cue and target priming. The experimental design for this study was essentially the same as their previously discussed study with three important differences: (1) in the priming phase cue words as well as target and neutral words were primed; (2) the duration between the JOL estimation for an item and the Final Recall test for that item was shortened from 9–11 to 4–7 minutes; and (3) the final recall for some items occurred before other items were learned.

In this study Lee et al. showed the following priming results:

1. Target priming produced higher recall than neutral priming.

2. There was no difference between cue priming and neutral priming on recall [$N = 42$; M(neutral) $= .391$, $SEM = .04$; M(target) $= .470$, $SEM = .04$; M(cue) $= .417$, $SEM = .04$; $F(2, 82) = 6.22$, $p < .01$, $MS_e = 0.01$].

3. Target priming yielded higher JOL ratings than either cue priming or neutral priming [Wilcoxon tests: $Z = 2.697$, $p = .004$, and $Z = 2.549$, $p = .01$, respectively].

4. Cue and neutral priming produced no difference in JOL ratings.

Note that the finding of Lee et al. (1993) described in the previous section that target priming produced higher JOL ratings than neutral priming is replicated in the current experiment.

The findings also showed that cue priming did not increase JOL with respect to neutral priming [Wilcoxon test: $Z = -0.525$, $p = .30$]. Other data of Lee et al. (1993) also showed that this was the case when the items were analyzed separately, based on type of final recall performance (correct/wrong). Cue priming did not increase JOL for either final recalled items or final nonrecalled items. In fact, the trends were in the other direction [Wilcoxon tests: $Z = -0.550$ and

L. Narens, K. A. Jameson, and V. A. Lee

$Z = -1.919$, respectively]. This latter finding runs counter to results of Reder (1987, 1988), Schwartz and Metcalfe (1992), and Schwartz (1992). However, because of the many differences in paradigms between studies we draw no conclusions about this.

Summary

The several studies described in the previous sections show that priming can influence the metacognitive judgments FOK, FOK/C, and JOL. It is natural to ask what aspects of the primed material are being monitored when making a given metacognitive judgment. Although the studies presented above are not rich enough to give a definitive answer to this question, they bear on two important aspects of it: (1) Is the information contained in the prime being monitored? (2) Is target retrievability or cue familiarity being monitored? We will now consider these two issues in the context of the presented findings.

In the Nelson et al. (1984) study, the subthreshold target prime — and consequently the information contained in it — was presented after the metacognitive FOK judgment, and therefore the information contained in the prime could not have been monitored by the FOK judgment. In the Jameson et al. (1990) study, subthreshold target priming increased recall but did not influence the metacognitive FOK/C judgment. Therefore there is no reason to expect that the information presented by the target prime was monitored in that study. In the Lee et al. (1993) study, subthreshold target priming had an effect on JOL estimations, but this effect was attributable to monitoring the state of the item, that is, monitoring whether or not the item was recallable, rather than monitoring the information contained in the target prime. In theory, the information contained in the target primes changed the states of some items from "nonrecallable" to "recallable" without the information contained in the primes or the changes in item states being monitored.

Schwartz and Metcalfe (1992), and Schwartz (1992) showed positive effects of cue priming on the metacognitive FOK judgment, and Reder (1987, 1988) showed a positive effect of cue priming on a related metacognitive judgment. These researchers consider that "familiarity" is a feature that is being monitored in making the relevant metacognitive judgments, and they concluded that the observed effects of priming on the judgments were due to cue priming increasing familiarity. However they provided no theory about (1) how cue priming increased familiarity, and (2) whether the information contained in the cue prime was being monitored as part of the metacognitive judgment. Metcalfe (1993) does provide an explicit theory of how cue familiarity is computed and monitored. According to Metcalfe's theory the information contained in the prime is being monitored.

The studies on cue priming discussed in this chapter provide evidence for the cue familiarity hypothesis for the metacognitive judgment FOK — that in making FOK judgments the familiarity or recognizability of the cue is assessed. No evidence that cue familiarity affects the metacognitive judgments JOL and LFOK was found by Lee et al. (1993). The study by Nelson et al. (1984) involving target priming provided indirect evidence for the target retrievability hypothesis by showing that FOK judgments are based on partial retrieval information about the target. Portions of studies by Schwartz and Metcalfe (1992) and Schwartz (1992) concerning the effect of target priming on FOK had methodological difficulties, and because of this, they were not good tests of the target retrievability hypothesis for FOK. Jameson et al. (1990) provided evidence against the target retrievability hypothesis for the metacognitive judgment of FOK/C. For Lee et al. (1993), results concerning the metacognitive judgments of JOL and LFOK are interpreted in a way that makes the target retrievability hypothesis untestable.

Conclusions

The empirical studies discussed in this chapter showed varied patterns of relationships between priming and metacognitive judgments, as summarized above. With occasional theoretical interpretations, the patterns boil down to the following: (1) For both superthreshold and subthreshold priming, target priming increased retrievability of targets but did not increase judgments of knowing or learning for those items whose targets were not retrievable at the time of judgment. (2) For superthreshold priming, cue priming increased judgments of knowing of items whose targets were not retrievable at the time of judgment, often without an increase in retrieval. (3) For subthreshold priming, cue priming did not increase JOLs.

Despite many empirical findings and some theorizing, there are still gaps in the discussed research. At the empirical level, two loose ends need to be resolved. First, a better paradigm is needed for testing the effect of superthreshold target priming on the FOK for items for which subjects attempted recall but failed. Second, the effects of subthreshold cue and target priming on the JOL needs to be examined under a wider range of contexts, for example, for rapid judgments like those used in Reder's "game show" paradigm (1987). At the theoretical level, our understanding of the issues and implications of the major concepts discussed in this chapter would be enhanced by additional mathematical and formal models.

Acknowledgments

This research was partially supported by National Institute of Mental Health Grant MH32205. We thank Nancy Alvarado, Janet Metcalfe, and Thomas O. Nelson for helpful comments.

Notes

1. Reminiscence is the subsequent correct recall of nonrecalled items without priming. Reminiscence needed to be taken into account because high FOK items are more likely to be recalled without priming than low FOK items (Gruenberg et al., 1973; Hart, 1967; Read & Bruce, 1982).

2. Nelson et al.'s (1984) results showed a correlation only between FOK and ease of identification.

3. Due to small variations in presentation times resulting from properties inherent in their equipment, Jameson et al. (1990) conservatively described their presentation times and method of priming as "near threshold" rather than "subthreshold."

4. In this instance the methodological pitfall discussed earlier is avoided because recall was not significantly influenced by target priming and more neutrally primed items were recalled than target primed items.

5

Methodological Problems and Pitfalls in the Study of Human Metacognition

Bennett L. Schwartz and Janet Metcalfe

In this chapter, we discuss several methodological issues concerning metacognitive accuracy. These issues are of importance because they could serve to qualify interpretation of experimental findings concerning the nature of and mechanisms underlying people's metacognitive abilities. First, we show how the nature of the final test itself, and, in particular, the number of alternatives in that test, influences assessed accuracy of prediction. A review of the literature is given showing that accuracy of metacognitive prediction increases along with the number of alternatives at time of second test. The reasons for this strong relation are discussed. Second, we discuss how restricted range on either the judgments themselves or on the criterion variable can influence the accuracy of metacognitive predictions. We present an experiment that illustrates the impact of this potential confound. Third, we discuss problems that may arise when comparing groups that show a different mean level of problem solving, recall, or recognition. Dissociations in metacognition, occurring among such groups, may have implications for our understanding of the architecture of cognition. But we need to be confident that the dissociations are real and not a mere consequence of the methods of measurement. The use of nonparametric as compared to parametric statistics for measuring accuracy when the level of memory performance varies radically between patient groups is discussed, as are other methods of control that have been used by various researchers. Finally, following Glenberg and his colleagues we stress the importance of informing the subject as to the nature of the upcoming memory test prior to making judgments. Given that there is no general pervasive metacognitive knowledge that is equally useful on all tests, then subjects' lack of appreciation of the nature of the test they are about to take can lead to serious distortions in assessment of their metacognitions. Subjects may know what they know, but unless they also know what kinds of questions they will be asked they may not be able to assess how well that knowledge will serve them. This lack of knowledge about the nature of the test may occur because the test conditions are not specified, because they are incorrectly specified, or because the skill level of the subject is not adequate to understanding the task.

One would like to be able to interpret differences in the accuracy of metacognitive judgments in terms of differential cognitive processes, differences in the transparency of certain tasks to conscious inspection, or differences, perhaps, among different patient groups, in mechanisms by which judgments are made. However, such cognitive interpretation may not always be straightforward because some methodological issues may cloud the results. In the studies that we discuss here subjects make one or more predictive judgments about their own future performance on a test of memory, problem solving, or comprehension. They are then given the final test and the relation between the predictive judgments and the final test results are the metacognitive "accuracy" measure of interest. We will deal mainly with experiments that investigate micropredictive accuracy or discrimination, that is, does the subject know on which questions he or she will do well or poorly? This micropredictive accuracy is often measured by a correlation coefficient, such as the nonparametric Goodman-Kruskal gamma measure, that relates the ranking of the questions to the correctness of response on the final test. In some instances, though, we will refer to studies in which macroprediction, or calibration, is of interest. In this case the prediction is one of how good performance will be, overall, without respect to which particular questions contribute in which way to that performance. Micro- and macroprediction are both metacognitive indices, but measure aspects that may be but are not necessarily linked (see Yates, 1990, p. 57). In this first section we discuss several factors concerning the relation between the judgments and the subsequent test that, failing careful consideration and control, could produce spurious results.

Number of Test Alternatives

A simple factor that can influence the micropredictive accuracy of feeling-of-knowing (FOK) judgments, for reasons having little to do with the mechanisms underlying human metacognition, is the number of alternatives presented in the final test. Suppose the subject does not know the answer to a particular question and knows that he or she does not know, and hence gives the question a very low FOK rating. If he or she then gets that question wrong on the final test, this correspondence between the low rating and the incorrect performance will contribute to a positive correlation. This would be an appropriate demonstration of accurate metacognition. However, the chance that the person will get such a question wrong depends on the number of alternatives presented at the time of test. If the test is a two-alternative recognition test, then the odds of picking a correct answer with no knowledge are quite high. As the number of alternatives becomes large, the chances of guessing the correct answer become increasingly small. Insofar as these correct guessing responses should decrease the correlation, which is the measure of metacognitive accuracy, and insofar as more of these correct guesses are expected with fewer test alternatives, we would expect to find lower gamma correlations with few than with many alternatives.

Leonesio and Nelson (1990) noted this possibility, and hence constructed a 19-alternative forced choice test. They say: "The large number of alternatives helped to reduce the noise that necessarily occurs in a forced-choice recognition test; that is, the greater the number of distractors, the less likely an item is to be correct by chance alone. In turn, this reduces the noise in the measures of metamemory accuracy by reducing the likelihood of chance recognition performance on items that the person does not know" (pp. 465–466). The rationale seems reasonable, but the experiment used only a fixed-number-alternative forced-choice test so the empirical validity of this idea was not, thereby, demonstrated. In an earlier study, Nelson, Leonesio, Landwehr, and Narens (1986) compared a four-alternative to an eight-alternative forced-choice test on what was otherwise the same task. Numerically, the gamma values were higher on the eight-alternative task (.33) than on the four-alternative task (.28). However, the researchers were interested in other effects, and the significance level of this variable was not explicitly mentioned. So, although it seems reasonable to suppose that the number of test alternatives matters to the accuracy of prediction, we do not know whether this factor really has a detectable effect on the data, and if so, how important it might be. To investigate this question in more detail we conducted a survey of the literature. The results for recognition and for recall are presented below.

Recognition

We were able to find 26 recognition experiments in which the gamma statistic was reported as the measure of metacognitive accuracy. These studies are listed in table 5.1. There were several additional experiments that report other correlation coefficients or methods of expressing the accuracy of metacogniton, but because a number of factors affect these measures differently we decided to restrict the pool to experiments using gamma. The number of alternatives varied from yes/no (which we coded as if it were a two-alternative task) to 19. The left panel of figure 5.1 plots the gamma correlations reported in these studies against the number of alternatives. (The 19-alternative task is not plotted, though those data were entered into the regression equation.) The tasks on which subjects made predictions and were tested included general-information retrieval, picture identification, paired-associate recall, and sentence completion. There was a significant correlation between the number of alternatives and the magnitude of gamma ($r^2 = .21$).

The tasks, in the initial analysis, were rather diverse. It would be expected, then, that factors other than just the number of alternatives would be contributing to the magnitude of the accuracy effects — diluting the correlation between accuracy and the number of alternatives. However, there were 14 experiments in which the same test — general information questions — made up the target material. In most of these experiments, subjects were tested on the same same pool of materials — a set of general information question devised by Nelson and Narens (1980a). Subjects were given a sequence of questions until they had made a certain number of errors. Then they were asked to make FOK judgments on how likely it was that they would later be able to recognize the answer to the question from an

Table 5.1
Accuracy versus number of alternatives in feeling-of-knowing studies

Study	Alternatives[a]	Accuracy[b]	Type of material[c]	Notes[d]
Costermans et al. (1992) exp 1	Yes/no	.11	G.I.	
Butterfield et al. (1988)	Yes/no	.18	Picture identification	Adults
Nelson et al. (1982)	4	.17	P.A.	
Carroll & Simington (1986)	4	.22	P.A.	
Nelson et al. (1984) exp 1	4	.29	G.I.	
Nelson et al. (1984) exp 2	4	.28	G.I.	
Nelson et al. (1986) exp 1	4	.28	G.I.	
Nelson & Narens (1990) exp 1	4	.23	G.I.	
Costermans et al. (1992) exp 2	5	.27	G.I.	
Schwartz & Metcalfe (1992) exp 1, 2	6	.03	P.A.	
Metcalfe et al. (1993) exp 2	6	.18	P.A.	
Prevey et al. (1991)	6	.53	G.I.	Controls
Janowsky et al. (1989) exp 2	7	.42	G.I.	Control
Shimamura & Squire (1986) exp 2a	7	.7	Sentence	Control
Shimamura & Squire (1986) exp 2b	7	.2	Sentence	Delayed
Janowsky et al. (1989) exp 1a	7	.6	Sentence	Controls
Janowsky et al. (1989) exp 1b	7	.5	Sentence	Delayed
Schwartz & Metcalfe (1992) exp 4	8	.27	P.A.	
Metcalfe et al. (1993) exp 1	8	.17	P.A.	

Table 5.1 (continued)

Study	Alternatives[a]	Accuracy[b]	Type of material[c]	Notes[d]
Metcalfe et al. (1993) exp 3	8	.2	P.A.	
Metcalfe (1986) exp 1	8	.45	G.I.	
Nelson et al. (1986) exp 2	8	.33	G.I.	
Nelson & Narens (1990) exp 2	8	.33	G.I.	
Shimamura & Squire (1986) exp 1	8	.50	G.I.	Controls
Schwartz & Metcalfe (1992) exp 3	8	.46	G.I.	
Leonesio & Nelson (1990)	19	.2	P.A.	
Metcalfe et al. (1993) exp 4	Recall	.39	P.A.	
Metcalfe (1986) exp 2	Recall	.52	G.I.	
Jameson et al. (1990)	Recall	.65	G.I.	
Reder & Ritter (1992) exp 1	Recall	.75	Arithmetic	
Reder & Ritter (1992) exp 2	Recall	.76	Arithmetic	

[a]Yes/no indicates yes/no recognition procedure; numbers indicate how many choices given in N-alternative forced-choice recognition; recall indicates that recall was final test.

[b]In some cases these numbers are means collapsed across conditions.

[c]G.I. indicates general information questions, P.A. means simple paired associates, others as indicated.

[d]Controls indicate that only gamma correlations for normal control patients are reported.

N-alternative forced-choice recognition test. Subjects were then given the recognition test. Among the 14 experiments there was a reasonable range in the number of alternatives presented. Within this set, there were a variety of differences, including things like delay in testing, other than in just the number of alternatives, but presumably this smaller set was more homogeneous than the total set of 26 in which radically different cognitive tasks and types of materials were included. Therefore we did a second analysis on the general information studies. In this case the correlation between number of alternatives and gamma was sizable ($r^2 = .63$). These data are presented in the center panel of figure 5.1. It seems quite clear from these studies that the number of alternatives is of critical importance to the appearance or nonappearance of a positive FOK-to-knowing correlation.

Recall

If our reasoning, and that of Leonesio and Nelson, about the number of alternatives and the relationship of that variable to observed micropredictive accuracy is correct, then it also follows that the correlations should be higher yet when recall is the second test than when forced-choice recognition is the second test. Recall implies an extremely large number of potential alternatives. We surveyed the literature and found that the correlations are higher in recall than recognition. For example, in one experiment using paired associates (Metcalfe, Schwartz, & Joaquim, 1993), subjects were asked to predict future recognition performance. In an otherwise identical experiment, they were asked to predict future recall performance. Correlations between feeling of knowing and recall (.39) were higher than were those between FOK and recognition (.20). We have reanalyzed these accuracy data (which were not of focal interest in the original article) and found that the difference between these two experiments in gamma correlations was significant, $t(46) = 2.25, p < .05$.

There are only five studies in the literature (that we were able to find) that used recall and reported gamma correlations. A mean gamma of .61 was found for those five studies, while a mean gamma of .31 was calculated for the 26 recognition studies shown in the left panel of figure 5.1. This difference in the accuracy of prediction when the final test was recall rather than recognition was significant, $t(29) = 3.83$, $p < .01$. The recall gammas are plotted in the right panel of figure 5.1.

The results of the review of the literature presented here and of the reanalysis of those data that we had available bearing on the issue are unequivocal in pointing to the importance of the number of test alternatives as a factor determining the magnitude of observed feeling-of-knowing correlations. This is not just a hypothetical confound, which potentially could have some effect. Rather it is a factor that accounts for a considerable proportion of the variability across studies. It seems likely to be a contributing factor leading to some failures to uncover robust and accurate microprediction in humans.

The Hazards of Restricted Range

The restricted range problem occurs when one or both of two to-be-correlated variables represents a restricted or truncated range of the variability of that measure. It results in an observed sample correlation that may be lower than the "real" correlation. If there is little or no difference in the levels found in one variable, then it is impossible to show a correlation with that variable. This is a potential problem with all correlations, and can be acute in studies in which feeling-of-knowing judgments are related to later memory performance. Sup-

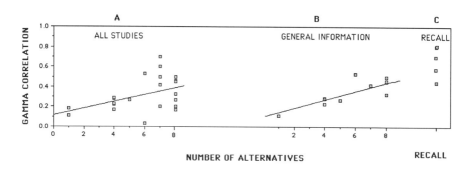

Figure 5.1
Feeling-of-knowing accuracy as a function of the number of alternatives presented in recognition. (A) Plots all studies; (B) plots the general-information studies; (C) shows the five studies using recall as the final test.

pose that the items about which subjects are making FOK judgments are the same in difficulty. Performance scores will tend to cluster around a particular value, and they are therefore restricted. This will obscure a real correlation that might be found in more heterogeneous data. Note that the scores need not be on ceiling or floor for restricted range effects to occur, though these would comprise special cases. When the items are more varied in difficulty, subjects should be better able to discriminate among the items. This should increase the chance of correctly observing accurate judgments given good metacognitive ability on the part of the subject.

Nelson et al. (1986) looked at feeling-of-knowing accuracy when subjects rank ordered a variety of questions relative to each other. In one analysis, they compared the predictive accuracy of two questions that were at the opposite extremes of the ranking (i.e., that enjoyed a considerable range on the scale) to two that were closer together (i.e., that were more restricted in range). The number of intervening questions was important in determining the predictive accuracy for FOK ranking. For questions ranked adjacently (and presumably closest in subjective difficulty), the gamma correlation was only .10, whereas for pairs with six or more intervening items (greater differences in subjective difficulty), the gamma correlation was .45. When they compared only the highest and lowest FOK rank, the gamma improved to .77. Thus it appears that a restricted range on the rating scale, or on the predictive variable, diminishes the correlation observed.

We hypothesized that differences in gamma correlations would also result when the range of item recognition difficulty was varied. To test this idea an experiment was conducted in which two groups of subjects were asked general-information questions with different item-difficulty ranges, as given by Nelson and Narens' (1980a) norms. The restricted variance materials (Narrow) had an initial standard deviation of .18, while the less restricted variance materials (Wide) had a normative standard deviation of .30. They were matched in mean difficulty (.50). Our hypothesis was that correlations giving the accuracy of the judgments would be lower in the Narrow than in the Wide group. Alternatively, though, it was possible that subjects could adjust their level of "tuning" of the judgments to the level of variance in the material, and no differences would be seen.

Subjects read the general-information questions, answered the questions aloud, and an experimenter recorded their responses, until each subject had made 10 errors. Then the 10 cards were reshuffled and subjects were requested to give FOK judgments, on a 0 to 10 scale, about the likelihood that they would later be able to choose the correct answer from among eight alternatives. Then, the recognition test, using the materials of Wilkinson and Nelson (1984), was conducted.

Because subjects only made judgments on the unrecalled items, whereas the norms included all items in the set, we checked to see that the means and variances maintained the same relation for the unrecalled items as they did the original pool in both conditions. The two conditions maintained equivalent mean difficulty for non-recalled items (Narrow = .24, Wide = .21, $t(38) = 1.40$, n.s.). The standard deviations — giving the manipulated difference in range that was the main experimental variable of concern — were still significantly different, in keeping with the initial manipulation (Narrow = .07, Wide = .24, $t(38) = 8.16$, $p < .05$).

The mean gamma correlation for the Wide condition (.72) was higher than that of the Narrow condition (.43), $t(38) = 3.02$, $p < .05$. Both correlations were significantly greater than zero (i.e., better than chance). The conclusion is straightforward: Restricted range effects can substantially alter the magnitude of an observed correlation, and might obscure a real correlation. This danger is especially important when comparisons across different treatment combinations or different subject populations are of interest in the experiment. If a researcher is investigating the possibility that there are different cognitive operations implied by a difference in the correlations across tasks (see Metcalfe, 1986a, for example) or that different patient groups exhibit selective deficits in a particular kind of ability, as measured by a difference in the correlations (see Shimamura & Squire, 1986b; Janowsky, Shimamura, & Squire, 1989, for example) it is of considerable importance to ensure that the groups being compared are using the same range of scale on the judgments task, and also that they exhibit the same magnitude of variability on the criterion (recognition) task. Otherwise, the observed differences may be attributable to restricted range effects rather than to the more interesting cognitive variables under study.

Different Levels of Performance on Criterion Tasks: Dissociation Studies

Accuracy differences in metacognitive judgments across patient groups with different focal lesions or with different neuropsychological syndromes could be of enormous importance for our understanding of the structure and function of the systems and the interrelation among the systems involved in human cognition. A number of studies have been directed at investigating such differences in underlying systems or processes (Janowsky et al., 1989; Lupker, Harbluk, & Patrick., 1991; Metcalfe, 1986a; Nelson, Leonesio, Shimamura, Landwehr, & Narens, 1982; Prevey, Delaney, Mattson, & Tice, 1991; Shimamura & Squire, 1986b). In this section we discuss problems (and methods of solution to those problems) that, while not necessarily isolated to these kinds of studies, nevertheless are salient in them. The possibility of restricted range confounds, as discussed above, is, of course, one such possible pitfall.

A second possible confound, noted by Shimamura and Squire (1986b), is an item selection effect. If, for some reason, one group of subjects ends up with a set of items that are easier or more difficult than another group, differences between the two groups might be due to item differences, rather than to differences in the underlying cognitive structures of the two groups. Shimamura and Squire (1986b) investigated whether certain kinds of amnesic patients would show selective deficits in metacognition, that could be teased apart from general impairments in memory. In experiment 1, Korsakoff amnesics, amnesics of varied etiologies other than Korsakoff's syndrome, and control patients were presented with general-information questions and asked to recall them. Both control patients and the non-Korsakoff amnesics showed normal above-chance micropredictions. By contrast, the Korsakoff patients were impaired. Unfortunately, they were also impaired relative to both controls and other amnesics in recall of the general information. Presumably that information was learned before the onset of the amnesia, and hence was somewhat spared from the memory impairment. As a result of the differences in recall, though, the pool of questions the Korsakoff patients failed to answer, and hence the questions that they made judgments on, was on average easier than that of the other subjects, since the Korsakoff patients did not skim off the easy questions by recalling them in the first phase of the experiment. Shimamura and Squire (1986b) suggested that the decreased accuracy seen in the Korsakoff patients might have been due to a specific metacognitive deficit for Korsakoff patients, but alternatively that it could have resulted because of differences in the question pools.

Accordingly, in experiment 2 they used questions that had to be newly learned in a successful effort to equate recall on the initial test among the different amnesics. "Facts" such as "At the museum, we saw ancient relics made of clay" were used. At test, subjects were shown the sentence with a word missing: "At the museum, we saw ancient relics made of _____." Metacognitive accuracy was still impaired only for the Korsakoffs patients. There are really two possible factors that could have been contributing to Shimamura and Squire's results, other than the factor of interest. One is an item selection effect. The other is simply that metacognition might necessarily be correlated with goodness of memory (or indeed, they might be causally connected). By equating the initial level of recall, though, it is difficult to argue that either of these effects was responsible for the metacognitive differences seen. This leads to the interesting conclusion that Korsakoff patients suffer a real impairment in metacognition, dissociated from other cognitive operations. This finding has been followed up by Janowsky et al. (1989) with frontal patients, and has far reaching theoretical implications for the relation between metacognitive and control processes and basic memory (Metcalfe, 1993).

Given that different patient groups may have different base levels of final recognition, as well as initial recall, it is important that the statistic used to measure metacognition not be sensitive to differences in the absolute level of recall. The nonparametric gamma correlation measure, preferred by many researchers, has the desirable characteristic of being independent of absolute performance in the final test. Table 5.2 gives several examples of patterns of data that could easily result were the baseline performance across subject groups different. Intuitively one would say that the correlation should be

Table 5.2.
Hypothetical cases demonstrating differences between r and g^a

Case 1		Case 2		Case 3	
Judgment	Recognition	Judgment	Recognition	Judgment	Recognition
100	C	100	C	100	C
90	I	60	C	90	I
90	I	50	C	90	I
90	I	40	C	90	I
90	I	30	C	90	I
90	I	20	I	10	I
	$G = 1.00$		$G = 1.00$		$G = 1.00$
	$r = 1.00$		$r = 0.52$		$r = 0.32$

[a] C indicates correct response, I indicates incorrect response, G indicates Goodman–Kruskal gamma correlation, r indicates Pearson product–moment correlation.

perfect in all three cases. The gamma correlation exhibits such a perfect correlation, whereas the parametric Pearson r shows differences. On the other hand, the gamma correlation obscures magnitude information that in some cases could be revealing real judgmental differences, so some caution is needed in its use. A subject might be revealing something real and interesting about the set he or she is judging and/or about the judgment processes themselves by giving values of .49, .50, and .51 for the three items in one list and .01, .50, and .99 in another. But the gamma statistic, treating only rank, discards this information. Nelson (1984) argued that gamma is preferable to parametric signal detection theory analysis because it does not require the data to be normally distributed, and is preferable to nonparametric signal detection analysis because gamma does not require as many observations. However, Swets (1986) showed that for 2 × 2 contingency tables, that gamma (identical in this case to Yule's Q) yields equivalent outcomes to signal detection analysis.

As described above, Shimamura and Squire (1986b) were concerned that an item selection effect might somehow lead to very low predictive accuracy in a low-functioning group. But there is a reverse side to the item selection that leads us to suppose that just the reverse would be expected to occur. Consider a situation in which an extremely bright and well-informed subject participates in a general information study and answers most of the questions in the pool. It may be surprising, at first, that such a subject does not invariably show good micropredictive accuracy, since we tend to expect that good performance will be related to good metacognitive ability (though see the section below on skills for some counter examples). The reason for poor microprediction given exceptional memory performance is straightforward, and combines item selection effects with restricted range effects. The extremely good subject necessarily limits the pool of items to those that are very difficult, and hence operates within a restricted range. The more mediocre subject is tested on a broader mix of easy and difficult questions. As we showed above, the chance of revealing a high correlation between prediction and performance decreases under restricted range conditions. Thus, because of self-imposed item selection effects, the extremely good subject is operating within a restricted range of question difficulty and is liable to show worse micropredictive accuracy than the more mediocre subject. This effect should occur at all levels of performance with the better subjects showing worse micropredictive accuracy than the poor ones, all else being equal.

Nature of the Test: Subjects' Expectations and Subjects' Skills

Knowledge of the Test

One might hope that some metacognitive judgments or feelings reflect a stable familiarity with or propensity toward certain items — a propensity that would have predictive accuracy about performance on a variety of tasks. Unfortunately, a number of studies suggest that the tasks and the metacognitive judgments are much more specific. If the test is different from that which the subject expected when making the judgment, the correlation between the judgment and test, whether positive, negative, or zero, is suspect. It follows that if subjects do not have a full appreciation for what the final test will be, or if they can enact the test by using a different strategy than that implied as being necessary when they were making the judgment, then inferences about the goodness of metacognition with respect to that test cannot be made. For example, in one experiment investigating the relation between feeling-of-knowing judgments, recognition, and perceptual identification, Nelson, Gerler, and Narens (1984) asked subjects to provide FOK judgments about later recognition. The results showed that these judgments did, modestly, predict recognition, gamma = .29, and that they also predicted perceptual identification, gamma = −.16. (The negative correlation resulted because a low rather than a high number of perceptual recognition trials implied good performance.) The absolute values of the correlations were not significantly different from each other. Unfortunately for the stable propensity idea, there was no correlation between the absolute values of the gammas relating the FOK judgments and recognition and the gammas relating the FOK judgments to perceptual identification, based on these scores for each subject. So one is not justified in concluding that the FOK judgments are based on simple strength of memory trace and that that strength influences both recognition and perceptual identification in the same way. It is not clear what one should conclude. As Nelson et al. (1984) discussed, though, there does not seem to be a stable unidimensional FOK ability that applies to all tests.

Sometimes experimenters inadvertently construct a test situation in which the subject can make the response in a manner other than that which is expected when they are making the judgment. For example, in one experiment in Metcalfe et al. (1993) subjects were given a list of paired associates to study. They were asked to give judgments about the likelihood that they would be able to choose the correct associate to the cues. However, only one of the alternatives presented at test (the correct one) had been presented in the initial list. To do the task, subjects needed only to assess the familiarity or oldness of the alternatives; no associative knowledge was necessary. As has been pointed out by Blake (1973) the inclusion of other old items among the lures is needed to make the test one of association, rather than just of familiarity. Some of the other experiments in the Metcalfe et al. (1993) study included within-list lures. Unfortunately, in some conditions the gammas were better with intralist lures, whereas in other conditions they were worse, so a clear systematic factor cannot be isolated.

Glenberg and his colleagues examined how knowledge about the structure of the test affects accuracy of judgments (Epstein, Glenberg, & Bradley, 1984; Glenberg, Wilkinson, & Epstein, 1982; Glenberg & Epstein, 1985, 1987; Glenberg, Sanocki, Epstein, & Morris, 1987; Morris, 1990). Their interest was in how well people understood text they had just read, and thus, they asked subjects to make judgments of comprehension. These were correlated then with performance on various objective tests of comprehension.

Glenberg et al. (1982) and Epstein et al. (1984) investigated the relation between self-assessment of comprehension and objective performance on a contradiction detection task. They asked subjects to read short passages of text as if they were preparing for an exam. Subjects were also informed that inconsistencies in the text could occur, and that it was their job to detect these contradictions. They were instructed to indicate contradictions in the text, and then rated their confidence that they understood the texts. Presumably, if subjects understood the text they should be able to pick out the inconsistencies. The results showed that subjects frequently reported high confidence of comprehension, but nevertheless failed to detect the contradictions contained in the passages. Glenberg et al. (1982) labeled this phenomenon an "illusion of knowing."

Similarly, Glenberg and Epstein (1985) asked subjects to read a brief passage of text and to judge their confidence in being able to correctly draw inferences from that text (on a 1–6 scale). They were then asked to verify whether inferences drawn from the text were true or false. The inferences were new statements whose truth value could be determined by the information provided in the text. For example, after reading a passage entitled the "Detection of Black Holes" and making a confidence judgment, subjects were given one of two sentences, "A black hole which exists in the region of the universe many light years removed from any other matter has a high probability of going undetected" (true), or "A black hole which exists in a region of the universe many light years removed from any other matter has a low probability of going undetected" (false). Then they indicated whether they thought their choice was correct or incorrect.

In the first two experiments using this procedure, the judgments of comprehension failed to predict performance on the inference verification task (but see Weaver, 1990, for better accuracy in a similar paradigm). Subjects were, however, able to assess the correctness of their answers, after the fact. It is possible that subjects were simply unable to assess their comprehension. The third experiment, in the series, however, suggests a different possibility.

In the third experiment, Glenberg and Epstein (1985) modified their procedure by adding an additional confidence judgment and inference verification. Subjects judged whether they would be correct on the objective inference test, were given a test question, and judged the correctness of their answer (so far identical to the first experiments). Then they made a second confidence judgment about how likely they would be to correctly answer a second objective inference test. They then answered the question and judged the correctness of their second answer. On second metacognitive prediction, subjects showed a modest ability to predict their performance. Apparently, the reason that subjects were able to accurately judge their performance on the second question but not the first lies in the fact that experience with the first question gave them a feel for the nature of the test. They were, by and large, correct in saying whether they got the answer correct on the first question, and so had some (better) basis for saying whether they would get a similar second question correct.

Glenberg et al. (1987) found a similar pattern for other kinds of judgments. In a series of experiments, poor predictive accuracy resulted in tests of verbatim recognition, idea recognition, and inference-making, regardless of whether the tests were given immediately or after a delay. But, when subjects were given a second test, predictive accuracy improved. Glenberg et al. (1987) suggested that the first test provided the subject with needed feedback on the nature of test, as well as feedback on his or her actual comprehension of the text. Knowing the structure of the test, subjects were in a better position to make accurate metacognitive judgments.

Skill or Knowledge in the Domain

There are those who might say that the relation between people's skill and their metacognitive ability should not be treated as a methodological problem, since skill is a psychological/cognitive variable of great interest in its own right. While we certainly agree with this sentiment, we could not resist the temptation to include a brief section on skill. Our rationalization for doing so is that as a person gains skill in a domain he or she may have a better knowledge of the nature and difficulty of the test. Thus skill may be seen as a corollary of the idea that, in order for a fair assessment of metacognitive ability to be possible, the subject must have some idea of what the structure of the test questions might be. Of course, other arguments for increases in metacognitive performance with skill can be made, and we do not wish to discount their importance. For example, people may become highly skilled and able to cope with problems in a particular domain because they have good metacognitive abilities (rather than the reverse). In short, then, when compared to more straightforward and clearly methodological issues like the number of alternatives at test, or restricted range effects, including "skill" as a methodological confound is borderline.

The idea that increasing experience, skill, or knowledge within a particular domain should result in increasingly accurate metacognitive judgments seems intuitively obvious. Some studies reveal an effects of skill. Maki and Berry (1984) asked subjects to read sections out of an introductory psychology text. They then made judgments as to how well they thought they would do on multiple-choice questions for that text. In one condition, subjects returned 24 hours later and were given a four-alternative choice test. Those subjects who performed above the median on the test showed good predictive ability; those below the median showed no predictive ability. In addition, the studies of Glenberg et al. (1987) and Glenberg and Epstein (1985) discussed in the preceding section, in which subjects' performance improved with self-generated feedback, or with additional testing, could be considered to be due to skill.

On the other hand, Nelson and Narens (1990) found no improvement in the accuracy of FOK judgments when subjects were given feedback on an earlier session. Subjects were informed of what their judgment had been and of whether they had given the correct answer in recognition. But this feedback had no effect. Similarly, in one experiment reported in Metcalfe et al. (1993) subjects participated in four sessions of learning, initial recall, FOK judgment, and final recognition. The sessions were structurally identical. There was no improvement in accuracy over sessions.

Glenberg and Epstein (1987) examined the relation between judgments of comprehension and inference verification in a group of music or physics "experts" (students who had completed two or more courses in at least one of the topics). Subjects read a number of passages concerning both music and physics, made judgments about how well they understood the passage, and then were given sentences to verify. The physics students gave higher judgments to the physics than the music passages and tended to be more correct on the physics passages. The reverse was found for the music students. Thus both groups showed reasonable macropredictions. However, none of the students was able to predict which passages would be easiest, either within their own speciality domain or in the other domain. Thus the micropredictions were near chance. Glenberg and Epstein (1987) suggested that subjects use a system of self-classification (as expert or nonexpert) to determine their overall confidence. This accounts for both the good accuracy across domains, although the failure to find discrimination is perhaps surprising. It might be noted, however, that the criterion test was a simple true/false test, so there were few alternatives, and a low predictive accuracy might have resulted for that reason alone, as illustrated in the first section of this chapter. Alternatively, the effect of skill on metacognition might be overrated.

Despite the negative results of Glenberg and Epstein (1987), Nelson and Narens (1990), and Metcalfe et al. (1993), discussions of the nature of the novice/expert shift in problem solving (see, for example, Wiser & Carey, 1983) would lead one to suspect that if novices were requested to give rankings of problem difficulty they would be rather poor at doing so. Experts, though, understanding the nature of the concepts underlying various problems, should be better able to assess problem difficulty. As before, though, the exact nature of the test, and the relevance of the skill possessed by the expert and not possessed by the novice, is likely to be critical.

An experiment conducted by J. Krause, in the second author's laboratory, provides a clear example of how skill or knowledge in the task domain may impact on metacognitive judgments. Krause constructed a set of crypt arithmetic problems somewhat similar to the famous DONALD + GERALD = ROBERT problem. The subject's task was to assign a digit to each letter, such that the arithmetic worked out correctly. The twist in Krause's experiment was that he constructed the easiest problems to look like they were long and complicated, and the difficult problems to appear perceptually simple. So, for example, the problem:

```
  H H H H H H H H H
+ S A A A A A A A A S
  R A A A A A A A A A
```

looks fairly difficult, but in fact is easy.[1] Krause constructed, and subjects were tested on, two sets of such problems that varied in their real difficulty in a way that, in his subjective impression, was negatively correlated with their perceptual complexity. The structures of the problems in the two sets were identical. What varied were the actual letters that each problem was assigned. Before solving, subjects were asked to make judgments about how difficult each of the problems would be, as measured by how long it would take to solve it. These predictions were then correlated with the actual time to solve. The difference in the accuracy of the predictions from the first to second trial was dramatic. Correlations, giving subjects' micropredictive accuracy, were near zero on the first trial and near perfect on the second. Of course, this was an extreme situation, where the rules and difficulties of each problem were easily and immediately assimilated during the solving process. The requisite skill needed to understand the structure of the crypt arithmetic problems presented was gained in a single trial, with a corresponding increase in metacognitive "ability." Despite the transparency of this situation, it provides a demonstration of the kind of increase in metacognitive judgment one might expect to accompany an increase in skill in other well-defined situations.

It appears likely that the nature of the task may interact with the efficacy of feedback or skill in improving predictive judgments. In some situations subjects may learn the structure of the task. When they do so their predictive ability may improve dramatically. In other situations, however, such as memory predictions, the structure of the final test may be less learnable, and the improvement in predictive ability with experience in the task less obvious.

Conclusion

The study of human metacognition and its relation to other cognitive processes seems fraught with technical and methodological difficulties. We think that these problems are solvable and that, with careful experimental and theoretical techniques, valuable and valid results can be attained that will advance our understanding of human cognition.

Acknowledgments

We gratefully acknowledge the support of NIMH grant R29 MH48066-03 to J.M. We thank Robert A. Bjork, Arthur M. Glenberg, Thomas O. Nelson, and Arthur Shimamura for helpful comments on the manuscript. The order of authorship was determined by a coin flip, since both authors contributed equally.

Note

1. The solution is:

```
    9 9 9 9 9 9 9 9 9
+ 1 0 0 0 0 0 0 0 0 1
  ───────────────────
  2 0 0 0 0 0 0 0 0 0
```

6

Memory's Knowledge of Its Own Knowledge: The Accessibility Account of the Feeling of Knowing

Asher Koriat

This chapter contrasts two theoretical approaches to the feeling of knowing. According to the commonly held trace-access approach, when people fail to recall a target from memory, they can nevertheless provide feeling-of-knowing (FOK) judgments by monitoring the presence of the target's trace in store. This approach assumes a two-stage, monitoring-and-retrieval process, where people first ascertain the availability of the target in store before attempting to retrieve it. An alternative single-process account advocated in this chapter is that FOK is computed during the search and retrieval process itself, relying on the overall accessibility of partial information about the target. The implications of this approach for the analysis of the accuracy and inaccuracy of FOK are discussed, and some supportive experimental evidence is presented. This evidence suggests that people have no privileged access to information about the target's presence in store that is not already contained in the output of the retrieval attempt.

What Do We Know When We Don't Know?

There are two general properties of memory that are readily demonstrated both in everyday experience and in the laboratory. First, the information that we can retrieve at any one moment represents only a fraction of what we actually know. In the terminology of Tulving and Pearlstone (1966), more information is *available* to people than is *accessible* to them. The second property is that memory is not an all-or-none matter. Thus, even when we fail to retrieve a specific target from memory, we may still be able to say something about it. The information that we can often supply about an unrecallable target is of two different sorts. First is a *feeling-of-knowing* (FOK) judgment, conveying our subjective assessment that we "know" the target to the extent of being able to recall or recognize it in the future. The second consists of some *partial* or *generic information* about the target. For example, even when we fail to recall the name of a person, we may still be able to tell what it sounds like.

A question that naturally arises concerns the *validity* of the information supplied regarding the unrecallable target. Interestingly, both FOK judgments and partial information tend to be quite accurate, suggesting that people can somehow "get a glimpse" of the unrecalled target. Consider FOK judgments first. Many studies confirmed that these judgments are accurate in predicting the likelihood of recalling the target in the future, producing it in response to clues, or identifying it among distractors (e.g., Freedman & Landauer, 1966; Gardiner, Craik, & Bleasdale, 1973; Gruneberg & Monks, 1974; Gruneberg & Sykes, 1978; Hart, 1965a, 1967a, 1967b; Leonesio & Nelson, 1990; Nelson & Narens, 1990; Schacter, 1983).

With regard to partial information, the classic study by Brown and McNeill (1966) has indicated that the information that comes to mind in the tip-of-the-tongue (TOT) state tends to be accurate. Thus, subjects were able to guess various features of the inaccessible word, such as the initial letter, the number of syllables, the location of the stress, and so on (see also Brown, 1991; Koriat & Lieblich, 1974; 1975; Smith, this volume). Other studies still indicate that subjects can also gain accurate information about some of the word's *semantic* attributes (Schacter & Worling, 1985; Yavutz & Bousfield, 1959). For example, in an unpublished study in our laboratory (Erdry, 1990), subjects unable to recall the translation of a so-called Somali word were accurate in judging its connotative meaning with regard to the three dimensions of the semantic differential, good-bad, active-passive, and strong-weak. Their judgments were accurate even after a 1-week period.

The present chapter focuses on FOK judgments, but I shall use some of the observations regarding partial information to help clarify the mystery surrounding the FOK phenomenon. Two questions about the FOK suggest themselves. First, what is the *basis* for the feeling of knowing? Second, what makes such subjective feelings *valid predictors* of objective memory performance? These two questions are, of course, related, because a satisfactory model of the basis of FOK judgments must also provide an explanation for their validity.

What Is the Referent for FOK and Partial Information?

I would like to relate a personal experience and use it to highlight some of the issues pertaining to FOK and partial information: During one of the conferences on memory, I tried to recall the name of the author of a particular book, a book that I had read many years earlier. I tried hard, but for some strange reason I could not retrieve it. Only some letters came to mind, and these made me all the more frustrated for not being able to home in on the name: I felt quite sure that the name contained *W* and *N*, and was somewhat less confident about a third letter, *S*. I struggled with the name for a whole day, trying to play with various permutations of the letters to help retrieve the entire name.

In the evening, I went for a walk with a friend, an expert on the TOT phenomenon, who saw me in my anguish and offered his help. I described to him what I knew about the book — that it was a Penguin book on thinking, with a bluish cover — and also communicated to him the letters that I was able to access. Luckily, he remembered a Penguin book that roughly fits the description, as well as the name of the author: Wason! At that point I had some insight about what was happening: I knew the Penguin book edited by Wason (Wason & Johnson-Laird, 1968), and it was immediately clear to me that it was *not* the book I had in mind, and Wason was *not* the name that I was searching. However, I also realized where the partial information was coming from: It was most probably coming from *Wason!* I made an effort to put aside the letters that came to mind, and after a while I successfully retrieved the name: It was McKellar!

This example illustrates one of the accounts of the TOT state. According to that account, the failure to retrieve the target in the TOT state stems, in part, from the interfering effect of "blockers" or "interlopers" that come to mind (Burke, MacKay, Worthley, & Wade, 1991; Jones, 1989; Reason & Lucas, 1984). Such interlopers represent plausible candidate answers that interfere with accessing the correct target.

Let us assume that "Wason" constitutes such an interloper, and "McKellar" represents the correct, ultimate target. The example described above then presents a dilemma: When we fail to access the full target, but are able to provide partial information and FOK judgments, which is the actual *referent* for these responses? In other words, when I cannot recall an item and yet can access some information, what is that information about? With regard to partial information, the example mentioned above indicates that the phonological clues that came to mind were quite accurate in predicting the *wrong* referent (Wason), and were way off as far as the correct target is concerned (the name "McKellar" does not contain any of the letters that came to mind). With regard to FOK judgments, however, it is not clear which of the two targets was being monitored. Evidently, throughout the entire search process I had a very strong positive FOK, and this turned out to be valid, because I ultimately succeeded in recalling the correct name (McKellar). Thus, is it possible that a *dissociation* exists between partial information and FOK, so that FOK continues to monitor the availability of the *correct* target in store, even when we receive "vibrations" from a related, but *incorrect* target?

To complicate the story further, when preparing the references for this chapter I discovered to my surprise that McKellar's book was *not* a Penguin book. I thought I had the book, so I went to look for it in the place where it was supposed to be, but the book I pulled out from the shelf was not McKellar's. Rather, it was a blue-cover Penguin book by Thomson entitled *The Psychology of Thinking*. So, perhaps, it was this book that gave rise to the partial attributes "bluish" and "Penguin" (I do not know even now what was the color of the cover of Wason's or McKellar's books). "Thomson" may have been also responsible for some of the letters accessed (S and N), though I must admit that I had no recollection of having ever read Thomson's book.

The example cited above helps illustrate some of the theoretical dilemmas raised by memory-blockage states such as those associated with a strong TOT and FOK. These states are of particular interest because they combine two conflicting features: the *subjective* conviction that I know the answer, and the actual, *objective* failure to retrieve it. The question that naturally arises is how does a person know that he/she knows the answer in the face of being unable to produce it? In what follows I shall contrast two general accounts of the FOK that attempt to address this question, the trace-access account and the accessibility account.

The Trace-Access Account of FOK

A simple and elegant model that explains both the *basis* of FOK judgments as well as their *accuracy* is the trace-access model. This model, first advocated by Hart (1965a, 1967a, b; see Nelson, Gerler, & Narens, 1984; Yaniv & Meyer, 1987), assumes that FOK judgments directly monitor the *availability* of the solicited target in store. These judgments are seen to represent the output of a specialized *memory-monitoring module* that can directly inspect the stored memory traces, and determine whether the target's trace is there or not. Thus, whenever a person is required to recall a target, the monitoring module is activated to make sure that the target is present in store before attempting to retrieve it. Such a monitor, then, can save the time and effort looking for a target that is not there.

This monitor-and-retrieve model can best be illustrated by drawing an analogy to the manner in which information is organized in computerized systems. If you have had some experience with computers you must have some knowledge about *directories*. A directory is a file that catalogues other files; it contains a listing of the *names* of the files stored in a computer's memory as well as their addresses. Thus, when the computer is requested to retrieve a file from memory (analogous to a memory query), the process is something like that depicted in figure 6.1. First, the *directory* is inspected to see whether it contains the *name* of the file. If the name cannot be located, the computer returns the response "File not found" (analogous, perhaps, to "I don't know"). Note that this "don't know" response is outputted without having to search the contents of the memory store. Only when the name of the file is found in the directory, will an attempt be made to retrieve the *file itself*.

Although it is not claimed that human memory is organized in a similar manner, the directory analogy contains the basic ingredients of the trace-access model: First, this model postulates a special mech-

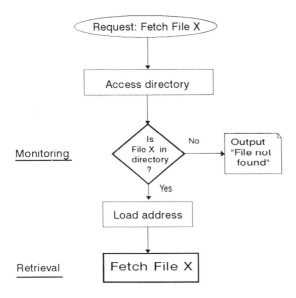

Figure 6.1
Retrieving a file in a computerized system: An illustrative implementation of a two-stage monitoring-and-retrieval process.

anism for detecting the presence of the sought for item *without having to retrieve it*. This mechanism also allows the person to reach a "don't know" decision in a way other than by failing to retrieve the target. Second, the process of answering a question is conceived as a *two-stage* process: The person first ascertains that the solicited target is available in store (analogous to consulting the directory listing) and only then embarks on an attempt to retrieve it (analogous to accessing the file itself). Such utilization of the memory-monitoring mechanism can save the time and effort searching for something that is not there. Thus, while a positive FOK can drive the search process, a negative FOK would discourage it (see Nelson & Narens, 1990; Reder, 1988). Finally, because FOK judgments rest on a process that is *independent* of that required to retrieve the target itself, a *dissociation* may be expected between the outputs of the two processes. Such dissociation should possibly be more prevalent in the fallible human memory than in computerized systems. Consider, for example, what happens when retrieval is misled by "interlopers." The dissociation between retrieval and monitoring implies that although such inter-lopers (like "Wason," in the example cited above) may lead the search astray, the monitoring process continues to detect the *correct* (eventually retrieved) target ("McKellar"), despite the misleading clues that come to mind.

The strongest support for the trace access view comes precisely from the *accuracy* of FOK judgments in predicting correct recall or recognition of the target. How else would people know that they know the correct target if they cannot retrieve it, or worse, when the partial information that they access is wrong? Thus, evidence indicating that FOK is accurate in predicting target recognition is normally seen to also constitute support for the trace-access account of FOK.

FOK as Based on Inference

The trace-access model assumes that the information pertaining to the feeling of knowing is directly available in a *ready-made* format. An alternative view, however, is that FOK judgments, like many judgments concerning future events, rest on an *inferential* process, conscious or unconscious, where several cues are utilized to assess the likelihood that a momentarily inaccessible target will be recalled or recognized at some later time. Nelson et al. (1984) listed a number of cues that can feed into the FOK, such as familiarity with the general topic and retrieval of pertinent episodic information.

Inference-based mechanisms underlying the FOK may be roughly classified into two general types, analytic and nonanalytic (see Jacoby & Brooks; 1984; Jacoby & Kelley, 1987). Analytic inferences are those in which a variety of considerations are explicitly considered and weighed to reach a probability estimate that the solicited target will be subsequently recalled or recognized. For example, in trying to recall the name of a person, I may retrieve the episode in which that person was first introduced to me, or in which I later introduced that person to a friend, and *deduce* that I must have known the name at some time. Such analytic inferences are possibly not very different from those underlying probability judgments in general. In fact, in such cases subjects may prefer to phrase their judgments as "I *must* know" or "I *believe* that I know" rather than as "I *feel* I know" (see also

Costermans, Lories, & Ansay, 1992). Such responses are better classified as *"judgments* of knowing" rather than *"feelings* of knowing."

If the FOK were always based on an analytic, educated inference, perhaps it would not have attracted any special attention. However, it did attract some interest precisely because the subjective experience associated with a strong positive FOK or TOT state is that of an *unmediated feeling* that the sought-for target is "there." This is, perhaps, why studies of the FOK phenomenon have confined themselves to a very specific type of memory task, one where the memory cue presented to the subject constitutes a "memory pointer" (see Koriat & Lieblich, 1977), i.e., serves to specify a particular *memory entry* (a "target") such as a name or a word. Possibly, this is the situation most likely to activate a positive FOK or TOT state when retrieval fails. In contrast, consider the question "what is the width of the Nile in its widest point?" Even if you do not know the correct answer, you can still make an educated guess regarding the likelihood of selecting the correct answer from among distractors. However, it is hard to think of such a judgment as being based on an immediate *feeling* of knowing. The point that I wish to emphasize here is that "knowledge" comes in many different forms: We know the names of people and the words designating various concepts, but we also know that canaries are yellow, what the map of Italy looks like, and when America was discovered. Note, however, that the latter type of questions are not typically included in FOK studies (though they are included in studies of subjective confidence, see, e.g., Koriat, Lichenstein, & Fischhoff, 1980). This should, perhaps, be telling about the FOK phenomenon itself.

In fact, from a phenomenological point of view, the experience associated with a positive FOK or TOT is often quite similar to what is implied by the trace-access view (see James, 1890): We sometimes *sense* the unrecalled target, and can even *feel* its emergence into consciousness. Therefore, if the *feeling* of knowing is based on an inference, possibly that inference must be nonanalytic in nature, involving a global, automatic, and effortless process, where several inarticulate and undifferentiated cues contribute en masse to the FOK. Indeed, two of the accounts of FOK that have been considered in recent work represent nonanalytic heuristics, cue familiarity and accessibility. According to the cue-familiarity hypothesis (see Metcalfe, 1993; Metcalfe, this volume; Metcalfe, Schwartz, & Joaquim; 1993; Miner & Reder, this volume; Nelson et al., 1984; Reder & Ritter, 1992; Schwartz & Metcalfe, 1992) when a person is presented with a memory query that is intended to cue a particular target, FOK is based not on the availability or retrievability of the target, but on the familiarity of the cue itself. This view has been supported by several findings indicating that FOK judgments can be enhanced by advance priming of the cues, but not by the priming of the target (Reder, 1987, 1988; Reder & Ritter, 1992; Schwartz & Metcalfe, 1992). The accessibility hypothesis, which will be presented in detail below, assumes that FOK monitors the overall accessibility of the information pertaining to the target.

The Accessibility Account of the Feeling of Knowing

According to the accessibility model there is no need to invoke a separate monitoring module that taps directly the presence of the solicited target in store when retrieval fails. Rather, the cues for the FOK are to be found in the products of the retrieval process itself. Whenever we search our memory for a solicited target, a variety of clues often come to mind (see Lovelace, 1987). These may include fragments of the target, semantic attributes, episodic information pertaining to the target, and a variety of activations emanating from other sources. Such clues are often not articulate enough to support an analytic inference. Furthermore, they tend to have a "nonaddressable" quality that makes it difficult to attribute them to their proper source, or to judge their dependability, for example, by pitting them against each other (e.g., think of the letters that come to mind during the TOT state). However, they may act en masse to give rise to the subjective feeling that the target is "there," and is worth searching for. Thus, even when retrieval of the target fails, the scattered debris that is left behind can foster a positive feeling of knowing, a feeling that the target will be recalled or recognized in the future. The feeling of knowing, then, is based on a nonanalytic inference that considers the *overall accessibility of partial information* pertaining to the target, i.e., the overall amount and intensity of the clues that come to mind. Essentially, this accessibility heuristic represents an attempt to extrapolate from the processes that occur during the early stages of one retrieval episode to future retrieval episodes: If a memory pointer activates many associations, it is likely to eventually lead to the recollection of the target. If it leaves one "blank," chances are that it will continue to bring nothing to mind. This account of FOK is similar to the availability heuristic postulated by Tversky and Kahneman (1973) to explain how people estimate proportions or frequencies.

In sum, in contrast to the trace-access model, which implies a dissociation between monitoring and retrieval, the accessibility account assumes a *single* retrieval-and-monitoring process: It is through the process of attempting to search for the solicited target that one assesses the likelihood that it is available in store and can be recollected. FOK judgments, then, do *not* monitor memory *storage* (see Hart, 1967a). Rather, they are *computed and updated on-line,* on the basis of clues accumulated during the initial stages of search and retrieval. The monitoring process, then, is *not* independent of the retrieval process; if the latter goes astray, so will the former.

We are now in the position to take up the questions raised earlier in connection with the McKellar–Wason example. As noted earlier, according to the trace-access model, the feeling of knowing continues to tap the trace of the *correct* target (McKellar) even when the partial information that comes to mind emanates from other, misleading sources. The target that I eventually recalled, and that I recognized as the correct one was "McKellar," rather than, say, "Wason," or "Thomson." Therefore, if the feeling of knowing monitors storage rather than retrieval, it must be this target that has served to drive FOK throughout the entire search process. In contrast, according to the accessibility position, the partial information accessed in the course of the retrieval process *is* the very basis for the FOK. Because the FOK is computed on line, it must reflect the overall accessibility of information *at every point in time.* Therefore, every clue that comes to mind will tend to contribute to the enhancement of FOK unless (and until) it is proven to be wrong or irrelevant. This implies, in a sense, that the strong feeling of knowing that I had about McKellar stemmed, in fact, from the partial information accessed about Wason!

According to the accessibility account, then, the FOK is based on the overall accessibility of information, *regardless of its source.* Thus, both *correct* and *incorrect* clues contribute equally to the FOK. This assumption of the accessibility account distinguishes it from the *target retrievability* explanation of FOK. According to this explanation (see Nelson et al., 1984; Schwartz & Metcalfe, 1992), FOK is based on partial recall of the *target proper*. The assumption is that although subjects sometimes fail to retrieve the entire target, they may retrieve parts of it, and these are sufficient to activate a positive FOK. This can also explain the *accuracy* of the FOK, because FOK is seen to be narrowly tuned to the partial recall of the actual, *correct* target. In terms of the example used above, this would mean that the FOK emanates specifically from those clues that pertain to McKellar, implying that subjects can monitor directly the *accuracy* of the information that comes to mind.

Explaining the Accuracy and Inaccuracy of FOK

Let me now turn to the question of the *validity* of FOK in predicting actual memory performance. As noted earlier, a desirable feature of the trace-access model is that it affords a straightforward account of the *accuracy* of FOK: FOK is assumed to tap directly the trace of the inaccessible target, and hence its accuracy in predicting subsequent recognition memory. This is also true of the target retrievability account just described, where FOK is seen to tap the partial information that is specifically due to the correct target.

In contrast, it is not immediately clear how the accessibility account can explain the accuracy of FOK in predicting *correct* memory performance. In fact, the basic tenet of this account is that not only are subjects incapable of monitoring the *availability* of information in store, but they are also incapable of monitoring directly the *accuracy* of the accessible information. Therefore, if monitoring is based on the by-products of the retrieval process, then one must seek an explanation for its validity in the nature of the partial information that comes to mind during a retrieval episode.

As indicated in the introduction of this chapter, when unable to retrieve a target from memory, subjects can sometimes provide partial information about it, and this information tends to be *accurate* (e.g., Erdry, 1990; Schacter & Worling, 1985; Yavutz & Bousfield, 1959). It is proposed that the validity of FOK in predicting future memory performance stems directly from the validity of the partial information recollected. Assuming that FOK judgments rest on the mere *amount* of partial information retrieved, it can be shown that such judgments would tend to be valid as long as that information contains more correct than incorrect elements.

Indeed, the typical result with most free-report memory tests is that correct responses represent a much larger proportion of the total number of responses reported than incorrect responses (see Koriat & Goldsmith, 1993). This is also true of the partial information retrieved. This, of course, derives from a fundamental property of memory, that an item that has been committed to memory is more likely to give rise to correct than to incorrect (full or partial) reports. Under such conditions, a monitoring mechanism that relies on the mere accessibility of information is bound to be predictive of subsequent recall or recognition performance, because most of that information is correct. Of course, there are "deceptive" items that tend to produce more incorrect than correct responses (see Fischhoff, Slovic, & Lichtenstein, 1977; Koriat, 1976; Nelson et al., 1984), and these may result in an unwarranted feeling of knowing (Koriat & Lieblich, 1977). However, these (perhaps, like the McKellar-Wason example) are the exception, not the rule.

This brings us to the question of the *inaccuracy* of feeling of knowing. The trace-access account implies that FOK judgments would be highly accurate in predicting recognition performance. However, the correlations reported in the literature, although generally positive, are low to moderate in size (Nelson & Narens, 1990). Therefore we must examine the conditions that contribute to FOK's *inaccuracy*. These can be derived from figure 6.2. As sketched in this figure, the validity of FOK in predicting subsequent memory performance depends on the correlation between (1) the *quantity* of information accessible at time *t1* and (2) the *accuracy* of memory performance (e.g., recognition) at time *t2*. Thus, there are two factors that should contribute to the inaccuracy of FOK: the discrepancy in the *property* concerned (accessibility vs. accuracy) and the *time lag*.

Consider the first factor. As noted above, the accuracy of FOK judgments depends largely on the *correctness* of the partial information retrieved. Therefore, *monitoring accuracy* should be intimately tied to *memory accuracy,* so that conditions that improve memory ac-

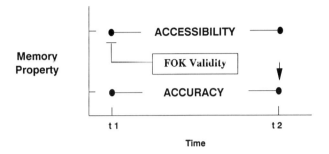

Figure 6.2
A conceptual framework for the analysis of FOK accuracy and inaccuracy.

curacy should tend to enhance monitoring accuracy (Carrol & Nelson, 1993; Lupker, Harbluk, & Patrick, 1991; Nelson & Narens, 1990). Note that what matters according to the present formulation is not how many of the partial attributes of the target are recalled, but how many attributes recalled are correct (in the terminology of Koriat & Goldsmith, 1993, these two indices correspond to input-bound and output-bound measures of memory performance, respectively). Indeed, the analysis of memory pointer (word definitions) reported by Koriat and Lieblich (1977) supports this contention. This analysis was motivated by the observation that the exact same memory pointers tended to precipitate a TOT state in many subjects. Therefore, it seemed important to investigate the nature of these pointers. In their study, subjects were presented with word definitions, and were asked to recall the corresponding word. The word definitions were then classified in terms of the memory states that they tended to precipitate. These memory states (e.g., "don't know," "know-incorrect," "TOT-got it-correct") were defined in terms of both subjective and objective indices of knowing. Some of the word definitions were found to consistently elicit *accurate* positive or negative feelings of knowing across all subject. Examination of these definitions indicated that they typically provided an articulate specification of the target through a set of converging operations that allowed the search process to zero in on the target (or on the memory region where it resides). Such "focused" memory pointers, then, induce selective tuning to the correct target, resulting in a larger ratio of correct to incorrect partial clues. Therefore, they allow subjects to know that they know the answer when they actually know it, and to know that they do not know, when the target is not available to them.

Other memory pointers, in contrast, tend to produce a wealth of partial clues early in the search process, many of which are incorrect. This may occur either because the word definition itself is not focused or specific enough, or because the lexical entry corresponding to the solicited target is difficult to single out from other potential candidates. With such memory pointers the high accessibility of information does not guarantee the subsequent recall or recognition of the correct target. Therefore, such pointers tend to foster a false positive feeling of knowing.

With regard to the effects of *time lag*, one source of inaccurate FOKs derives from the systematic changes that occur over time in the amount and kind of information accessed. The search for a solicited memory target apparently begins with a rapid, shallow analysis of the question or word definition (see Reder & Ritter, 1992), which gives rise to a diffuse, nondeliberate summoning of pertinent clues from a broad memory region (see Kohn, Wingfield, Menn, Goodglass, Gleason, & Hyde, 1987). Gradually the search becomes more focused and controlled, and entails a more detailed evaluation of the information retrieved. These systematic differences between the information that comes to mind when memory is first queried and that which is ultimately used to support target retrieval will generally contribute to FOK's inaccuracy. In the analysis of Koriat and Lieblich (1977), pointers that resulted in a discrepancy between knowing and feeling of knowing were typically of two types, those that activated rich associations early in the search process, which later proved ineffective in supporting retrieval, and those that brought to mind few associations initially, followed later by a spontaneous retrieval of the answer.

Consider the former first. Because the initial inspection of memory covers a broad region, some of the clues that come to mind originate from misleading "interlopers" in the entire region. Such clues are difficult to discard because their source cannot be specified (unless the "interloper" itself — like "Wason" — is retrieved and identified). Therefore, their accessibility inflates preliminary FOK, even if the correct target is eventually recognized or retrieved. Thus, a critical determinant of FOK accuracy is the "density" of memory entries in the broad memory region initially inspected. Indeed, on the basis of their analysis of word definitions, Koriat and Lieblich (1977) concluded:

> The presence of responses which approximately satisfy the definition seems to raise the rate of false positive feeling of knowing even when the correct target is zeroed in on. This latter effect may suggest that the preliminary analysis of the definition involves a cursory inspection of a broader region of memory including many entries, some of which satisfy the definition only grossly. The ease with which entries from this region come to mind then affects the estimate that the correct target will be found. (p. 161).

Interestingly, a false positive feeling of knowing was also precipitated by short definitions, as well as by the presence of redundant information in the word definition. Both of these were seen to affect FOK through the same mechanism mentioned above — by facilitating the emergence into mind of likely candidates during the stage of preliminary analysis.

In contrast, other memory pointers tend to be associated with a positively accelerated rate of information accrual, resulting in a false preliminary "don't know" response. Such pointers induce a search process similar to that involved in solving insight problems (see Metcalfe, 1986a; Metcalfe & Wiebe, 1987): The information does not accumulate gradually, but rather the answer appears to pop up suddenly, sometimes because of a spontaneous restructuring or paraphrasing of the question (see Koriat & Lieblich, 1977). Such word pointers may lead to the peculiar sequence of events characteristic of the "*don't know-got it-correct*" state (Koriat & Lieblich, 1974).

In general, then, FOK is assumed to be computed and updated on-line according to the information accessible at that point in time. However its accuracy will depend on the correlation between (1) the accessibility of information at the time of soliciting FOK judgment, and (2) the accuracy of memory performance at the time of administering the criterion test (e.g., recognition). Systematic differences that are due to memory property (accessibility vs. accuracy) and time lag may contribute to the impression that monitoring and retrieval are dissociable, independent processes.

One implication of the results of the analysis of memory pointers is that characteristics of the *question* (e.g., the amount and kind of initial activations it precipitates) may sometimes be more critical for preliminary FOK judgments than the recallability of the *answer*. This implication is consistent with that which derives from the cue familiarity hypothesis (Metcalfe et al., 1993; Reder, 1987; 1988, Reder & Ritter, 1992; Schwartz & Metcalfe, 1992).

An Accessibility Model of FOK and Some Empirical Evidence

In the present section I shall briefly sketch a process model of the feeling of knowing, and present some illustrative results of experiments designed to test it (figure 6.3). The model and the experimental work are described in detail elsewhere (Koriat, 1993), and here only a brief report will be included.

The model assumes that when searching memory for a solicited target a variety of clues come to mind. Some of these emanate from the target proper and represent "correct partial information," while others represent "wrong partial information" that may stem from a

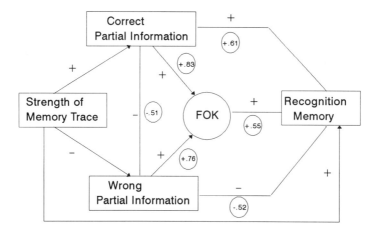

Figure 6.3
An accessibility model of the feeling of knowing. The positive and negative correlations postulated by the model are denoted by plus and minus signs, respectively. The correlations marked within circles are based on the results of experiment 1 of Koriat (1993).

variety of sources. In general, the higher the memory strength of the target, the more likely it is to give rise to correct partial or full recall, as well as to accurate recognition. In contrast, the stronger the memory trace, the lesser the likelihood that misleading clues will intrude. Thus, positive correlations are expected between the three components representing "objective knowing" (memory strength, correct partial information, and recognition), and all should be negatively correlated with the accessibility of wrong partial information.

Turning next to the *feeling* of knowing, the core assumption of the model is that FOK depends on the accessibility of partial information *regardless of its correctness*. Accessibility includes two factors, the *amount* of information retrieved, as well as its *intensity* (its ease of access, its persistence, etc.). FOK is assumed to increase with increasing accessibility of *both* correct as well as incorrect partial information. It is important to stress that the distinction between these two components is assumed *not* to be directly available to the subject, i.e., subjects cannot directly monitor the *accuracy* of the partial information that comes to mind. Therefore what matters is only the overall accessibility of information.

The pattern of relationships noted above between partial information, FOK, and recognition memory implies that the dependence of FOK on the accessibility of *correct* partial information is responsible for its *success* in predicting correct recognition, whereas its dependence on the accessibility of wrong partial information is responsible for its *inaccuracy*.

This pattern raises the question of why FOK is nevertheless generally *accurate* in predicting recognition? There are two main reasons for that. First, as noted earlier, under most common conditions, the partial or full information that comes to mind is more likely to be correct than incorrect. Therefore, correct partial information tends to constitute the largest portion of the total amount of accessible information, and to account for the bulk of its variance. The overall result is that of a *positive* correlation between the *total amount* of accessible information and recognition memory.

The second reason has to do with the *intensity* of the information recalled. Not only does a memory target tend to give rise to more correct than incorrect partial clues, but also correct clues tend to emerge into consciousness with a greater *intensity*. Therefore, although subjects may not be able to monitor *directly* the accuracy of the partial information retrieved, they can do so *indirectly* on the basis of its intensity. An important intensity cue that is utilized by subjects is the *ease* with which information comes to mind (see Jacoby, Kelley, & Dywan, 1989; Jacoby & Kelley, 1991; Jacoby, Lindsay, & Toth, 1992), and this cue can be expected to contribute to both the FOK as well as its accuracy.

I shall now present some illustrative results from experiment 1 of Koriat (1993), which is a modification of that employed by Blake (1973; see also Hart, 1967a). In each trial, subjects memorized a four-letter string (e.g., *TLBN*). They were then presented with a filler task for 18 seconds, and were then asked to report the full target or as many letters as they could remember. Finally they provided FOK judgments about the probability of identifying the target among distractors, and their recognition memory for the target was tested. Thirty subjects participated in the experiment, and each was presented with 40 such trials.

A methodological note is in order. Although this procedure generally conforms to the recall-judgment-recognition paradigm (Hart, 1965a) that has been typically used in most FOK studies, some of its unique features should be noted, because they are critical for the accessibility account of FOK. First, unlike most previous studies, FOK judgments were always solicited here regardless of the subject's performance on the initial recall test. The common practice of soliciting FOK judgments only when the subject's answer is incorrect (or when the subject fails to produce any response) reflects the assumption that the subject has direct access to the correctness of his/her answer. From the point of view of the accessibility model, however, it would seem odd to eliminate from the study of FOK all of the subject's responses which the *experimenter* knows are right. Second, unlike some of the previous studies that tested the partial-recall hypothesis (Blake, 1973; Eysenck, 1979; Schacter & Worling, 1985), where partial knowledge was assessed through a forced-report procedure, here subjects were allowed the option to report as many letters as they could remember. This was necessary to allow assessment of the *amount* of partial information accessible to them. When a forced-choice procedure is used, it is the *experimenter* who must determine how many of the letters reported by the subject are *correct*, and it is not clear at all that that information is accessible to the subject. In fact, a finding that FOK ratings rest on the number of correct letters retrieved provides little insight into the basis of FOK judgments, because it leaves us with a no less intriguing question: How does the subject know how much he or she knows?

The procedure described above allows evaluation of some of the predictions of the model pertaining to the amount of partial information retrieved. Figure 6.3 also includes (in circles) the estimated correlations between some of the components of the model. These estimates were derived from the empirical data using complex procedures that will not be described here (see Koriat, 1993). Note that correct partial information was defined in terms of the number of correct letters reported by the subject, whereas wrong partial information was defined in terms of the number of incorrect letters reported. Each of these could range from 0 to 4, with their sum never exceeding 4. It can be seen that the correlational pattern conforms to the model. Notably, FOK increased as a function of increasing number of correct letters recalled (+.83), but it also increased with increasing number of *wrong* letters accessed (+.76). While the former was positively correlated with recognition (+.61), the latter was negatively correlated (−.52). Thus, it would seem that the number of correct letters retrieved should contribute to the *accuracy* of FOK, whereas the number of incorrect letters should contribute to its *inaccuracy*.

However, despite the conflicting contributions of correct and wrong partial recalls to the validity of FOK, the overall correlation between FOK and recognition was positive (+.55; figure 6.3). The reason is that the great majority (89%) of the letters recalled were correct. Therefore the mere number of letters recalled is a sufficiently good predictor of recognition memory even if subjects cannot tell correct from incorrect recalls.

If monitoring effectiveness derives from the effective retrieval of correct partial information, then subjects exhibiting better memory accuracy should also evidence better metamemory (see Lichtenstein & Fischhoff, 1977). Indeed, when subjects were divided in terms of their overall recognition memory performance into a High-Recognition and a Low-Recognition group, the average correlation between FOK and recognition performance was significantly higher

(+.67) for the former group than for the latter (+.40). Examination of the partial recall performance of the two groups explained why: high-recognition subjects produced a higher proportion of correct to incorrect letters than the low-recognition subjects, and this was probably responsible for the higher validity of their FOK judgments.

The results presented above support the claim that the predictive validity of FOK derives solely from the diagnostic value of total partial information. If such is indeed the case, then the latter should be no less predictive of recognition memory than the subject's own feeling of knowing. Indeed, the correlation between number of letters recalled (regardless of their correctness) and recognition memory was .58, which is about the same as that between FOK and recognition (.55). Thus, the feeling that one "knows" the target, was not any more diagnostic of the "availability" of the solicited target than the mere amount of information accessed. This implies that subjects' monitoring responses do not have privileged access to information that is not already contained in the output of the retrieval attempt.

Additional results (experiment 2; Koriat, 1993) indicated that subjects can further improve their monitoring by taking into account factors having to do with the *intensity* of the partial information retrieved. When ease of access was indexed by the latency of recalling the letters of the target, it was found, first, that ease of access is diagnostic of the *correctness* of the information retrieved. That is, recall latency was shorter for correct than for incorrect partial recalls, even when the total number of letters recalled was held constant. Second, FOK judgments increased with increasing ease of access, suggesting that the feeling of knowing rests not only on the amount of partial information recalled, but also on its ease of access. Thus, reliance on ease of access can also contribute to FOK validity in predicting recognition.

In conclusion, the present chapter contrasted the trace-access model of FOK with the accessibility model. The former model postulates a special monitoring mechanism that taps directly the presence in memory of an unrecallable target. This mechanism provides for the validity of FOK judgments. The accessibility account, in contrast, denies the necessity of invoking such a mechanism, and shows how both the accuracy and inaccuracy of FOK judgments can be explained by assuming that FOK judgments merely monitor the overall accessibility of partial information regarding the target in question.

Acknowledgments

The research reported in this chapter was supported by the Israel Science Foundation administered by the Israel Academy of Sciences and Humanities. The experiments were conducted at the Institute of Information Processing and Decision Making, University of Haifa.

7

A Computational Modeling Approach to Novelty Monitoring, Metacognition, and Frontal Lobe Dysfunction

Janet Metcalfe

Most researchers agree that the human episodic memory system (or, in the framework of Nelson & Narens, this volume, the "object-level") requires, for its optimal functioning, a subsidiary monitoring and control system (see, for example, Atkinson & Shiffrin, 1968). Nelson and Narens call this system the 'meta-level.' This meta-level has different properties and functions than does the basic system, and it may influence memory in a manner that is distinct from that of the associative and storage mechanisms per se. One function of the monitoring and control system may be to assess the novelty or familiarity of incoming events, and to adjust the attention, effort, or cognitive energy assigned to those events as they are entered into memory. Such a monitoring and control device contributes to the adaptive nature of human memory and cognition insofar as it allows us to devote little energy or attention to old and already well-known events, and much attention to novel events. Of course, the monitoring and control system, taken as a whole, may have a variety of other functions as well — allowing the selection of retrieval strategies (see Miner & Reder, this volume), allowing us to make assessments of learning (see Bjork, this volume; Narens, Jameson, & Lee, this volume) that may determine study time, and providing us with assessments on which to base our cognitive performance. In this chapter, however, I shall focus on novelty and familiarity monitoring and the relation of this kind of monitoring to feeling-of-knowing judgments. The novelty or familiarity assessments made by such a monitoring-control system may be thought of as *feelings* that are available to consciousness and which people may use for making feeling-of-knowing (FOK) judgments, that is, subjective assessments of how likely it is that they will be able to later remember the answers to questions to which they cannot, at time of judgment, retrieve the answers.

If subjects do use a fast and hard-wired novelty-detection system as the informational basis for at least some metacognitive judgments, it would suggest that the familiarity of the cue (rather than retrieved information about the target) should be related to FOK judgments. Some experimental literature relevant to this hypothesis will be reviewed shortly. Other evidence concerning the cue familiarity hypothesis, and a different explanation of its function, is given by Miner and Reder (this volume). The conjecture that FOK judgments depend on a functioning novelty monitor implies that deficits in feeling-of-knowing judgments should be linked to impairments in novelty monitoring and control — in short, a syndrome should be observable. Cognitive neuroscience data (see, Shimamura, this volume) and some clinical literature (Moscovitch, 1989; Stuss, 1991a, b) bearing on the possible frontal locus of this novelty monitoring and control function are summarized and some implications are discussed.

Traditionally, within the field of cognitive psychology (though, interestingly, not behaviorism, see, for example, Berlyne, 1960) the concept, mechanisms, and implications of habituation and novelty detection have been downplayed. Habituation or novelty measures have been used as markers for certain kinds of knowledge. For example, release from proactive inhibition (which may well be attributable to novelty responding) has been used as a measure of the stimulus dimensions the person encodes (Wickens, 1972). But little attention has been paid to why changing the dimensions results in an improvement in recall. People's electrophysiological responses to novelty have been studied intensively (e.g., Hillyard & Picton, 1987, Picton, 1992), and relations of these responses to memory have been pointed out (Donchin & Fabiani, 1993), but the reasons for the memory effects are not well delineated. We would have little information about perception during early infancy if we were to give up the idea that even newborn babies respond to novelty and habituate to similarity. For example, our knowledge of the content of phonological perception in infants, which does not always correspond to that of adults, depends on this assumption. But even within the realm of early infant development neither the theoretical status of the concept nor its implications have been emphasized. As Jeffrey (1976), one of the leaders in using habituation and novelty responding as a tool for discovering what infants perceive, aptly put the situation: "I realized that I have been less interested in what I could do for habituation than in what habituation could do for me" (p. 279).

It is possible that our past reliance on the computer metaphor of memory and cognition is responsible, at least in part, for the lack of focus on people's adaptive responding to novelty. Computers, unlike humans, are insensitive to the content of the information they are given. Computers do not habituate when the same bit sequence is given to them again and again, nor do they respond to novelty. Computers get neither bored nor excited. In contrast, patterns of habituation and responses to novelty are characteristics of a dynamic system, capable of changing, learning, and adapting. With the recent excitement in the field of cognitive psychology about the structure, processes, and implications of adaptive filtering/neural network models (Elman, 1990; Hinton, 1989; Kohonen, 1982; Levine & Prueitt, 1989; Lewandowsky & Murdock, 1989; Murdock, 1990; Nowlan & Hinton, 1991; Schley, Chauvin, Henkle, & Golden, 1991), though, with their inherently dynamic, adaptive, and interactive characteristics, and also with the recent cognitive neuroscience findings indicating the dissociability of certain control functions, we find a renewed attention to and interest in people's adaptive responding to novelty and their use of control processes, that is, to meta-level functioning.

The idea that I will outline here, that feeling-of-knowing judgments and other memory phenomena derive from a novelty-monitoring system that controls the basic memory system, stems, in part, from investigations of a particular computer simulation neural-network model of human memory — CHARM (composite holographic associative recall/recognition model). It is likely that many of the patterns of data generated by CHARM would result from other adaptive neural network models as well, but because I have worked most with the CHARM model, I shall focus on it here. As has been previously illustrated (Metcalfe, 1990, 1991, 1993), the CHARM model breaks down unless a novelty monitoring and control system is implemented. The postulate of a novelty-monitoring system, then, both solves an inherent problem in the basic (object-level) memory model and allows the modified model to account for a variety of phenomena concerning metacognitive functioning as well other memory data related to the meta-level system.

The Model

CHARM is a computational neural model of human episodic memory. An overview is presented in figure 7.1. Events (which have been perceived via a preepisodic semantic memory "lexicon") are represented as vectors, which may be associated with one another, episodically, by the operation of convolution. This operation completely intermeshes every element of one event with every element of the other event (or in the case of an autoassociation, with itself), resulting in a thoroughly interactive association. The form of this particular association, as distinguished from other types of proposed

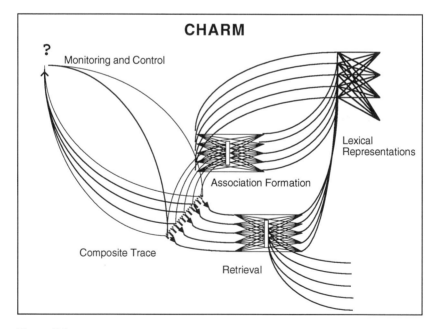

Figure 7.1
An overview of the CHARM model.

connectionist associations (see, for example, Anderson, 1977; Mc-Clelland & Rumelhart, 1986; Rumelhart & McClelland, 1986), is responsible for psychological effects such as those revealed by episodic memory studies. Other models, particularly those that learn slowly with many repetitions or epochs (e.g., Elman, 1990; Rumelhart, Hinton, & Williams, 1986), are probably better suited for conceptual and language learning phenomena. Other models, also, do a better job than CHARM in handling implicit memory data (see, Metcalfe, Cottrell, & Mencl, 1993). Episodic memory results such as the facilitative effects of similarity between the two associated items, bidirectional associations, encoding specificity effects, associative context effects, the effects of misinformation on later memory in the eyewitness testimony paradigm, and interactions between recognition and recall giving rise to the Tulving/Wiseman recognition-failure function, are handled well by CHARM.

In CHARM, successive associations are stored by being superimposed or added into the same single composite memory trace, which is itself a vector — the sum of successive associations. The composite trace causes interactions among the various items and associations, and is responsible for many of the important, and confirmed, psychological predictions of the model. Because of its psychological and neurological plausibility, the idea of a composite memory trace is an attractive concept. However, each time a new association is entered into the trace, the variability of the trace, (i.e., the absolute values of elements of the trace) tends to increase. Without some kind of control, there are no bounds on this increase. If the trace is considered to be a real system — say a neural system — then this boundless increase in the values is impossible. For example, suppose that the values on the elements of the trace mapped to firing frequencies of neurons. These frequencies must be limited, and cannot increase without bounds without destroying the neurons themselves. There are a number of possible solutions to this problem, but the one I have investigated is to suppose that there is a homeostatic mechanism that keeps the values within dynamic boundaries, such that over the entire trace, the variability is locked to a constant value. In more sophisticated future treatments of this issue, this value might be allowed to vary somewhat according to generalized arousal, or other factors. But, as a start, a simple assumption of stable trace variability seems reasonable.[1]

It can be shown that the variability of the trace increases more, on average, the more similar is the incoming association to the information that is already stored in the trace. Without knowing anything explicit about the content (or the values of particular elements) of the incoming event, one can say that it is similar or dissimilar to what is stored previously in the trace by measuring how much the incoming event increases the variability of the trace. To keep the potential explosion from happening and to stabilize the composite memory trace it is necessary to quickly measure the increase in variability in the trace. The problem cannot be solved by simply adding a decay parameter to the model, because it cannot be known, in advance, what the similarity characteristics of the new incoming event, either in isolation, or, more importantly, in relation to the composite trace already existing at time t, will be. Events in the world are unpredictable, and different events have different impacts on the variability. Therefore, a monitor is needed. Note, though, that the monitor is approximately as simple as a thermometer. No complex or mystical qualities are assumed. The reading given by the monitor is used to modify or renormalize the trace to an appropriate stable value.

Because the monitor gives high values for high matches between the incoming event and the trace, and low or zero values for mismatches between the incoming event and the trace, it could be considered to be a quick prestorage familiarity (or at the other end of the dimension — novelty) monitor. The process of squeezing down the variability of the trace according to the familiarity of the incoming event (based on the monitored value) could be considered to be novelty/familiarity filtering. The novelty filter, then, differentially weights events being entered into memory according to their familiarity or novelty with the former getting low weightings and the latter getting high weightings. The monitoring and feedback devices are enacting quite different operations from association formation (convolution) and storage in a composite trace (addition), and thus, by any criterion should be considered to comprise a different system that interacts with and modulates the basic memory system.

The novelty/familiarity monitoring mechanism proposed to account for the exploding variance problem in CHARM bears some resemblance to an orienting reflex theory proposed many years ago, by Sokolov (1963, 1975), especially insofar as the mechanism is separable from the more basic cognitive process itself. Sokolov's theory is usually applied at a sensory level, where the stimuli are of an elementary form — sensations. The feedback loop that reacts to novelty is an orienting reflex. Although, in his 1975 paper, Sokolov does state that such a mechanism could apply to verbal stimuli, most attention and applications of Sokolov's ideas have been at the level of sensory discrimination and targeting (Konorski, 1967) .

In contrast, the novelty monitor and filter considered here are assumed to operate at a cognitive level, where the events, being processed by the episodic memory system, are complex and meaningful. It is likely that other feedback loops and monitoring mechanisms are used at different levels of analysis within the human cognitive/perceptual system. Contrast enhancement, for example, is an early sensory form of novelty filtering operating at a peripheral level of the nervous system. Contrast is, after all, a *change* in the brightness, and a novelty detector has the function of picking out and emphasizing change. The mechanism of lateral inhibition, though, is quite different from the novelty filter proposed in the present context. My concern, in this chapter, is not with novelty detection and filtering in general, but only with the implications of the monitoring and control functions on semantically interpreted representations just prior to their being entered into episodic memory storage.

Novelty Monitoring and Control in Selected Cognitive Paradigms

Feelings of Knowing

The feeling perceived as a result of the novelty monitoring process may be, literally, a feeling of knowing or not knowing — knowing when the monitor indicates familiarity and not knowing when it indicates novelty. The monitor gives no other information about the item. It does not say what aspects of the event are old, why an event is old, where it was experienced, under what circumstances it became known, how frequently an event was experienced, how recently, or whether it might not have been precisely that event that is causing a feeling of familiarity, but rather, perhaps just some other event that was fairly similar. None of these things is revealed. The value yielded up by the monitor is simply a scalar, corresponding to an unanalyzable feeling (magnitude is given, but the circumstances contributing to that magnitude are unknown) — removed from content knowledge, declarative knowledge, or "knowledge about." A scalar is not representational, just as a feeling is not representational. It is simply a strength signal. More detailed evidence on the possibility that feeling-of-knowing judgments are based on these feelings will be reviewed shortly.

Buildup and Release from Proactive Inhibition

In this paradigm subjects are presented successive lists of items that are drawn from the same category. With each successive list, people's recall performance decreases. This decrease in recall is easy to understand as habituation. In the model, with an intact monitoring and control device, with each successive highly similar event the variability of the trace, which is monitored by the familiarity monitor, will increase, and hence the feedback weighting will be less and less. When the category is shifted people's recall performance rebounds to its initial high level. This rebound in recall seems very much like a response to novelty. In the model, when the new category is presented, it is unlike that which was already in the trace, and hence is novel. Thus the feedback control registers this novelty and assigns a high weighting — resulting in a modeled release from proactive inhibition.

Experimental evidence qualifying the idea that the buildup of proactive inhibition is due to habituation and the release is due exclusively to a novelty response comes from a study by Gardiner, Craik, and Birtwistle (1972). Subjects were presented with lists from two categories — wildflowers and garden flowers, for example — that would not normally be distinguished by college students. If subjects were told nothing about this subtle shift, they did not show release from proactive inhibition. However, if they were told about the distinction either at time of encoding or at time of retrieval, then they showed an improvement in recall. The fact that subjects showed release when the distinguishing information was given only at time of retrieval suggested to the authors that the release from proactive inhibition phenomenon might be retrieval based, and that the category cue might be used to restrict the subjects' search set. In their situation, though, subjects would not normally notice the change in category. It is not known whether or to what extent retrieval factors are at work in the situation in which (normal) subjects do notice a category change, since they did not examine this situation. It seems most likely that both factors are normally operative in this paradigm.

Cue Overload

If subjects are asked to remember a list of words, blocked into different taxonomic categories, the number of exemplars given in each category is important in determining performance. With an increase in the number of exemplars comes a decrease in memory performance. Results of this kind have been explained by the concept of cue overload. The basic idea is that a retrieval cue — the category name — has only so much power or efficacy to evoke its exemplars. If too many exemplars are attached to the same cue, the cue becomes diluted by expending this power among them, and hence its effectiveness is decreased. Alternatively, though, subjects might habituate as more and more highly similar exemplars are presented.

The Von Restorff Effect

If subjects, in a memory experiment, are presented with a list of items from one category, but embedded in the center of the list is a member of a different category, recall of the unusual word will be better than would be expected as compared to nearby items from within the category. One might evoke the idea of cue overload as an explanation — the cue of the oddball item certainly would be overloaded less than that of the rest of the list. Alternatively, the oddball effect might be attributable to an encoding-level novelty filter.

This paradigm has been investigated by electrophysiologists studying event-related potentials (erps). The oddball, or Von Restorff item, has associated with its presentation a particular averaged potential called a P300 (see Hillyard & Picton, 1987; Picton, 1992). In order to produce a P300, the stimulus must be novel and relevant to the task at hand (Courchesne, Hillyard, & Galambos, 1975). The amplitude of the P300 varies inversely with stimulus probability, and occurs at many levels of meaningfulness of the stimuli, including sensory beeps and boops, visual targets, as well as semantic stimuli such as male versus female names (Kutas, McCarthy, & Donchin, 1977), and pictures of politicians versus nonpoliticians (Towle, Heuer, & Donchin, 1980). When words are presented in a series, the isolated, Von Restorff word evokes a P300 (Karis, Fabiani, & Donchin, 1984; Fabiani, Karis, & Donchin, 1990), though only if subjects were using a rote rather than an elaborative strategy (Fabiani, Karis, & Donchin, 1986) perhaps because under elaboration the oddballs are not so odd. There is controversy over whether there are two memory-related erp waveforms — one occurring earlier, and related to more sensory distinctions, and one occurring later and related to more semantic aspects of the stimuli. There is agreement, though, that these erp tracings linked to task-relevant novelty and to later memory reflect an encoding difference.

Spacing Effects

The spacing of repetitions of to-be-remembered material has a consistent and impressive effect on the memorability of that material. Since Melton's (1967) and Madigan's (1969) investigations of the spacing effect, it has been known that the further apart are two repetitions, the more effective will be the repetition for later recall, so long as the recency effects due to the last presentation, that is, the lag between last study and test, are controlled. Massed practice has little beneficial effect on memory, whereas spaced practice can be very helpful. Explanations for this effect include the "encoding variability" idea given by Bower (1972) that the further spaced the repetitions are, the greater will be the difference in context, and different contexts provide better retrieval cues. Number of rehearsals (Rundus, 1971) has also been implicated as an explanation of the effect. Recently, Bjork and Bjork (1992) suggested that differential retrieval difficulty, and the memorial benefits attendant on difficult retrievals, might underlie the spacing effect.

A simple novelty/familiarity difference in the processing of the repeated item might also underlie the spacing effect, as has been suggested by Hintzman (1974). Consider the massed practice case. When the second repetition of the to-be-remembered item is presented, the composite memory trace is still strongly weighted by the first presentation. Thus, the familiarity monitor will give a high familiarity value, and the weighting that the new incoming (repeated) item is assigned will be low. At a long lag, though, when the repeated item is presented, its similarity to the trace is low. The many intervening items have lessened the proportional weighting of the first repetition. The familiarity monitor will therefore give a 'novelty' reading, and assign the incoming item a high weighting. At a sufficient delay in testing, the memorability could be expected to be a function of the first and second weightings. This value will be greater in the spaced than the massed condition, simply because the second weighting was greater for the repeated item. While acknowledging other theoretical possibilities, it is plausible that spacing effects may be attributed in part to habituation and novelty monitoring mechanisms.

Feeling-of-Knowing Judgments

The evidence that feeling-of-knowing judgments might be based on a novelty/familiarity detector has been presented in Metcalfe (1993). If these judgments are based on the novelty monitoring, this would imply that a quick assessment of the familiarity of the cue is made, an assessment that forms the basis of the judgment. Miner and Reder (this volume) provide an extensive review of the literature on the cue-familiarity hypothesis, though they advocate a different function for this cue-based monitoring. An alternative view of the mechanism underlying FOK judgments — the target-based accessibility heuristic — is given by Koriat (this volume). His argument is that instead of evaluating the familiarity of the cue, subjects make their judgments by trying to retrieve, and that the judgments are based on what and how much they are able to retrieve. Although Koriat's hypothesis makes some overlapping predictions with the cue-familiarity hypothesis, the underlying mechanisms are quite different. A number of other researchers, including Connor, Balota, and Neely (1992), Costerman, Lories, and Ansay (1992), Glenberg, Sanocki, Epstein, and Morris (1987), and Reder and Ritter (1992), have proposed cue-familiarity explanations of FOK judgments.

Metcalfe (1993) suggested that since the feeling of knowing procedure is typically enacted on only those items that the subject cannot remember at the time of initial test it is plausible to suppose that the judgments are made on the basis of information other than that which is explicitly retrieved. It is of some interest that in other metacognitive paradigms, where subjects do have retrieved information concerning the to-be-judged items, they seem to make their judgments on the basis of that information (see Narens, Jameson, & Lee, this volume). In the FOK paradigm, incorrect information can be separated into two types: errors of commission and of omission. Krinsky and Nelson (1985) found that the ratings given to the former were much higher than were those given to latter errors. If people were basing their judgments on what is retrieved but knew that what had just been retrieved was wrong, as in the case of errors of commission, one might expect especially low ratings, rather than the high empirically observed ratings. However, if the judgments were based on the value returned by the novelty-familiarity monitor, the familiarity measure returned by the cues producing commission errors should be high. Hence, the FOK judgments for commissions should be high. The cues for omission errors were so unfamiliar that they produced no response, and so the omission FOK judgments should be low, as Krinsky and Nelson's data showed. Interestingly, Koriat (this volume) argues that this same pattern of data provides evidence for the accessibility heuristic.

If feeling-of-knowing judgments were based on a preretrieval familiarity monitor, one would expect these judgments to be made quickly — more quickly than the actual retrieval of the information (as has been found by Reder, 1987, 1988). She and her colleagues (Miner & Reder, this volume; Reder & Ritter, 1992) suggest that fast feeling of knowing judgments might provide the basis for deciding whether to initiate retrieval (or some other question answering strategy). In addition, if feeling of knowing judgments were based on a novelty monitor that assesses the familiarity of the cue, then manipulations that increase cue familiarity should increase feeling of knowing ratings. A number of studies stemming from the original work of

Reder (1988) have now shown this effect. In Reder's (1988) study, before being given general information questions in a feeling of knowing task, subjects (in an ostensibly unrelated task) rated a list of words for frequency of occurrence . Embedded in the frequency-rating task were some of the words that occurred later in one third of the feeling of knowing questions. Priming the cues increased subjects' feelings of knowing without increasing their ability to retrieve the answers to the questions. Schwartz and Metcalfe (1992) and Metcalfe, Schwartz, and Joaquim (1993) have found similar cue-familiarity effects. They also found that tip-of-the-tongue feelings (see Smith, this volume) depended on the repetition (or familiarity) of the cues and not on the memorability of the targets. Converging evidence comes from a sequence of experiments by Glenberg, Sanocki, Epstein, and Morris (1987). Typically, subjects were given a number of short informative paragraphs to read, each on different topics. They were then given the titles of the stories and asked to predict either their specific recall of aspects of the content of the stories or their ability to make appropriate inferences about each story. Subjects' micropredictive accuracy in these experiments was near zero (see Schwartz & Metcalfe, this volume). But, there was a substantial positive correlation between the subjects' domain knowledge, or the 'familiarity' of the cues, and their confidence ratings.

Jameson, Narens, Goldfarb, and Nelson (1990) in experiments in which the targets were primed (subliminally) found an increase in recall combined with no discernible effect on feeling-of-knowing judgments. Thus, while cue priming consistently affects FOK judgments, target priming does not . There are cases where target priming has affected FOK judgments, however. Schwartz and Metcalfe (1992, experiment 3) showed a target-priming effect on FOK judgments with general-information questions. They thought that this effect might have been attributable to covert recall of the targets, in the target-primed conditions. If subjects could recall the targets, then high FOK judgments on those items would be a reasonable response. As Narens, Jameson, and Lee (this volume) point out, the possibility of target priming and retrievability effects on FOK judgments has not yet been ruled out.

An initial result by Yaniv and Meyer (1987) was thought to favor the target retrievability hypothesis, but has recently been reexamined

(Connor, Balota, & Neely, 1992) and reinterpreted as cue-familiarity effect. Yaniv and Meyer (1987) gave subjects word definition problems, such as "A statement that is seemingly contradictory or opposed to common sense and yet is perhaps true? (paradox)." Feeling-of-knowing and tip-of-the-tongue judgments correlated with quickened reaction time on a subsequent lexical-decision task, and to later recognition reaction time, suggesting that FOK judgments were based on partial information that was also responsible for the fast reaction times. However, Connor et al. (1992) found a similar effect even when the question and the FOK judgments were made 1 week after the tests of lexical decision and recognition. Connor et al. (1992) suggested that the FOK judgments probably were made on the basis of familiarity with the domain of the cues.

People often know what they do not know. In addition, they can sometimes report that they do not know very quickly (Kolers & Palef, 1976). Because these judgments can be quick it does not seem that people first retrieve and then piece together the don't know judgment from (the lack of) partial information. It is more plausible to assume that the value from a preretrieval familiarity monitor is used. Glucksberg and McCloskey (1981) conducted an investigation in which instead of having subjects rely only on implicit don't know information, they specifically gave statements indicating that certain information was not known. In contrast to what one might expect if the 'don't know' judgments were based on retrieving such explicit information, the explicit answers hurt subjects' performance. If the judgments were based on a quick familiarity monitor that did not analyze the content of the information but only gave a gross measure of similarity, then the presentation of the explicit information, which was highly similar to the cue, would be expected to hurt performance, as was found in the data. Overall, then, it seems reasonable to conclude that at least some and possibly most feeling of knowing judgments are based on an assessment of the familiarity of the cue, such as may be available via a novelty-monitoring system.

Cognitive Neuroscience of Novelty Detection and Metamemory

If novelty monitoring, habituation, and metacognition stem from the same system, and if that system is distinct from the basic memory system, one might expect to find certain linked deficits. Patients who exhibit an impairment in one task based on this proposed system should also show an impairment in the others. There are several studies, using patient groups having the same diagnosis, that suggest such a linkage.

Korsakoff patients are alcoholics who have suffered damage to the diencephalon and the frontal lobes as a result of a thiamine deficiency associated with alcohol abuse. These patients differ from other amnesic patients and from normals along a number of possibly related dimensions. They have difficulty making estimates about everyday objects or events. They tend to be apathetic. They sometimes show poor performance on categorization tasks such as the Wisconsin Card Sorting Task. Some researchers have argued that at least some of the deficits associated with Korsakoff syndrome are attributable to frontal lobe damage, rather than to damage to the diencephalon (which is more directly connected to the basic memory system, though, note that the frontal lobes are also connected rather directly to the hippocampus, which appears to be the major site of episodic association formation). Shimamura and Squire (1986b) found that Korsakoff patients are selectively impaired in making feeling-of-knowing judgments. Their experiments compared Korsakoff amnesic patients with other amnesic patients — ECT patients and four patients with organic amnesia not attributable to Wernicke-Korsakoff's syndrome. The major finding of interest was that the Korsakoff patients were severely impaired on the feeling-of-knowing task, while the other patients performed at the normal level on the metacognitive task, despite memory impairments.

Many researchers have found impairments, with Korsakoff amnesia, in the release from proactive inhibition (PI) paradigm (Cermak, Butters, & Morienes, 1974; Kinsbourne & Wood, 1975; Moscovitch, 1982; Squire, 1982; Warrington, 1982; Winocur, 1982; Winocur, Kinsbourne, & Moscovitch, 1981). Squire (1982) investigated a variety of patient populations — depressed subjects, ECT patients, a left-diencephalic amnesic — contrasted to a normal control group. All of the patients showed some decrement in overall memory performance. However, only the Korsakoff patients failed to release from PI.

In an effort to become more specific about the location of the deficit leading to metacognitive impairment, Janowsky, Shimamura, and Squire (1989) tested a small group of patients whose only deficit was frontal lobe damage. The extent and the site of the lesions varied greatly over this small group. These patients experienced little memory impairment, and so provide a contrast to the Korsakoff patients who had both metacognitive and memory impairments. Like the Korsakoff patients, these patients manifested selective impairment in their feeling of knowing judgments, though the extent of the impairment was not as pronounced as found with the Korsakoff patients.

There is a suggestion that frontal patients may fail to release from proactive inhibition, and to show other inappropriate novelty-monitoring responses. Moscovitch's (1982) data indicate that most patient groups (control subjects, temporal lobe patients, including those with pronounced hippocampal damage and severe memory deficits, and even right frontal lobe patients) released from PI. But patients with marked left frontal lobe damage showed an impairment. These data are suggestive but *not* yet conclusive (Moscovitch, personal communication, July 1992; Shimamura, personal communication, January 1992). Certainly, if it turns out that the frontal lobes are critically involved in monitoring and control functions that modulate memory, this would comprise a substantial advance in our knowledge about the architecture of mind and brain.

Conclusion

In this chapter people's ability to make feeling-of-knowing judgments has been related to the functioning of a novelty/familiarity monitor. The possibility was suggested that the novelty monitor used in conjunction with human episodic memory may be primarily frontal in nature, with a feedback loop that modulates the hippocampus — the location where episodic associations are formed. The feedback from the novelty monitor controls the weighting of events being entered into memory — resulting in enhanced memory for novel events (to which the person pays attention). The idea that such a monitor might involve the frontal lobes is, of course, consistent with the widely accepted idea that the frontal lobes are responsible for control processes. There are a number of other investigators who point to such strategic, monitoring, and control function for the frontal lobes, though often the kind of monitoring suggested is more complex than that proposed here.

For example, Moscovitch (1989) describes a patient with frontal lobe damage, H.W., who appeared to be unable to control and order his memory. A peculiar kind of confabulation, overlaid with a logic that revealed that the patient realized that the confabulation had to be incorrect, was manifested. And yet, unlike normal people who are troubled by inconsistencies between what they remember and what they know must be the case, this patient appeared unconcerned. For example, when asked how long he had been married (the correct answer being over 36 years), he replied 4 months. When asked, in the next breath, how many children he had, and their ages, he replied four. Then he remarked: "Not bad for 4 months." H.W. was not concerned when he gave the age range of his children as somewhere between 20 and 32. Moscovitch suggests that the hippocampal memory system may retrieve information in an fairly automatized manner. But the normal person, with intact frontal monitoring processes, will check and monitor automatically retrieved information, while a frontally damaged patient such as H.W. does not. Moscovitch suggested, then, that the bizarre confabulations seen in some patients are not due to a basic memory problem, but rather to a control process disturbance. The control processes outlined in this chapter are an order of magnitude simpler than those proposed by Moscovitch. However, the basic idea, that the frontal lobes are responsible for control of many varieties, and that disturbances in metacognitive functions are characteristic of frontal lobe disturbances, is widely accepted.

Suppose one had an impairment in one's ability to detect and appreciate novelty. Suppose one were unable to have (or had distorted) feelings of knowing, that is, not the judgments that subjects make in the experimental tasks that we study, but rather the more basic but rather undifferentiated *feelings* that a particular situation, happening, word, statement, person, is familiar. If one did not have these feelings, then, presumably one would have great difficulty in modulating the hippocampal memory system. But there would be other repercussions. It seems plausible that people use these feelings to appropriately apportion attention or cognitive energy — paying attention to the things that are new and unknown and ignoring those things that are old and well known. Curiosity is aroused when events are novel; restlessness and boredom occur when nothing new is happening. If a person had a breakdown in the ability to distinguish what is familiar from novel it might appear to others as an attentional deficit. It might look like the person were apathetic. It might sometimes seem as if such a person were distractible. It might even look like a failure of drive. Normal people desire to discover what they do not know. But if one had no notion of what one knew or did not know — if one lacked these feelings of novelty — how could one possibly have such a desire? Everything would be, quite literally, the same to such a person — flat. Such symptoms are classic clinical markers of frontal impairments (see Prigatano, 1991).

There are case studies of patients who exhibit a deficit in the phenomenology that may underlie such feelings. They may have the cognitive information (that in the model would result from retrieval) but lack the feelings of familiarity. Stuss (1991b), for example, described one very interesting frontal patient, R.B., who exhibited a rare syndrome called reduplicative paramnesia. This patient believed that a new second wife and family — astonishingly similar to his first wife and family — had been substituted for his first wife and family (who in his mind continued to exist, though he did not make any attempt to find them). He considered that he had eight sons and two daughters with both of the wives having had five children each. These two families were virtually identical, except that the children in the second family were one year older than in the first. (He had been hospitalized for 10 months following the automobile accident that had been the cause of his head injury.) He had no feeling of familiarity, even though he cognitively knew that many, indeed all, features such as the age, height, haircolor, and age were very similar between his first and "second" wife. In discussing his first wife's role in his current situation he said: "She set up the second wife. It was her say-so, her doing that the second girl was at the hospital on the Friday." E: "You're kidding, she brought in the whole family the same. That is very thoughtful of her, and she even got a girl who is just like her." R.B.: "Yes. This is the irony of the whole thing is the girl is very similar to her own appearance and she went out and did it herself." When questioned about the credibility of the story, R.B. said: "I would find it extremely hard to believe, and I probably should be defending myself more so. I have not to date, I have not tried in any way shape or manner or tried to divorce the first wife" (Stuss, 1991b, p. 73).

One possible explanation of R.B.'s unusual belief system is that he experienced a lack of a feeling of familiarity (given by the frontal familiarity monitoring system) when he first encountered his "second" wife. The identity match of that person to the remembered first wife by mere similarity of the cognitive content — representational similarity — in the absence of the reassurance given by the novelty monitoring system was insufficient to allow him to sustain the belief that this first and second were one and the same. Perhaps the frontal damage that R.B. had sustained temporarily took with it his *feeling* of knowing, even though the cognitive information or the knowledge itself could still be retrieved. Perhaps the early, automatic scalar that gives the *feeling* of familiarity is needed for our sense of the rightness or the realness of identity. Conversely, one might suppose that déjà vu presents just the opposite phenomenon — the familiarity monitor spuriously gives a strong feeling of familiarity even though the representational content, on further inspection, belies it.

I do not wish to claim that novelty/familiarity monitoring (and the control attendant on such monitoring) is the only frontal function. There are many theories about the role of the frontal lobes in human cognition (Damasio, 1985; Fuster, 1980; Jouandet & Gazzaniga, 1979; Knight, 1991; Luria, 1966; Shallice and Burgess, 1991; Stuss & Benson, 1986), and most of these include some kind of control function. But many of them include other functions as well (including working memory, see Goldman-Rakic & Friedman, 1991), a point I certainly do not wish to dispute. The conjecture here, though, is that what seems to be a trivial ability — an ability to reliably, immediately, and automatically detect familiarity or novelty prior to associative memory storage — could have major implications for the patterns of results seen in the memory tasks that we study as well as for the person's predictions and metacognitions about those same patterns. More importantly, an impairment in such an ability may have a profound impact on the real world memory functioning, the phenomenology, the ability to get on in the world, the awareness, and the motivation of the human beings who suffer it.

Acknowledgments

This research was supported by National Institute of Mental Health grant MH48066-03. I thank Bennet B. Murdock, Bennett Schwartz, and the Dartmouth cognitive group for their helpful comments.

Note

1. In my first work on this problem, I assumed that the entire trace, including the just-encoded event, was renormalized altogether, but there are some peculiar repercussions of that obligatory "all at once" assumption. For example, an event highly similar to previous events in memory would cause all of the previously stored events to be weighted less than would a novel item. This severe retroactive effect seems unlikely, and so I am presently investigating formulations that stabilize the variability by allowing a combination of decay on the variability of the trace combined with selective weighting of the new association, at time of entry into the trace.

8

Viewing Eyewitness Research from a Metacognitive Perspective

Kenneth R. Weingardt, R. Jacob Leonesio, and
Elizabeth F. Loftus

Over a century of research has established that human memory is
far from the precise, permanent, and objective recorder of information that it is sometimes believed to be. We may forget information
that we have learned (Ebbinghaus, 1885, 1964; Linton, 1982). We
may actively reconstruct events that we have forgotten (Bartlett,
1932). We may even change our memories to accommodate new
information added after the original experience (Carmichael, Hogan, & Walters, 1932; Loftus, Miller & Burns, 1978; Spiro, 1977;
Weingardt, Toland, & Loftus, 1993)

The processes by which we monitor our cognitive processes, particularly that by which we monitor our memory, are also far from
perfect. We may be confident that the response we have selected is
the correct one, when in fact we are wrong (Lichtenstein, Fischhoff,
& Phillips, 1977). We may think that we are fast approaching the
solution to a problem, when in fact we are speeding towards a dead
end (Metcalfe, 1986). We may be certain that our memory for a
particular event or item was the product of our perceptual system,
when in fact the memory in question was the result of a past act of
imagination (Johnson & Raye, 1981).

Nowhere can the imperfect nature of memory and memory monitoring processes have more of an adverse impact as when they must
be relied on by people who have witnessed events of legal significance
such as crimes or accidents. It has long been argued that the testimony of an eyewitness has an enormous impact on the outcome of
a trial. Some have gone so far as to say that "aside from a smoking

pistol, nothing carries as much weight with a jury as the testimony of an actual witness" (Loftus & Ketcham, 1991, p. 16). Given the importance of eyewitness testimony in the legal system, and the questions that psychological research has raised concerning the accuracy of memory and the metacognitive processes by which we monitor it, it is not surprising that many researchers have focused their energies on the applied study of eyewitness perception, memory, and metamemory.

The idea of utilizing the tools of psychology to evaluate the validity of eyewitness testimony is not a new one. The perception and memory of eyewitnesses were the subject of considerable research during the early 1900s (e.g., Munsterberg, 1908; Whipple, 1909). Although eyewitness testimony did not receive much attention from experimental psychologists from the late 1900s until the mid-1970s, vigorous research on this topic during the last decade "has resulted in an applied cognitive psychology of eyewitness behaviour that is a rapidly maturing body of knowledge" (Deffenbacher, 1991, p. 377).

The "rapidly maturing body of knowledge" refers to research examining a plethora of factors that can affect eyewitness performance. Some of these factors, referred to by Wells (1978) as "estimator variables," are not under the control of investigators in a legal case. Estimator variables that have been examined include (1) characteristics of the suspect (e.g., sex, race, physical distinctiveness, and transformation of appearance through disguise), (2) characteristics of the witness (e.g., race, sex, age, and personality traits), and (3) characteristics of the criminal event (e.g., exposure duration, capacity to elicit arousal) (see Deffenbacher, 1991 for a review).

Other factors affecting eyewitness performance, referred to as "system variables" (Wells, 1978), are under the control of investigators in a legal case. Considerable research has explored the system variables that can negatively impact storage of eyewitness memories (for example, material encountered subsequent to an event that may interfere with the witness's accurate recall of that event), as well as those system variables that negatively impact retrieval of such memories (for example, biased versus unbiased procedures for eliciting eyewitness identifications, such as lineups and showups).

It would certainly do the eyewitness literature a great disservice to attempt its comprehensive review in the limited space available here.

In this chapter, we briefly present some of the major findings from but two of the most heavily researched areas in the eyewitness literature — the effects of misleading postevent information and the relationship between witness accuracy and confidence. We then explore how a metacognitive perspective can enhance our understanding of both bodies of literature. Finally, we report the results of a recent experiment using a metacognitive perspective to address the confidence and accuracy of eyewitnesses in the face of misinformation. The reader interested in an in-depth discussion of other areas of the eyewitness literature is referred to Deffenbacher (1991) and Wells and Turtle (1987), both of which are excellent reviews.

The Effects of Misleading Postevent Information

Considerable research has established that new information encountered after witnessing an event can lead to changes in people's recollection of that event. If the new information is misleading, it can cause errors in an eyewitness's account of an event. For example, exposure to misleading postevent information has caused subjects to recall stop signs as yield signs (Loftus, Miller, & Burns, 1978), to recall hammers as screwdrivers (Belli, 1989), and even to recall objects that were not present in the event at all (Loftus, 1975). This phenomenon, by which new information leads to errors in eyewitness reports, has been referred to as the "misinformation effect" (Loftus & Hoffman, 1989).

Most of the research on the misinformation effect (e.g., Lindsay, 1990; Loftus, Donders, Hoffman, & Schooler, 1989; Loftus, Miller, & Burns, 1978; McCloskey & Zaragoza, 1985; Tversky & Tuchin, 1989) has employed a three-stage procedure in which subjects first witness an event by means of a slide sequence or videotape. Then subjects receive new information about the event, often in the form of a written narrative or embedded in questions. Finally, subjects take a test of their memory for the event (figure 8.1). Typically, people in such studies report that they have seen objects or actions as part of an event, when in fact those objects or actions came from other sources, such as the written narrative.

Research on the misinformation effect conducted over the past two decades has provided insights into the conditions under which

K. R. Weingardt, R. J. Leonesio, and E. F. Loftus

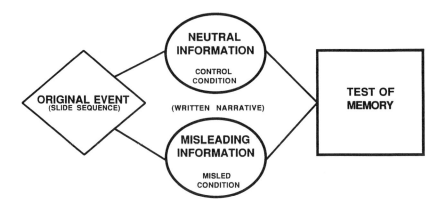

Figure 8.1
The three-stage procedure typically employed in misinformation experiments. In stage one, subjects witness an event, usually in the form of a slide sequence with an accompanying tape-recorded narrative. In stage 2, subjects read a written narrative describing the event they have just witnessed. In this narrative, some subjects encounter misleading information, while other subjects do not. Finally, in stage 3, subjects take a written test of their memory for the events that they saw in the slide sequence.

misinformation is incorporated into eyewitness reports. For example, Dristas and Hamilton (1977) report that subjects' memories for peripheral details of events are more susceptible to the influence of misleading postevent information than memories for more central or salient details. Loftus and Greene (1980) found that misleading suggestions have a more deleterious effect when they are embedded in complex sentences rather than in transparent ones.

In addition to describing the conditions under which misinformation impairs memory performance, misinformation researchers have actively investigated the mechanism by which this impairment occurs. While some researchers (e.g., Lindsay, 1990; Loftus, Schooler, & Wagenaar, 1985) argue that misinformation can irreversibly distort a witness's memory of the original event, others (e.g., Bekerian & Bowers, 1983; McCloskey & Zaragoza, 1985) contend that a misinformation experiment in which a subject witnesses an event, and subsequently receives misleading suggestions about it, results in two memories — one for the event they actually saw and one for the misinformation. As Wells and Turtle (1987) put it, "This co-existence idea speculates that one or the other memory will be retrieved by the person depending on the relative availability of one or the other as determined by such things as recency or context" (p. 373).

The Misinformation Effect as a Metacognitive Monitoring Error

If memories for both the event and the misleading suggestion coexist in the mind of an eyewitness, then perhaps the misinformation effect is a result of witnesses confusing their memory of an event with that of a misleading suggestion. In other words, perhaps the misinformation effect results from eyewitnesses confusing the sources of these two memory traces (Lindsay & Johnson, 1989).

The term metamemory monitoring has been used to describe the process by which individuals make judgments about information in their memory (Hart, 1967a). One type of metamemory monitoring concerns people's ability to monitor the source of their memories. Such judgments about the source of one's memories may involve discriminating "a past perception from a past act of imagination, both of which resulted in memories" (Johnson & Raye, 1981, p. 216). The process by which individuals make such specific discriminations between the products of perception and imagination has been termed "reality monitoring" (Johnson & Raye, 1981), and has been the subject of intense investigation over the past decade (e.g., Foley, Johnson, & Raye, 1983; Johnson, Raye, Foley, & Kim, 1982; Johnson, Foley, Suengas, & Raye, 1988).

In a sense, reality monitoring is a specific type of source monitoring. While reality monitoring refers to the process of discriminating between internally generated and externally derived memories, source monitoring is a more general term that refers to the process of determining the source of one's memories. In the psychological literature, however, source monitoring has taken on a more specific meaning, and is customarily used to refer to the process of distinguishing between memories derived from two externally perceived sources. For example, a typical source monitoring experiment might require subjects to identify who said what in a conversation (Foley & Johnson, 1985; Lindsay & Johnson, 1987), or to determine whether a particular item or event was either seen in a slide sequence or read about in written form (e.g., Lindsay & Johnson, 1989; Zaragoza &

Koshmider, 1989). When a subject misattributes a memory derived from one external source to another external source, a source monitoring or source misattribution error is said to have occurred (e.g., Lindsay & Johnson, 1989; Hashtroudi, Johnson, & Chrosniak, 1989).

Metamemory monitoring judgments such as those required of subjects engaged in source monitoring tasks are thought to be based primarily on metacognitive knowledge consisting "of knowledge or beliefs about what factors or variables act and interact in ways to affect the course and outcome of cognitive enterprises" (Flavell, 1979, p. 4). Briefly, monitoring the source of one's memory is thought to be affected by two different types of metacognitive knowledge (Johnson & Raye, 1981). One type of metacognitive knowledge consists of people's beliefs about the different attributes or class characteristics that can be used to guide their judgments about the origin of memories. According to source monitoring theorists (e.g., Johnson & Raye, 1981; Lindsay & Johnson, 1989), attributes such as the amount of spatial and temporal information associated with a memory trace, or the amount of sensory detail a memory trace contains, convey information about the conditions under which a particular memory was acquired. When required to determine the source of a particular memory, individuals are thought to rely primarily on an evaluation of the attributes associated with that memory. For example, one may decide that a particular memory was externally derived because it contains a lot of spatial and temporal information, has many sensory attributes, and is semantically detailed (Johnson & Raye, 1981).

Another type of metacognitive knowledge that affects source monitoring decisions consists of people's knowledge of how their memories work (i.e., their metamemory assumptions). An example of one such assumption, termed the "it-had-to-be-you" effect, was discovered by Johnson, Raye, Foley, and Foley (1981) in some of their early work on reality monitoring. These authors found that "people seem to assume that they will remember what they themselves have generated and hence, if they do not remember producing a familiar thought, conclude that it must have originated elsewhere" (p. 62), saying in a sense, "I don't remember generating that memory, so it had to be you."

The use and misuse of metacognitive knowledge of the first type discussed, concerning the various attributes of memories derived from different sources, have been used to explain the misinformation effect (e.g., Lindsay & Johnson, 1989; Zaragoza & Koshmidcr, 1989). The general argument is that the memories for the witnessed event and the misleading postevent information are similar with regard to so many of the attributes that people use to determine the source of their memories, people often get the sources of the two memories confused, and source misattribution errors result. As Lindsay and Johnson (1989) put it:

> The procedures used in studies of eyewitness suggestibility create ideal conditions for source monitoring errors. Both the original information and the postevent information concern the same topic, and both are typically presented close together in time, in the same environment, by the same experimenter, and so forth. These similarities make it difficult for subjects to later discriminate between memories derived from the postevent information and memories derived from the original depiction of the event (p. 350).

The operation of the second type of metacognitive knowledge outlined above, namely the various metamemory assumptions that people bring with them into the laboratory, may also be used to explain the misinformation effect. Probably one of the most prevalent assumptions that people make about the nature of their own memories is that there is something innately inferior about their memory ability (Higbee, 1988). Although, as Higbee points out, this belief is almost always unfounded, a subject's belief that "I have a bad memory" may contribute to the misinformation effect in the following manner.

McCloskey and Zaragoza (1985) point out that subjects in most misinformation experiments are led to believe that the written narrative is an accurate description of the events that they have just witnessed. Consequently, they argue that when subjects are tested on their memories for the witnessed event, they may base their responses on information that they know was obtained from the narrative. Subjects' faith in the accuracy of the narrative may interact with their lack of faith in their own memories (i.e., their metamemory assumptions) resulting in a bias toward attributing a memory of uncertain origin to the visual event. Although there is virtually no direct empirical evidence concerning the role that subjects' metamemory assumptions may play in the genesis of the misinformation effect, our current hypotheses seem to us intuitively satisfying and may well be the topic of future research.

In sum, viewing the misinformation effect as an error resulting from the imperfect operation of metamemory monitoring systems has undoubtedly enhanced our understanding of the effect. Considering how fruitful the metacognitive approach has been in this area, research on the source monitoring of subjects in studies of eyewitness suggestibility seems likely to continue. At this point we shall digress briefly from the misinformation effect, and turn our attention to a second area of the eyewitness literature that could profitably be examined through a metacognitive lens — the relationship between eyewitness confidence and accuracy.

The Relationship between Witness Confidence and Accuracy

There are few pieces of evidence more convincing to a jury than an eyewitness who takes the stand and confidently identifies a defendant. Research on this issue has conclusively established that the confidence with which a witness makes such an identification is a strong determinant of whether people believe that the eyewitness's testimony is accurate (Cutler, Penrod, & Stuve, 1988; Lindsay, Wells, & Rumpel, 1981; Wells, Ferguson, & Lindsay, 1981).

Unfortunately, jurors' strong reliance on witness confidence as a measure of accuracy seems to be unjustified. Although some studies have found an appreciable relationship between confidence and accuracy, (e.g., Brigham, Maas, Snyder, & Spaulding, 1982), as a whole, much research on eyewitness identification has consistently found very weak correlations (see reviews by Deffenbacher, 1980; Wells & Murray, 1984).

A metaanalysis of numerous staged-event studies that measured both confidence and accuracy provides the evidence for this assertion (Bothwell, Deffenbacher, & Brigham, 1987). Across 35 studies, this metaanalysis found that the correlation between witness confidence and accuracy was a modest .25 ($d = .52$) (with the 95% confidence interval ranging from .42 down to .08). The Bothwell et al. metaanalysis thus supports Wells and Turtle's (1987) conclusion that the relationship between confidence and accuracy is probably in the positive direction, but nonrobust.

Having established that the correlation between accuracy and confidence is not a robust one, most of the recent research on this relationship has sought to describe the conditions under which it may be stronger. In other words, research in this area has concentrated on identifying variables that moderate the confidence-accuracy relationship. Some moderator variables that have recently been identified include personality variables (Bothwell, Brigham, & Pigott, 1987), feedback about the accuracy of preceding confidence judgments (Sharp, Cutler, & Penrod, 1988), and disguise of the perpetrator (O'Rourke, Penrod, Cutler, & Stuve, 1989).

Deffenbacher (1980) proposed a framework, called the "optimality hypothesis," that he used to predict the conditions under which the relationship between confidence and accuracy will be stronger. Briefly, this hypothesis asserts that the correlation between accuracy and confidence will be stronger when the witnessing conditions are more optimal. The interested reader is referred to Deffenbacher (1980, 1991) for an explication of this hypothesis and the evidence that supports it.

In addition to their interest in identifying the moderators of the accuracy-confidence relationship, researchers have recently become interested in describing this relationship more precisely. The correlation coefficient (the measure of association commonly used in studies of confidence and accuracy) certainly provides us with a comprehensive, overall picture of the relationship between two variables. However, researchers eager for a more precise picture of the accuracy-confidence relationship need more resolution than it can provide. To that end, several researchers (e.g., Wagenaar, 1988) have borrowed a methodology and technique of analysis known as "calibration" from the area of decision making.

The construction of calibration curves, which we describe later, allows one to visually depict the relationship between a subject's confidence in a response and an objective measure of accuracy. As such, the calibration graph perspective enables researchers to quantify the nature of the confidence-accuracy relationship more fully.

The Calibration of Eyewitnesses

In many respects, asking people to provide confidence ratings, like asking them to determine the source of their memories, is a retrospective metamemory monitoring task (Nelson, 1992). As is the case when subjects are engaged in a source monitoring task, subjects who rate the confidence of their answers are making retrospective judgments about information in memory. The calibration perspective provides a valuable tool in the description and explanation of how a subject's metamemory monitoring judgments in the form of confidence ratings relate to the accuracy of report.

In the type of calibration study that has long been popular in studies of decision making (see review by Lichtenstein, Fischhoff, & Phillips, 1977), confidence ratings provided by subjects are treated as probability judgements. The appropriateness of confidence is then measured by comparing these assessed probabilities with the observed relative frequencies of being correct (Koriat, Lichtenstein, & Fischhoff, 1980).

This comparison of probability judgments and actual outcomes is often expressed using calibration graphs. An example of this type of graph is shown in figure 8.2. In such a display of data, the subjects' probability judgment (i.e., confidence judgment) is plotted on the horizontal axis. The proportion of correct responses (i.e., accuracy) is plotted on the vertical axis.

Using this graph then, one can determine the proportion of times the target event actually happened (the accuracy level) when a particular probability judgment (i.e., confidence judgment) was offered (Yates, 1990). For example, say a subject is 100% confident in her responses to 10 questions, and we want to determine the proportion of times she was actually correct (i.e., how accurate she is). If a calibration graph has been constructed, this determination is easy to make. We simply find the point on the graph corresponding to a probability judgment of 1.0, and examine the vertical axis to find the average confidence rating for that probability judgment (in this case, 80%).

The diagonal line in figure 8.2 represents what is known as "perfect calibration." Note that for each point on this line, the probability judgment (or confidence) is exactly equal to the proportion correct

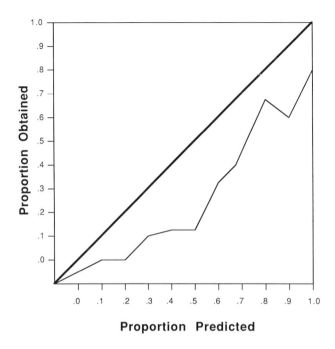

Figure 8.2
A typical calibration graph. "proportion predicted" refers to subjective confidence judgments, while "proportion obtained" refers to the objective probability that subjects will respond correctly and is thus a measure of accuracy. The dark diagonal line is the line of perfect calibration and the lighter line is the calibration line of a hypothetical subject or group of subjects

(or accuracy). Responses along this line of perfect calibration would be produced by a clairvoyant if she were to make confidence judgments about her responses. Since the clairvoyant can see the future, her confidence ratings would precisely predict the actual probability that the responses she selects are the correct ones.

The use of calibration curves rather than simple correlations as a means of describing the confidence-accuracy relationship has a number of distinct advantages. First, the calibration graph perspective allows one to visually determine the average accuracy score attained for subjects at each confidence level, and vice versa. For example, as was pointed out earlier, the calibration curve enables us to determine the average proportion of correct responses for subjects who claim to be 100% confident in their identification (again, refer to figure 8.2). This represents a distinct advantage over the correlation coefficient, which enables one to look at only the overall relationship between confidence and accuracy.

Second, calibration curves allow us to assess how "well calibrated" eyewitnesses are. Generally speaking, a subject is said to be well calibrated if "over the long run, for all answers assigned a given probability, the proportion correct equals the probability assigned" (Koriat et al., 1980, p. 172). In other words, "we say that an individual's probability judgments are well-calibrated to the extent that those judgments match the proportions of times that the target event actually occurs" (Yates, 1990, p. 50).

A well-calibrated individual tends to remain on, or near, the line of perfect calibration. Thus, we can conclude that their confidence ratings are good predictors of their accuracy. The same conclusion can be drawn if one was provided with a coefficient indicating a strong correlation between confidence and accuracy. But what if it is discovered that an individual's confidence judgments are *not* good predictors of their accuracy? In this case, a low correlation coefficient would certainly let us know that we should not trust that individual's confidence judgments as valid predictors of their accuracy scores. Unfortunately, for those interested in precisely describing the characteristics of the relationship in an effort to understand why it is so weak, the correlation coefficient is rather uninformative.

In contrast, the calibration graph perspective allows us to examine the pattern of responses that gives rise to a weak relationship between confidence and accuracy. To see this, recall the first advantage of using calibration graphs, namely that they enable us to determine an individual's average accuracy score for each confidence level. Using this information, we may find that subjects' confidence judgments are only weakly correlated with their accuracy because they are "overconfident," meaning that they consistently overestimate the probability of being correct in their identification (i.e., their confidence scores are consistently higher than their accuracy scores). Conversely, we may find that an individual's confidence judgments are weakly correlated with their accuracy because they are "underconfident," meaning that they consistently underestimate the probability of being correct (i.e., their confidence scores are consistently lower than their accuracy scores).

It is important to note that an individual's overall pattern of results need not be characterized by either overconfidence or underconfidence. In fact, an individual subject may exhibit both types of miscalibration in a single set of responses. For example, figure 8.3 represents the hypothetical responses of a single subject to a single set of stimuli. Notice that this subject exhibits marked underconfidence when his accuracy is high, while simultaneously exhibiting marked overconfidence when his actual accuracy is low. The ability to visually detect such varied patterns of miscalibration is perhaps the single most important advantage the calibration graph approach provides.

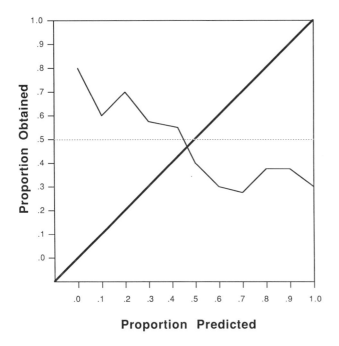

Proportion Predicted

Figure 8.3
The dark diagonal line is the line of perfect calibration. The lighter solid line is the calibration curve for a subject who is underconfident at low levels of confidence and overconfident at high levels of confidence. The dotted line is the line of nil discrimination.

A final advantage of using the calibration graph approach is that it provides us with the opportunity to look at subjects' discrimination as well as their calibration. Briefly, "discrimination concerns the ability of a person to distinguish instances when a target event is going to occur from those when it is not" (Yates, 1990, p. 57). In the context of eyewitness identification then, "discrimination concerns the ability of the witness to distinguish situations where his or her judgments are more likely to be accurate, from situations where they are less likely to be accurate" (Miyamoto, 1991).

On a calibration graph, discrimination is indicated by the extent to which the points deviate from the horizontal line of nil discrimination (see figure 8.3). If a subject is completely unable to distinguish situations in which her judgments will be accurate from those in which her judgments will be inaccurate (for example, if the subject is simply guessing), we would expect all of the points on her calibration graph to lie along a horizontal line at an elevation corresponding to the sample base rate for the target event (this is usually the probability that a subject who is guessing randomly will guess correctly).

Good discrimination can be revealed in a calibration graph by looking at "the extent that the vertical locations of the points deviate from the horizontal sample base rate line, and each tends toward either the top or the bottom of the figure" (Yates, 1990, p. 55). Consequently, if a subject were to exhibit perfect discrimination, as would be expected from the clairvoyant we referred to earlier, we would expect to see each of the points on the calibration graph at either the extreme top or extreme bottom of the graph.

In conclusion, it is important to point out that discrimination and calibration are quite different processes. While discrimination concerns an individual's capacity to distinguish instances when a target event is going to occur from instances when it will not, irrespective of the labels that one assigns to those instances, calibration reflects an individual's ability to assign numerical labels (i.e., probabilities) to those instances.

With this background information about the calibration graph approach behind us, we turn our attention to a series of experiments that have recently been conducted at the University of Washington. These experiments are among the first to have used the calibration approach to investigate the relationship between eyewitness confidence and accuracy (but see also Wagenaar, 1988). The background information provided in the preceding pages will hopefully be sufficient for readers to interpret our new findings. Those interested in a more in-depth discussion of calibration and discrimination are referred to J. Frank Yates' recent textbook on judgment and decision-making processes (Yates, 1990).

The Calibration of Eyewitnesses in the Face of Misinformation

As was discussed previously, the relationship between eyewitness confidence and accuracy has been the subject of intense empirical investigation in recent years (Deffenbacher, 1991). Several studies have sought to determine how this relationship is influenced by exposure to misleading postevent information. For example, Loftus, Donders, Hoffman, and Schooler (1989) conducted an experiment using the typical three-stage misinformation paradigm (subjects see an event, read a misleading written narrative, and take a memory test). For each question on the test, subjects rated the confidence in their response using a five-point rating scale. The primary finding of this experiment, for purposes of the present discussion, was that misled subjects exhibited as much confidence in their incorrect responses based on misinformation, as they did in their genuine memories based on information actually witnessed in the event.

This result leads to a number of questions that the calibration graph perspective can help us answer. An important question concerns *why* misled subjects exhibit as much confidence in their incorrect responses as they do in their correct ones. Are subjects overconfident in their misinformation-based responses? If so, are they more overconfident when the objective probability of being correct is low, when the objective probability of being correct is high, or across the board? Are they generally underconfident in their responses to items about which they did not receive misinformation? If so, when do they exhibit this underconfidence? In general, what patterns of miscalibration does exposure to misinformation engender? Does misinformation impair subjects' discrimination?

In an effort to address these issues, we conducted two experiments that examined the calibration of eyewitnesses who had been exposed to misleading postevent information, and those who had not. These experiments both employed the standard three-stage misinformation paradigm in which subjects were first shown a videotape depicting a robbery. Then, immediately after viewing the videotaped event, subjects read a narrative describing the event that they had just witnessed. This narrative contained either neutral or misleading information about four critical details that were seen during the videotaped robbery. Finally, subjects were tested on their memories for the robbery that they had previously witnessed. After each item on the test, subjects provided a confidence judgment, expressed as a percent chance that the answer they chose was the correct one. The results, interpreted using the calibration graph approach, revealed some distinctly different patterns of miscalibration exhibited by subjects who had been misinformed about the details seen in the event, and those who had not.

Experiment 1

Method

In the first experiment, 229 students watched a 4 minute videotaped portrayal of a robbery. The video depicts two police officers "walking their beat" who stumble on a robbery in progress at a liquor store. This film, which was originally developed for police training, has been used extensively by eyewitness researchers (e.g., Geiselman, Fisher, MacKinnon, & Holland, 1985).

Immediately after watching the video, subjects read a written narrative describing the events depicted in the video. This narrative, which was designed to look like a newspaper article covering the robbery that subjects had just witnessed, inaccurately described two of the four critical items, while describing the remaining two critical items in neutral terms. The items described inaccurately in the narrative thereby served as "misled" items, while those described neutrally served as "control" items.

The four critical items were (1) the number of suspects who committed the robbery (subjects saw two in the video, while some were misled to believe that there were three), (2) the race of the suspect who was shot down by the police during the course of the robbery (subjects saw a white perpetrator be slain in the video while some were misled to believe that the perpetrator was black), (3) the type of store robbed (subjects saw the robbery occur in a liquor store in the video while some were misled to believe that it was a drug store), and (4) the name of the street on which the robbery occurred (subjects saw Maple street on a sign in the video, while some were misled to believe that it was Elm street). Items were counterbalanced across subject groups such that for each item, half the subjects received misinformation about that item in the narrative and the other half received neutral information. More specifically, equal numbers of subjects were run in each of two conditions. In condition A, subjects received misinformation about items 1 and 3 while receiving neutral information about items 2 and 4. In condition B, subjects received misinformation about items 2 and 4, while receiving neutral information about items 1 and 3.

Finally, the subjects were administered a nine-item, two-alternative forced-choice recognition test. Of the nine items on the test, four were critical items. Each item was a brief question about information that was seen in the film, and required subjects to chose between two alternative responses. An example of one such question is "The officers walked down (1) Maple Street, (2) Elm Street."

Of course, the calibration approach requires that confidence judgments be elicited from subjects on each of the items to which they responded. Consequently, after each item, subjects were asked to provide a confidence judgment expressed as a percent chance (from 50% to 100%) that the answer they chose was the correct one.

For the calibration analysis to be meaningful, it must be established that subjects have a conceptual understanding of the probability judgments that they are asked to make, and that they know how to use confidence scale appropriately. Consequently, some rather explicit instructions were given in this regard. Specifically, subjects were told that

After each response express the degree of certainty that you have in your answer by recording the likelihood that your answer is correct. You may respond with any whole number between 50% and 100%. . . . Each of these percentages represents the number of times that you expect to be correct if you made 100 judgments at that same degree of certainty. For example, if your "chances that your answer is correct" is 73% then you expect to be correct 73 times out of 100 judgments that you gave this degree (73%) of certainty for. Because there are only two alternatives (one of which is correct) you have at least a 50% chance of being correct.

Another important part of the instructions emphasized that subjects should base their responses on what they *saw or heard in the film.* Without such an instruction, some might argue that subjects could be basing their responses on information that they know was obtained in the narrative in an effort to prove themselves vigilant, "good" subjects (Lindsay, 1990). Before allowing subjects to begin the test, the experimenter repeated and rephrased all of the instructions several times to ensure that subjects understood them.

Results and Discussion[1]

Was There a Misinformation Effect?
In any experiment using the misinformation paradigm, one of the first questions to ask is, "Was there a misinformation effect?" In other words, did subjects who received misleading postevent information perform more poorly on the test of memory than control subjects who were not exposed to misinformation? In this experiment, as in many others that have used this paradigm, subjects who were misled did in fact exhibit poorer recognition performance. While the mean proportion correct for control subjects was 92%, the mean proportion correct for misled subjects was only 45%. This difference is, of course, highly significant [$t(228) = 12.50$, $p < .001$].

The Confidence Data
Turning next to the confidence data, we first describe how the current results replicate and extend those of Loftus et al. (1989). Recall their finding that misled subjects exhibited as much confidence in their incorrect responses based on misinformation as they did in their genuine memories based on information actually witnessed in the event. In the current experiment, misled subjects' confidence in their incorrect memories not only met, but exceeded their confidence in their genuine memories. When they were incorrect in their responses, misled subjects had a median confidence rating of 90%. When they were correct, their median confidence rating was a full 10 percentage points lower (80%).

The next analysis compares the confidence ratings of misled subjects versus control subjects to explore the issue of "true belief." Considerable empirical evidence indicates that misled subjects often truly believe that they have seen items that in reality were only suggested to them (e.g., Lindsay, 1990; Loftus & Hoffman, 1989, see Weingardt, Toland, & Loftus, 1993, for a review) If confidence in one's response is a reflection of the degree to which one truly believes that one's response is correct, and misled subjects truly believe that they have seen suggested items, then one would expect misled subjects to exhibit a higher degree of confidence in their incorrect responses than control subjects.

This prediction was borne out in this experiment. On the average, subjects who received misinformation gave a median confidence rating of 90% for their incorrect responses. In contrast, subjects who did not receive misinformation gave a median confidence rating of 62% for their incorrect responses. This difference was found to be highly significant using a Kruskal–Wallace test [$X^2(1) = 6.92$, $p = .006$].

This last result indicates that misled subjects exhibited overconfidence in some sense of the word. When faced with misinformation, subjects consistently overestimated the probability of being correct in their responses. Are these subjects, however, overconfident in a stricter sense of the word? By this, we mean are their confidence scores consistently higher than their accuracy scores? Furthermore, do they exhibit overconfidence across the board, or only for very difficult items that they have a high probability of getting incorrect? How do these patterns of results compare to those of control subjects? These and other more detailed questions can be addressed by reference to the calibration graph depicted in figure 8.4.

The Calibration Graph
Recall from the previous discussion of calibration graphs that the "proportion obtained," which can be conceptualized as accuracy, is plotted on the vertical axis, while the "proportion predicted," in this case confidence judgments, is plotted on the horizontal axis. Recall further that the diagonal line represents the line of perfect calibration. Points lying below the diagonal are said to indicate over-

confidence, while points lying above the line are said to indicate underconfidence.

Notice that this graph differs in two respects from the calibration curves previously displayed. First, the calibration curves in figure 8.4 have numbers next to each of the points on them. These numbers indicate the number of observations that each point contains. We have included these numbers so that the reader can better judge the stability of the points (presumably the more observations per point, the more stable that point, and the more seriously we should take it). Because the last four points in each of the two curves (the segment of the curves above a proportion predicted of 0.7) contain a greater number of observations than the preceding two points, we focus our attention, and most of the comments that follow, on the latter portion of the two curves.

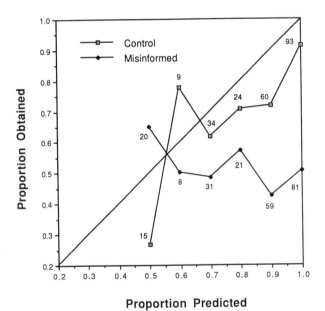

Figure 8.4
Calibration curve for experiment 1. The numbers indicate the number of observations. Proportion predicted refers to subjective confidence judgments, while the proportion obtained refers to the objective probability that subjects will respond correctly and is thus a measure of accuracy.

The second feature that differentiates figure 8.4 from the calibration graphs previously encountered is that it contains two different calibration curves on the same graph. One curve was generated for items about which subjects received misinformation (the "misinformed" curve), and one was generated for items about which subjects did not receive misinformation (the "control" curve). Plotting these two curves on the same graph facilitates comparisons between them.

There are a number of aspects of this calibration graph that warrant attention. First, consider the overall slopes of the control and misinformed lines. The slope of the control line is noticeably closer to the line of perfect calibration than is the slope of the misinformed line. This relationship implies that subjects calibration for control items is better than their calibration for misled items.

Furthermore, as we expected from our analysis of the confidence data reported earlier, an inspection of this graph indicates that the particular "brand" of miscalibration exhibited by subjects who received misinformation is overconfidence in their responses. As the graphs reveal, when misled subjects give very high confidence ratings (e.g., 70, 90, and 100%), their accuracy is only at or near chance (50%).

The fact that misled subjects' accuracy is at or near chance levels across the board indicates that misinformed subjects have poor discrimination (i.e., misled subjects are poorly able to distinguish situations where their judgments are more likely to be accurate from situations where they are less likely to be accurate). This lack of discrimination on the part of misled subjects stands in stark contrast to the relatively good discrimination evidenced by subjects on control items. Notice, for example, how the points on the control line, especially those that correspond to high levels of confidence, tend toward the top of the figure.

A final feature of this calibration graph that warrants comment concerns the levels of accuracy attained by subjects who were absolutely certain that their responses were correct (i.e., the accuracy of subjects who gave confidence ratings of 100%). Notice first that subjects who were certain about their responses to control items were in fact correct over 90% of the time. On the other hand, when subjects exhibited certainty that their responses on misinformation items were correct, they were actually correct less than 50% of the time (i.e., their performance was even slightly below chance).

In sum, subjects in this experiment who received misinformation exhibited marked overconfidence in their responses, particularly at certainty. It is tempting to conclude that this overconfidence on the part of misled subjects arose out of their erroneous belief that they saw the suggested item in the event. In other words, one could conclude on the basis of the results that misinformed subjects exhibit overconfidence in their incorrect responses (based on information contained in the narrative) because they truly thought that they saw the items that, in reality, were only suggested to them. However, what if subjects in this experiment had simply based their responses on information that they know was contained in the narrative? If this were the case, we would expect the same pattern of overconfidence to emerge, but we would not be able to draw any conclusions about how true belief in misinformation affects the relationship between confidence and accuracy.

In our second experiment, to be described below, we modified the critical test questions in an effort to ensure that subjects based their responses only on information that they knew was obtained from the videotape. If misled subjects in this second experiment continued to exhibit marked overconfidence in their responses, we could more confidently conclude that this overconfidence was reflective of true belief in the misleading suggestions, rather than demand characteristics or some other explanation.

Experiment 2

Method

As in experiment 1, the 202 subjects who participated in experiment 2 first viewed the videotaped liquor store robbery. As in the previous experiment, subjects then read the written postevent narrative describing the event. Finally, as in the first experiment, subjects took a recognition test of memory.

This recognition test was similar to that employed in the first experiment; the instructions that accompanied experiment 2 were virtually identical to those employed in experiment 1. The overall structure of the nine-item two-alternative forced-choice test was also preserved. Furthermore, the content of the questions was identical to those previously employed (i.e., subjects were asked questions about the same four critical items).

The structure of the questions, however, was somewhat different. To remind subjects that they should base their responses exclusively on information that they know was obtained from the videotape, each of the questions in the current experiment emphasized that subjects should base their responses on what they saw. For example, in the current experiment, subjects were asked "What street did you *see* the officers walk down? (1) Maple Street, (2) Elm Street." Questions employed in the first experiment did not have this same emphasis. For example, the corresponding critical question in experiment 1 was "The officers walked down (1) Maple Street, (2) Elm Street."

Given this modification, do subjects continue to exhibit the misinformation effect? Furthermore, do subjects who receive misinformation continue to be more poorly calibrated and more overconfident in their responses? Finally, does the discrimination of misled subjects improve when the questions force them to base their responses exclusively on information that they remember from the videotape?

Results and Discussion

The Misinformation Effect

Do subjects who have received misleading postevent information continue to exhibit poorer recognition test performance than control subjects when the questions focus them on information that they remember from the video? The data indicate that subjects in this experiment did indeed exhibit evidence of a misinformation effect. While the mean proportion correct for control subjects was 78%, the mean proportion correct for misled subjects was 62%. Although this difference is not as large as that obtained in experiment 1, it is statistically significant [$t(200) = 4.7$, $p < .05$].

The Confidence Data

Did the pattern of results that emerged from the confidence data in experiment 1 replicate when the emphasis of the questions was changed in experiment 2? First, recall that in experiment 1, subjects who received misinformation actually exhibited more confidence in their incorrect responses than they did in their correct responses. This result also emerged from experiment 2, but the difference was miniscule. While misled subjects assigned a mean confidence rating of 78% to their incorrect responses, the mean confidence rating assigned to their correct responses was 77%. This difference was obviously not statistically significant.

Did misled subjects in experiment 2 exhibit a higher degree of confidence in their incorrect responses than control subjects? As in experiment 1, the answer to this question was in the affirmative. While subjects who received misinformation gave a median confidence rating of 78% for their incorrect responses, control subjects who did not receive misinformation gave a median confidence rating of 68% for their incorrect responses. This difference was statistically significant using a Kruskal–Wallace test [$X^2(1) = 6.10, p = .01$].

The Calibration Graph

Two calibration curves were generated (see figure 8.5). Both of these curves have been plotted on the same graph to facilitate comparisons, and each point has been labeled with the number of observations it contains to enable the reader to better judge the stability of each point.

You may have noticed that the scales used in figures 8.4 and 8.5 are different. Neither of the scales ranges from 0.0 to 1.0, as is often seen on calibration graphs (see figure 8.2). Scales ranging from 0.5 to 1.0 are typically used when there is a two-alternative forced-choice test because the probability of being correct by chance on such a test is 0.5, and one would not expect subjects to perform below chance levels. Although we employed a two-alternative forced-choice test in our experiments, we were unable to use this 0.5 to 1.0 scale in reporting our results because subjects in both of our experiments performed below the chance level (0.5) on several of the judgments that they made. For example, control subjects in experiment 1 who were 50% confident in their responses were actually correct only 25% of

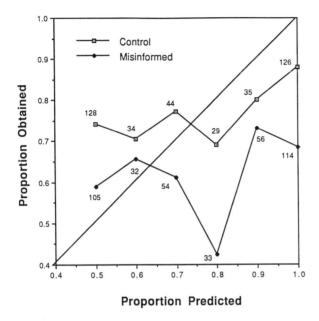

Figure 8.5
Calibration curve for experiment 2. The numbers indicate the number of observations. Proportion predicted refers to subjective confidence judgments, while the proportion obtained refers to the objective probability that subjects will respond correctly and is thus a measure of accuracy.

the time. Similarly, misled subjects in experiment 2 who were 80% confident in their responses were actually correct about 40% of the time. To plot these points, we had to extend the scales down to 0.2 in experiment 1 and 0.4 in experiment 2.

What then can be inferred from an examination of the calibration graph for experiment 2? To begin, consider the relative slopes of the two curves. As in experiment 1, it is clear that the control line is much closer to the line of perfect calibration than the misinformed line. Again, the implication is that subjects are much better calibrated when they do not receive misinformation.

Inspection of the misinformed line further tells us that when subjects do receive misinformation, they are often overconfident in their responses. Although subjects evidenced overconfidence on all of their confidence judgments above 70% (0.7 proportion predicted), the tremendous amount of variance in the degree of overconfidence exhibited makes generalization difficult. For example, when misled subjects expressed 90% confidence in a response, they were actually correct on average approximately 73% of the time. Compare this to responses for which misled subjects expressed 80% confidence. For this level of confidence, misled subjects were correct less then 50% of the time.

While subjects who received misinformation exhibited varying degrees of overconfidence at the "high end" (i.e., when subjects gave high confidence ratings), they simultaneously exhibited underconfidence at the "low end" (i.e., when they gave low confidence ratings). Control subjects exhibited this same pattern. However, they were less overconfident in their responses on the "high end" and *much* more underconfident in their responses on the "low end." For example, when control subjects expressed a mere 50% confidence in their responses, they were actually correct almost 75% of the time.

Briefly turning to the topic of discrimination, one might be tempted to conclude that the discrimination of misled subjects is better in experiment 2 than it was in experiment 1. After all, the points on the misinformed calibration curve do appear to tend toward the top and bottom of the figure more in figure 8.5 than in figure 8.4. Unfortunately, this conclusion is unjustified because, as was pointed out above, the axes of the two figures are scaled differently. While the axes in figure 8.4 range from 0.2 to 1.0, the axes in figure 8.5 range from 0.5 to 1.0. Thus, the same difference would appear larger in figure 8.5. When one takes this fact into account, it becomes apparent that the proportion obtained for misled subjects in experiment 2, as in experiment 1, tends to bounce around the target base rate of 0.5.

A final feature of this calibration graph worth mentioning concerns the points of the two curves at certainty (1.0 proportion predicted). As was the case in experiment 1, when control subjects were certain that their response was correct, they were actually correct nearly 90% of the time. In contrast, misled subjects who were 100% confident that their response was the correct one were actually correct only about 70% of the time. Again, it appears that subjects who received misinformation were more overconfident in their responses at certainty than were control subjects. Although the discrepancy is not as large as it was in experiment 1 (where misinformed subjects who were 100% confident in their response were actually performing at chance levels), the difference in the present experiment is still a large one.

General Discussion

What, then, can be said about the confidence–accuracy relationship in the face of misinformation? The primary conclusion that can drawn from the two studies reported above is that subjects who are exposed to misleading postevent information are more poorly calibrated than subjects who are exposed to neutral information. Furthermore, subjects who receive misinformation consistently demonstrate overconfidence in their responses. This overconfidence is most pronounced at the "high end," and is readily apparent even at certainty.

It should be noted that it would not have been possible to draw any of these conclusions had we not chosen to adopt the calibration graph approach. The research that we have reported demonstrates many of the distinct advantages that the calibration perspective can afford those interested in describing the confidence–accuracy relationship in detail.

Conclusion

Consider a typical situation in which an eyewitness is asked to report what he or she has seen. Whether the witness is asked to identify a perpetrator, describe the events leading up to an automobile accident, or discriminate between information actually witnessed in an event or read about in an newspaper article, he or she is required to make judgments about information in memory. In metacognitive terms then, eyewitnesses are often required to make metamemory monitoring judgments. As should be evident from our discussion of the misinformation effect as a metacognitive error, the literature on metamemory monitoring can provide valuable insights into the reasons for poor eyewitness memory performance.

The two experiments reported in this chapter clearly demonstrate that the concept of retrospective metamemory monitoring can also be profitably used to examine the relationship between eyewitness confidence and accuracy. The results of our experiments are certainly encouraging and suggest that the calibration graph approach can be a powerful tool in our effort to further quantify this relationship.

In sum, viewing the eyewitness literature from a metacognitive perspective has been quite a profitable undertaking. It is our hope that future eyewitness researchers will avail themselves of this perspective and all of the advantages that it can afford them.

Acknowledgments

Significant portions of the research described in this chapter were supported by a grant from the National Institute of Mental Health to E. F. Loftus.

Note

1. Due to an error in data collection, the following analyses are based only on subjects in condition B.

9

Memory and Metamemory Considerations in the Training of Human Beings

Robert A. Bjork

The conventialities of portrait painting are only tolerable in one who is a good painter — if he is only a good portrait painter he is nobody. Try to become a painter first and then apply your knowledge to a special branch — but do not begin by learning what is required for a special branch, or you will become a mannerist.

John Singer Sargent

The mistake we pop stars fall into is stating the obvious. "War is bad. Starvation is bad. Don't chop down the rain forest." It's boring. It's much better to hide it, to fold the meaning into some sort of metaphor or maze, if you like, and for the listener to have a journey to find it.

Sting

In recent papers, Christina and Bjork (1991) and Schmidt and Bjork (1992) have argued that training programs are often much less effective than they could be. A central part of the argument is that individuals responsible for training are often misled as to what are, and are not, effective conditions of practice. Conditions that enhance performance during training are assumed, implicitly or explicitly, to be the conditions of choice with respect to enhancing the goal of training: namely, long-term posttraining performance. That assumption, however, is frequently questionable and sometimes dramatically wrong. Manipulations that speed the rate of acquisition during training can fail to support long-term posttraining performance, while other manipulations that appear to introduce difficulties for the learner during training can enhance posttraining performance.

The goal of the present chapter is to examine two other contributors to nonoptimal training: (1) the learner's own misreading of his or her progress and current state of knowledge during training, and (2) nonoptimal relationships between the conditions of training and the conditions that can be expected to prevail in the posttraining real-world environment.

Memory Considerations

The Goals of Training

The principal goals of a typical training program are to produce optimal transfer of that training to an anticipated posttraining environment of some kind. With rare exceptions, then, the goals of training are long-term goals. We would like the knowledge and skills acquired during training to be durable, not only in the sense of surviving from the end of training to a later time when that knowledge or skill is demanded in a real-world setting, but also in the sense of surviving periods of disuse in the posttraining environment itself.

An equally important long-term goal of training is to produce a mental representation of the knowledge or skill in question that allows for flexible access to that knowledge or skill. We would like the learner to be able to generalize appropriately, that is, to be able to draw on what was learned during training in order to perform adequately in real-world conditions that differ from the conditions of training. Verifying that some individual has ready access to critical skills and knowledge in some standard situation does not, unfortunately, ensure that individual will perform adequately in a different situation, or on altered versions of the task in question. Even superficial changes can disrupt performance markedly. Perceived similarity, or the lack thereof, of new tasks to old tasks is a critical factor in the transfer of training (see, e.g., Gick & Holyoak, 1980). To the extent feasible, a training program should provide a learned representation that permits the learner to recognize when the knowledge and skills acquired during training are and are not applicable to new problems.

Stated in terms of human memory, then, we would like a training program not only to produce a stored representation of the targeted knowledge in long-term memory, but also to yield a representation that remains accessible (recallable) as time passes and contextual cues change. In general, it is explicit or conceptually driven processing of information that we want to optimize, not implicit or stimulus-driven processing (for discussions of the distinction, see Richardson-Klavehn & Bjork, 1988; Roediger & Blaxton, 1987; Roediger & McDermott, 1993; Schacter, 1987; Shimamura, 1986), and we want to optimize the ability to access knowledge and skills, not the ability to judge whether knowledge or skills produced by someone else seem appropriate to the situation. Such distinctions are discussed further in the metamemory section of this chapter.

Relevant Peculiarities of the Human as a Memory Device

Toward achieving the goals of training, it is important to remind ourselves of some of the ways that humans differ from man-made recording devices. We do not, for example, store information in our long-term memories by making any kind of literal recording of that information, but, rather, by relating that new information to what we already know — that is, to the information that already exists in our memories. The process is fundamentally semantic in nature; we store information in terms of its meaning to us, defined by its associations and relationships to other information in our memories. For all practical purposes, our capacity for such storage is essentially unlimited — storing information, rather than using up memory capacity, appears to create opportunities for additional storage. It also appears that once new information is successfully mapped on to existing knowledge in long-term memory, it remains stored, if not necessarily accessible, for an indefinitely long period of time.

The process of accessing stored information given certain cues also does not correspond to the "playback" of a typical recording device. The retrieval of stored information is a fallible, probabilistic process that is more inferential and reconstructive than literal. Information that is readily accessible at one point in time, or in a given situation, may be impossible to recall at another point in time, or in another situation. The information in our long-term memories that is, and is not, accessible at a given point in time is heavily dependent on the cues available to us, not only on cues that explicitly guide the search for the information in question, but also on environmental, inter-personal, mood-state, and body-state cues.

A final relevant peculiarity of human memory is that the act of retrieving information is itself a potent learning event. Rather than being left in the same state it was in prior to being recalled, the retrieved information becomes more recallable in the future than it would have been without having been accessed. In that sense, the act of retrieval is a "memory modifier" (Bjork, 1975). As a learning event, in fact, it appears that a successful retrieval can be considerably more potent than an additional study opportunity, particularly in terms of facilitating long-term recall (see, e.g., Gates, 1917, Hogan & Kintsch, 1971; Landauer & Bjork, 1978). Though not as relevant to the con-cerns of this chapter, there is also evidence that such positive effects of prior recall on the later recall of the retrieved items can be accom-panied by impaired retrieval of competing information, that is, of other items associated to the same cue or set of cues as the retrieved items (for discussions of such retrieval dynamics, see Anderson & Bjork, 1993; Bjork & Bjork, 1992).

In a very general way, then, creating durable and flexible access to critical information in memory is partly a matter of achieving a cer-tain type of encoding of that information, and partly a matter of practicing the retrieval process. On the encoding side, we would like the learner to achieve, for lack of a better word, an *understanding* of the knowledge in question, defined as an encoding that is part of a broader framework of interrelated concepts and ideas. Critical infor-mation needs to be multiply encoded, not bound to single sets of semantic or situational cues. On the retrieval side, practicing the actual production of the knowledge and procedures that are the target of training is essential: One chance to actually put on, fasten, and inflate an inflatable life vest, for example, would be of more value — in terms of the likelihood that one could actually perform that procedure correctly in an emergency — than the multitude of times any frequent flier has sat on an airplane and been shown the process by a steward or stewardess. Similar to the argument for mul-tiple encoding, it is also desirable to induce successful access to knowledge and procedures in a variety of situations that differ in the cues they do and do not provide.

The Need to Introduce Difficulties for the Learner

What specific manipulations of training, then, are best able to foster the long-term goals of training, whether stated in terms of measures of posttraining performance or in terms of underlying memory representations? Attempting to answer that question in any detail would involve prescribing a mixture of desirable manipulations, and there would clearly be some disagreement among researchers as to what set of manipulations constitute the optimal mixture. Any such prescription would also need to be tailored to the specifics of a given training mission. Whatever the exact mixture of manipulations that might turn out to be optimal, however, one general characteristic of that mixture seems clear: It would introduce many more difficulties and challenges for the learner than are present in typical training routines. Recent surveys of the relevant research literatures (see, e.g., Christina & Bjork, 1991; Farr, 1987; Reder & Klatzky, 1993; Schmidt & Bjork, 1992) leave no doubt that many of the most effective manipulations of training — in terms of post-training retention and transfer — share the property that they introduce difficulties for the learner. Some of the clearest examples of such manipulations are the following.

Varying the Conditions of Practice
It has now been demonstrated in a variety of ways, and with a variety of motor, verbal, and problem-solving tasks, that introducing variation and/or unpredictability in the training environment causes difficulty for the learner but enhances long-term performance — particularly the ability to transfer training to novel but related task environments. Where several differing motor-movement tasks are to be learned, for example, scheduling the practice trials on those tasks in random fashion, rather than blocking the trials by task type, has been shown to impair performance during training but enhance long-term performance (Shea & Morgan, 1979; Hall, Domingues, & Cavazos, 1992). Analogous results have been obtained with problem-solving tasks (e.g., Reder, Charney, & Morgan, 1986). Similarly, varying the parameters of a to-be-learned task — by, for example, varying the speed or distance of a target — impairs performance during

training but enhances posttraining performance (e.g., Catalano & Kleiner, 1984; Kerr & Booth, 1978). And the effects of increasing the variety, types, or range of exercises or problems (e.g., Carson & Wiegand, 1979; Gick & Holyoak, 1983; Homa & Cultice, 1984) tend to exhibit the same general pattern. Even varying the incidental environmental context in which learning sessions are situated has been shown to enhance long-term retention (Smith, Glenberg, & Bjork, 1978; Smith & Rothkopf, 1984).

Providing Contextual Interference

Such ways of making the task environment more variable or unpredictable can be considered one set of a broader category of manipulations that produce "contextual interference" (Battig, 1979). Other examples of contextual interference include designing or interleaving materials to be learned in a way that creates, at least temporarily, interference for the learner (e.g., Mannes & Kintsch, 1987), and adding to the task demands (e.g., Battig, 1956; Langley & Zelaznik, 1984). In Mannes and Kintsch's experiment, for example, subjects had to learn the content of a technical article (on industrial uses of microbes) after having first studied an outline that was either consistent with the organization of the article or inconsistent with that organization (but provided the same information in either case). The inconsistent condition impaired subjects' verbatim recall and recognition of the article's content (compared to the consistent condition), but facilitated performance on tests that required subjects to infer answers or solve problems based on their general understanding of the article's content.

Distributing Practice on a Given Task

In general, compared to distributing practice sessions on a given task over time, massing practice or study sessions on to-be-learned procedures or information produces better short-term performance or recall of that procedure or information, but markedly inferior long-term performance or recall. The long-term advantages of distributing practice sessions over time have been demonstrated repeatedly for more than a century, tracing back over the entire history of controlled research on human memory (for modern reviews, see Dempster, 1990; Glenberg, 1992; Lee & Genovese, 1988). The differing short-term and long-term consequences of distributing practice sessions are nicely illustrated by the results of an experiment by Bahrick (1979). The subjects' basic task was to learn the Spanish translations of a list of 50 English words. During each of several training sessions on the list, an alternating series of study and test trials were presented until a given subject had responded correctly in Spanish to every English word on the list (once a given Spanish word was given correctly that English-Spanish word pairing was dropped out of the next study trial). Successive training sessions were separated by 0, 1, or 30 days, and at the start of every training session after the first subjects were tested on their memory for all 50 words. Looking at those tests alone, performance was clearly poorest with the 30-day separation, was better with the 1-day separation, and better yet when the several training sessions were all on a single day (the 0-day separation). On a test of long-term retention, however, administered 30 days after the last training session, the levels of recall were dramatically reversed, with the 30-day spacing of training sessions yielding clearly superior recall (72% after three training sessions, versus 33% and 64% in the 0-day and 1-day conditions, respectively).

Reducing Feedback to the Learner
Until recently, a common generalization about motor skills was that providing external feedback to the learner facilitates the acquisition of skills, and that any means of improving such augmented feedback — by, for example, making it more immediate, more frequent, or more accurate — helps learning and performance. Recently, however, Richard Schmidt and his collaborators (see, e.g., Schmidt, 1991; Schmidt, Young, Swinnen, & Shapiro, 1989; Winstein & Schmidt, 1990) have found that — as in the case of the other manipulations summarized in this section — reducing the frequency of feedback makes life more difficult for the learner *during* training, but can enhance posttraining performance. They have demonstrated that providing summary feedback to subjects (after every 5 or 15 trials, for example), or "fading" the frequency of feedback over trials, impedes acquisition of simple motor skills but enhances long-term retention of those skills.

Using Tests as Learning Events
Such effects of reducing the frequency of feedback during the learning of motor skills are broadly consistent with a large verbal-memory literature on tests as learning events. As mentioned earlier, there is abundant evidence that the act of retrieval induced by a recall test can be considerably more potent than a study opportunity in facilitating future recall. Prior testing also appears to increase the learning that takes place on subsequent study trials (e.g., Izawa, 1970). Once again, however, using tests rather than study trials as learning events, or increasing the difficulty of such tests, may appear to be counterproductive *during* training. Hogan and Kintsch (1971), for example, found that study trials produced better recall at the end of an experimental session than did test trials, but that test trials produced better recall after a 48-hour delay. And Landauer and Bjork (1978; see also Rea & Modigliani, 1985) found that "expanding retrieval practice," in which successive recall tests are made progressively more difficult by increasing the time and intervening events prior to each next test of some target information, facilitates long-term recall substantially — compared to the same number of tests administered at constant (and easier) delays.

It is not the mission of the present chapter to put forth any detailed conjectures as to why each of the foregoing manipulations induces desirable encoding and/or retrieval operations. In a general way, it seems safe to say that in responding to the difficulties and challenges induced by such manipulations the learner is forced into more elaborate encoding processes and more substantial and varied retrieval processes. As Battig (1979) argued with respect to contextual interference, and Schmidt and Bjork (1992) have argued more broadly, such manipulations are likely to induce more "transfer appropriate processing" (Bransford, Franks, Morris, & Stein, 1979; Morris, Bransford, & Franks, 1977), that is, processing that will transfer to the posttraining environment. For present purposes, however, the central point is that the research picture is unambiguous: A variety of manipulations that impede performance during training facilitate performance on the long term.

Misperceptions of the Trainer

If the research picture is so clear, why then are massed practice, excessive feedback, fixed conditions of training, and limited opportunities for retrieval practice — among other nonproductive manipulations — such common features of real-world training programs? It is tempting to argue that there should be more venues for interaction, and vehicles of communication, between researchers and practitioners, and that might be true. More important than any underexposure to relevant research findings, however, is the fact that the typical trainer is overexposed, so to speak, to the day-to-day performance and evaluative reactions of his or her trainees. A trainer, in effect, is vulnerable to a type of operant conditioning, where the reinforcing events are improvements in the performance and/or happiness of trainees. Such a conditioning process, over time, can act to shift the trainer toward manipulations that increase the rate of correct responding — that make the trainee's life easier, so to speak. Doing that, of course, will move the trainer away from introducing the types of desirable difficulties summarized in the preceding section.

The tendency for instructors to be pushed toward training programs that maximize the performance or evaluative reaction of their trainees *during* is exacerbated by certain institutional characteristics that are common in real-world organizations. First, those responsible for training are often themselves evaluated in terms of the performance and satisfaction of their trainees during training, or at the end of training. Second, individuals with the day-to-day responsibility for training often do not get a chance to observe the posttraining performance of the people they have trained; a trainee's later successes and failures tend to occur in settings that are far removed from the original training environment, and from the trainer himself or herself. It is also rarely the case that systematic measurements of posttraining on-the-job performance are even collected, let alone provided to a trainer as a guide to what manipulations do and do not achieve the posttraining goals of training. And, finally, where refresher or retraining programs exist, they are typically the concern of individuals other than those responsible for the original training.

Metamemory Considerations

A second consideration in the training of human beings, arguably as important as the actual learning produced by a training program, is the extent to which trainees gain a valid assessment of their own state of learning or competence. Individuals who have illusions of comprehension or competence pose a greater hazard to themselves and others than do individuals who correctly assess that they lack some requisite information or skill. The reading we take of our own state of knowledge determines whether we seek further study or practice, whether we volunteer for certain jobs, whether we instill confidence in others, and so forth. In general, then, as argued by Jacoby, Bjork, and Kelley (1993), it is as important to educate subjective experience as it is to educate objective experience.

As it turns out, it is not just those individuals responsible for training who are susceptible to being fooled by the level of performance of trainees during training. Recent research suggests that the learner himself or herself is susceptible to the same type of inferential error. Rapid progress in the form of improved performance is reassuring to the learner, even though little learning may be taking place, whereas struggling and making errors are distressing, even though substantial learning may be taking place. Such a misreading of one's progress, together with the other types of misassessments discussed below, can lead trainees to prefer less effective training over more effective training. Baddeley and Longman (1978), for example, found that British postal workers who were taught a keyboard skill under massed-practice (and less efficient) conditions actually were more satisfied with their training than were workers taught under spaced-practice (and more efficient) conditions.

Relevant Peculiarities of the Human as a Memory Device

At the root of such problems is our misunderstanding of the complexities of our own memories. Human memory is multidimensional and multifaceted in ways that we apparently do not come to realize on the basis of the trials and errors of everyday experience alone. We seem to persist in holding to a kind of implicit assumption that what we can and cannot recall or recognize is governed by memory traces that vary on a unidimensional strength continuum — that past experiences of differing duration and intensity leave impressions or traces in the brain that are like footprints of differing depths in the sand. And such traces or footprints are subject to blurring over time, becoming harder to read as a function of retention interval and intervening events.

From a research standpoint, any such unidimensional idea, if ever plausible, is now preposterous. During the last decade particularly, the research of behavioral scientists, neuroscientists, and clinicians, employing subject populations ranging from animals and children to amnesic patients and normal adults has yielded a picture of human memory that is remarkably multifaceted. In response to an array of evidence of various types that implicate differing processes and types of memories, researchers have proposed a bewildering assortment of overlapping and nonoverlapping distinctions: short-term versus long-term memory, semantic versus episodic knowledge, declarative versus procedural knowledge, stimulus-driven versus conceptually driven knowledge, explicit versus implicit memories, controlled versus automatic processing, and memory as a tool versus memory as an object, to name a few.

Whatever the resolution of the current terminological turmoil, the important point for present purposes is that one subjective or objective measure of the "strength" of a memory representation may not correlate with the "strength" of a different subjective or objective measure. The research literature is now replete, for example, with a variety of dramatic interactions of encoding condition and test condition on performance. Encoding conditions or processes that yield good short-term performance can fail to support long-term performance as stressed above. Encoding conditions/processes that facilitate later recognition may not support later recall, and vice versa. And initial conditions of exposure that do and do not prime performance on indirect measures of performance, such as perceptual identification or word-fragment completion, can differ markedly from the conditions that facilitate performance on direct measures, such as recall and recognition (for some striking examples, see Roediger & Blaxton, 1987; for a review, see Richardson-Klavehn & Bjork, 1988).

Misperceptions of the Learner: Using One Index
to Predict Another

Failing to understand the multifaceted nature of human memory
opens the learner to a variety of misassessments of his or her state of
knowledge during training. As mentioned already, the learner may
be fooled by his or her own successes during training. Manipulations
such as blocking practice by subtask, providing continuous feedback
during training, and fixing the conditions of practice act like crutches
that artificially support performance during training. When those
crutches are absent in the posttraining environment, performance
collapses. The learner, however, will typically lack the perspective
and experience to realize that he or she has not yet achieved the
level of learning demanded by the posttraining environment. Conversely, the errors and confusion caused during training by spaced
practice, infrequent feedback, and variations in the task or task environment can lead trainees to underestimate their own state of
learning and comprehension.

At a somewhat oversimplified level of analysis, such misassessments
arise as a function of trainees observing their own objective performance during training. They then assume, implicitly or explicitly,
that successes predict future successes and failures predict future
failures. In effect, the learner relies too heavily on an unreliable
index — the current ease of access to a correct answer or procedure
— as a measure of the extent to which learning in a broader sense
has been achieved.

As an overall generalization from all of our past experiences, of
course, ease of retrieving some procedure or information *does* provide a measure of how well that procedure or information is regis-
tered in memory. The problem is that there are multiple
determinants of speed or ease of retrieval, only some of which are
commensurate with degree of learning. The type of training
"crutches" mentioned above increases the speed and probability of
retrieval via such mechanisms as constraining the possible responses,
multiplying retrieval cues, and tapping short-term memory — that is,
processes different from those that might truly build the long-term
representation of some procedure or knowledge. Apparently, however, we lack the type of understanding of our own memories that

would permit us to distinguish between the different sources of retrieval speed or probability.

A recent experiment by Kelley and Lindsay (1993) serves as a good illustration of that point. Using a general knowledge test, Kelley and Lindsay found, not surprisingly, that subject's confidence in the correctness of a given answer increased as a function of how rapidly that answer was given. They also found that having subjects read a list of answers prior to being given the general knowledge test increased the speed with which those answers were given, and the subjects' confidence in those answers — whether those answers were right or wrong. That is, if a closely related but incorrect answer (e.g., Hickock) to a given question (What was Buffalo Bill's last name?) had been read earlier, subjects gained an illusion of knowing: Such studied incorrect answers were not only given more frequently, they were given more confidently.

Speed or ease of retrieval access is only one type of index or measure that is subject to misinterpretation. A wealth of recent experimental evidence from several research paradigms suggests that the sense of familiarity or fluency during the encoding of retrieval cues can also be a source of illusions of knowing or comprehending. Reder (1987, 1988), for example, found that she could alter subjects' feeling-of-knowing judgments simply by making certain words in a general-information question more familiar. When key words in a question (such as "golf " and "par" in the question, "What is the term in golf for scoring one under par"?) were prefamiliarized by virtue of having appeared on an earlier experimental task, subjects were then more likely to judge the question as answerable.

Schwartz and Metcalfe (1992) and Reder and Ritter (1992) have demonstrated that not only is cue familiarity a factor in subjects' feeling-of-knowing judgments, it may be a more important factor than target familiarity. Schwartz and Metcalfe had subjects study a list of unrelated cue-target word pairs (such as OAK TURTLE) and then later tested subjects' cued recall of the target words. When subjects were unable to recall a given target (such as "TURTLE") in response to its cue ("OAK"), they were asked to give a feeling of knowing judgment, which took the form of rating their likelihood of being able to later recognize the correct target from among several alternatives. With certain types of general-information questions such judgments can be quite accurate (e.g., Hart, 1967a), though subjects tend to be overconfident (for a review see Nelson & Narens, 1990), and one theory is that it is recall of partial information — a first letter, for example, or whether the word is short or long — that is the basis for such judgments. Schwartz and Metcalfe found, however, that prefamiliarizing cue words increased subjects' feeling-of-knowing judgments without increasing the likelihood of recall of the targets associated with those cues, or having an effect on the accuracy of such judgments, whereas prefamiliarizing the target words had no effect on subjects' feeling of knowing. Consistent with that pattern, Reder and Ritter (1992) found that subjects' speeded judgments of whether they knew the answer to a given arithmetic problem (such as 13 times 27) was more heavily influenced by the frequency of prior exposures to the terms of the problem than by the actual degree of learning (as indexed by the frequency of prior exposures to the intact problem itself).

In terms of their real-world implications, a possible concern about the foregoing results is that the experimental tasks employed may be too artificial and/or simple to be compared to the types of tasks that are the typical objects of training. However, an impressive series of experiments by Arthur Glenberg, William Epstein, and their collaborators (Epstein, Glenberg, & Bradley, 1984; Glenberg & Epstein, 1985, 1987; Glenberg, Sanocki, Epstein, & Morris, 1987; Glenberg, Wilkinson, & Epstein, 1982) does much to allay that concern. The basic paradigm involves having subjects read expository text covering relatively technical content and then rate their comprehension of that material — in terms of the likelihood that they will later be able to answer questions on that material. In general, the subjects were poorly calibrated: The correlations of their judged comprehension and their later actual ability to answer correctly were surprisingly low. Consistent with the work of Reder (1987, 1988; Reder & Ritter, 1992) and Schwartz and Metcalfe (1992; see also Metcalfe, Schwartz, & Joaquim, 1993), subjects appear to be vulnerable to illusions of comprehension based on the general familiarity of the domain in question. Glenberg and Epstein (1987), for example, found that subjects' judgments were apparently more influenced by their self-classification of their own level of expertise than by their actual comprehension of the specific content of a text passage. Within a given domain, such as physics or music, level of expertise was actually inversely related to the calibration of comprehension! With a different paradigm, Costermans, Lories, and Ansay (1992) also obtained results consistent with the idea that subjects use one index, their general familiarity with a knowledge domain, to predict another, the degree to which the answer to a specific question exists in their memories.

A final important point, closely related to misreading the meaning of subjective familiarity, is that the learner is subject to hindsight biases (Fischhoff, 1975). Once an answer is provided or a solution is demonstrated, we appear unable to correctly assess the likelihood that we could have provided that answer or solved that problem ourselves. More specifically, we are subject to an "I knew it all along" effect. Given the nature of real-world instruction and training, the implications of the hindsight effect are profound. In a variety of ways we are put in the position of judging our level of comprehension on the basis of an exposure to the information or problem-solving procedure in question. As a student, for example, we make judgments of what we know and do not know (and, hence, how we should allocate our study time) based on reading a text or listening to an instructor. Such judgments, however, contaminated as they are by familiarity effects, hindsight biases, and other factors — such as the ease of following a "well polished" lecture — are a poor basis for judging one's ability to produce an answer or solve a problem.

The Need to Introduce Difficulties for the Learner

One implication of such misperceptions of the learner is that the conditions of training should provide meaningful rather than misleading subjective experiences. In designing training programs we are at risk of denying trainees the opportunity for certain types of feedback that are essential to their achieving a valid assessment of their current state of knowledge.

We can, in effect, inadvertently ruin the learner's subjective experience. Experiments by Jacoby and Kelley (1987) and Dunlosky and Nelson (1992; see also Nelson & Dunlosky, 1991) illustrate that point. Jacoby and Kelley presented a number of anagrams to subjects and asked the subjects to rate the difficulty of each anagram in terms of the likelihood that other people could solve it. In one condition, subjects had to first solve the anagram (e.g., FSCAR ?????), and in another condition the anagram was presented together with its solution (FSCAR SCARF). Subjects ratings in the former condition, presumably based largely or entirely on their own subjective solution experience, were considerably more accurate than subjects' ratings in the latter condition. Being given the solution to a given anagram apparently ruined a subject's opportunity to experience the solution process, which then forced them to use some less-predictive "theory" of what makes anagrams more or less difficult to solve.

Dunlosky and Nelson (1992) had subjects study a series of unrelated cue-target word pairs (e.g., WEED JURY). Interleaved among the study trials were judgments-of-learning (JOL) trials on which subjects were to judge their degree of learning of a particular pair presented earlier. Such JOL trials were immediate or delayed in terms of when they followed the study trial of the pair to be judged, and they consisted of the cue alone (WEED ????) or the intact cue target pair (WEED JURY). Subjects were asked to predict the likelihood they would be able, 10 minutes later, to recall the target when given the cue. Such predictions were unreliable for either type of JOL trial administered immediately, were not much better on delayed cue-target JOL trials, and were very good on delayed cue-alone JOL trials. One interpretation is that it is only on the delayed cue-alone trials that subjects get any kind of valid subjective experience as to their state of learning of a given pair (for an expansion of that argument, see Spellman & Bjork, 1992). On the immediate cue-alone JOL trials subjects can interpret ease of access from short-term memory as evidence of learning; on cue-target JOL trials, either immediate or delayed, subjects are vulnerable to the effects of familiarity and hindsight discussed in the preceding section.

In general, then, a major goal of training should be to inform the learner's own subjective experience. People need to experience the type of testing to which they will later be subjected (see Glenberg & Epstein, 1987), and, to the extent possible, questions embedded in training need to be phrased such that the processes tapped in answering those questions are the same processes that support long-term retention (see Begg, Duft, Lalonde, Melnick, & Sanvito, 1989). Stated more broadly, the conditions of training need to be constructed to reveal to the subject what knowledge and procedures are, and are not, truly accessible under the types of conditions that can be expected to prevail in the posttraining environment. Some of the best ways to achieve that goal involve making life seem more difficult for the learner. Manipulations such as varying the conditions of training, inducing contextual interference, distributing practice, reducing the frequency of augmented feedback, and using tests as learning events share the property that they act to better educate the learner's subjective experience.

It may be necessary, however, to educate the learner in another respect as well. For people to be receptive to the types of manipulations of training suggested herein, institutional and individual attitudes toward the meaning of errors and mistakes must change. People learn by making and correcting mistakes. We have known at least since an influential paper by Estes (1955; see also Cuddy & Jacoby, 1982) that it may be necessary to induce forgetting during training to enhance learning. Training conditions that prevent certain mistakes from happening (and give trainees a false optimism about their level of comprehension and competence) can defer those mistakes to a posttraining setting where they really matter. That is an especially important consideration in certain job contexts, such as police work, air-traffic control, and nuclear-plant operation, where society cannot afford the kind of on-the-job learning such mistakes might entail. Stated most strongly, when embarked on any substantial learning enterprise we should probably find the absence, not the presence, of errors, mistakes, and difficulties to be distressing — a sign that we are not exposing ourselves to the kinds of conditions that most facilitate our learning, and our self-assessment of that learning.

Should the Posttraining Environment be Simulated during Training?

A broad implication of the foregoing analyses is that training is frequently nonoptimal because it fails to incorporate the variability, delays, uncertainties, and other challenges the learner can be expected to face in a real-world job setting of some kind. It would seem, then, that optimizing training may be a simple matter — in principle, if not in practice — of simulating the posttraining environment during training. Such an assumption is clearly one rationale for spending massive amounts of money on high fidelity simulators in the aircraft industry and elsewhere.

At one level, it seems incontestable that the learner should experience conditions during training that are analogous or identical to those expected in the posttraining environment. But to what degree is it necessary to simulate the physical and social details of real-world settings in order to achieve that end? A strong position on that issue is staked out by advocates of the "situated learning" approach (see, e.g., Greeno, Smith, & Moore, 1993; Lave & Wenger, 1991). In that theoretical framework, it is critical to situate the learner in the context of application. The argument is that learning processes cannot be separated from contextual determinants of performance, particularly social aspects of context, and that learning by abstraction — as in a classroom — is ineffectual. That extreme position is the topic of considerable current debate among social scientists and educators (for an excellent review of the issues and relevant data, see Reder & Klatzky, 1993).

But is it really necessary to simulate the posttraining environment to induce processing that will transfer to that environment? It is an intriguing possibility that the conditions of learning should, in a sense, go beyond situated learning. That is, it may be optimal, from both a memory and metamemory standpoint, to introduce difficulties of certain types that are *not* anticipated in the real-world environment. Introducing more variability than one expects to be present in the real world, for example, or reducing the anticipated frequency of augmented feedback, may result in a more elaborated and internalized representation of knowledge and skills.

Such a possibility is suggested by the results of certain of the experiments on induced variability of practice cited earlier. Shea and Morgan (1979), for example, found that a random schedule of practice on several different motor-movement patterns — as opposed to blocked practice on those patterns — not only produced much superior transfer to a posttraining test carried out under random conditions, but also produced better transfer to a post-training test carried out under blocked conditions. That Shea and Morgan's results — which were obtained using relatively simple motor tasks in a laboratory environment — may well generalize to real-world settings is suggested by the results of a recent experiment by Hall et al. (1992). With the cooperation of the coaches of the varsity baseball team at the California Polytechnic University, San Luis Obispo, they arranged for extra batting practice to be given under either blocked or random conditions. Twice a week for 6 weeks, two matched subsets of players were thrown 45 pitches—15 fast balls, 15 curve balls, and 15 change-ups — under blocked or random conditions. Players in the blocked condition got those pitches blocked by type, whereas successive pitches in the random condition were determined by a random schedule. At the end of those 6 weeks, two transfer tests were administered, the first under random conditions and the second under blocked conditions. As in Shea and Morgan's experiment, random practice produced better transfer to blocked as well as random conditions than did blocked practice.

Using 8-year-old and 12-year-old children as subjects, Kerr and Booth (1978) obtained analogous results with a somewhat different paradigm. The task involved throwing miniature beanbags underhanded at a 4 inch by 4 inch target on the floor. In the case of the 8-year-old children, one group was given training at a fixed distance (3 ft), while another group was given the same number of training trials, half at 2 ft and half at 4 ft (but mixed across trials). On a posttraining transfer test carried out at a 3 ft distance, the group that practiced at 2 and 4 ft, but never at 3 ft, performed better than did the group that practiced *at* the criterion distance! With the same procedure, but with the distance increased by a foot, the outcome was the same for 12-year-old subjects.

Results of the foregoing type suggests that certain benefits that accrue from contending with variation and unpredictability may outweigh the benefits of having an exact match of the training and posttraining task environments. Another important consideration may argue against constraining the training environment to be the same as the anticipated posttraining environment: It may not be optimal to "contextualize" the learning process, even within the context that is the target of training. The problem is twofold. On the one hand, fixing environmental and task conditions during training, whether those conditions correspond to the posttraining target context or not, may reduce the frequency of the types of desirable processing induced by variation. On the other hand, the environmental, social, and task characteristics of any given job environment are not all that predictable. Equipment, physical settings, procedures, and co-workers usually differ across locations, or change with time. And emergencies and other unusual events are, almost by definition, hard to predict. It is in such special circumstances that the risk of having contextualized training may be greatest. If we want people to respond optimally to unanticipated novel conditions, such as emergencies and/or unique conditions of some other type, the evidence summarized in this chapter suggests that we do not want to have trained those people under fixed conditions.

Such issues are obviously crucial in the complex business of optimizing the design of simulators. Comparisons of high-fidelity (and high cost) simulators to simpler (and lower cost) simulators have often failed to demonstrate that high fidelity facilitates learning. It has been argued that high fidelity can even be detrimental early in learning by providing cues and complexities that are confusing in the early stages of learning (Andrews, 1988). Consistent with the theme of this chapter, it could also be argued that there are some benefits of *not* providing every bell and whistle present in the real-world apparatus. Simulators that require the learner to substitute imagery for external cues as a means of keeping track of the state of the system, for example, might facilitate higher levels of learning.

To argue that high fidelity is never necessary in a simulator is clearly unwarranted theoretically and empirically. Research with aircraft simulators has demonstrated that high fidelity can be very important for certain aspects of performance. But overall, as Patrick (1992) has argued, the most important determiner of transfer is likely to be psychological fidelity, not engineering fidelity. An extension of that argument may be the best single answer to the question raised at the start of this section. It is not the nominal overlap of the training and real-world environments that really matters, but, rather, the functional overlap. Our goal should be to best exercise during training the types of processing that performing at a high level in the posttraining environment will demand.

Concluding Comments

One implication of the considerations summarized in this chapter is that intuition and standard practice are poor guides to training. The body of research on human cognitive processes, though far from fully developed, has grown to the point where it provides a far better guide. A second implication is that, as a guide to training, research on the learner's metacognitive processes is as important, and inseparable from, research on the objective consequences of training.

Acknowledgment

This chapter was written while the author, as a Visiting Scholar, enjoyed the support and hospitality of the Department of Psychology, Dartmouth College.

10

The Role of Metacognition in Problem Solving

Janet E. Davidson, Rebecca Deuser, and
Robert J. Sternberg

Consider the following problems: (1) How many uses can you find for a plastic bag? (2) A man of mass M1 lowers himself to the ground from a height X by holding onto a rope passed over a massless frictionless pulley and attached to another block of mass M2. The mass of the M1 is greater than M2. What is the tension on the rope? (3) How can you make money in the stock market during an economic recession? (4) How can you arrange a dinner party so that everyone sits next to someone they do not know? On the surface, these problems are quite different. The first one requires divergent and creative thinking, the second measures convergent thinking and domain-specific knowledge, the third problem involves practical problem-solving skills, and the fourth requires deductive reasoning. What these problems have in common is that their solution requires behavior that is directed toward achieving a goal (Anderson, 1985). Metacognition, or knowledge of one's own cognitive processes, guides the problem-solving process and improves the efficiency of this goal-oriented behavior.

All problems contain three important characteristics: givens, a goal, and obstacles. The givens are the elements, their relations, and the conditions that compose the initial state of the problem situation. The goal is the solution or desired outcome of the problem. The obstacles are the characteristics of both the problem solver and the problem situation that make it difficult for the solver to transform the initial state of the problem into the desired state. Problem solving is the active process of trying to transform the initial state of a prob-

lem into the desired one. Metacognition helps the problem solver
(1) recognize that there is a problem to be solved, (2) figure out
what exactly the problem is, and (3) understand how to reach a
solution.

This chapter focuses on four metacognitive processes that are important contributors to problem-solving performance across a wide
range of domains. These processes are (1) identifying and defining
the problem, (2) mentally representing the problem, (3) planning
how to proceed, and (4) evaluating what you know about your performance. Successful application of these metacognitive processes
depends on characteristics of the problem, the problem solver, and
the context in which the problem is presented. The first four sections
of this chapter will discuss each of the four metacognitive processes.
The fifth section focuses on individual differences in the use of these
processes. The sixth section considers the role of the situational
context in problem solving. Finally, the main points will be summarized and areas for future research will be discussed.

Identifying and Defining the Problem

As obvious as it may sound, individuals must recognize that a problem
exists before they can solve it. In other words, individuals need to
identify and define the givens and goals of the situation. Sometimes
the givens and goals of a problem are well defined and obvious; often
they are not.

The first step in problem definition is to encode the critical elements of the problem situation (e.g., Newell & Simon, 1972). Encoding involves storing features of the problem in working memory and
retrieving from long-term memory information that is relevant to
these features. Consider the following example:

A car in Philadelphia starts toward New York at 40 miles an hour. Fifteen
minutes later a car in New York starts toward Philadelphia — 90 miles away
— at 55 miles an hour. Which car is nearest Philadelphia when they meet?

If this problem is encoded correctly, the solver quickly realizes that
the cars must be the same distance from Philadelphia when they
meet. Unfortunately, incomplete encoding leads many adults to solve

this problem by computing distance, rate, and time for each car (Davidson, in press).

After a problem is encoded, the solver must determine what is known, what is unknown, and what is being asked in the situation. Problems vary in how well the goals and procedures are specified (see, e.g., Greeno, 1980). As the name implies, well-structured problems have well-defined initial states and goal states. In other words, the givens and goals of these problems are usually easy to identify and specify. Consider the following example:

A mother sends her boy to the well to get 3 quarts of water. She gives him a 7-quart bucket and a 4-quart bucket. How can the son measure out exactly 3 quarts of water using nothing but these two containers?

Most adults quickly define this problem as being one of how 7 and 4 can lead to 3. The problem's difficulty lies not in problem definition but in deciding which transformations to make (Davidson, in press). (The correct answer is to fill the 7-quart bucket and pour from it into the 4-quart bucket until the 4-quart bucket is full. The 7-quart bucket will now contain 3 quarts of water.) Other examples of well-structured problems are school-like problems such as those found on standardized tests. Even if individuals do not know how to solve school-like problems, they generally know what is being asked.

In contrast to well-structured problems, ill-structured ones do not have well-defined given and goal states. Many of the insight problems studied by the Gestalt psychologists are of this nature (Duncker, 1945; Kohler, 1969; Maier; 1930; Wertheimer, 1959). The difficulty in solving these problems often lies in defining the problems in novel ways. Consider the following example:

A man was working on his house and realized that he needed something from the hardware store. He went to the hardware store and asked the clerk, "How much will 150 cost me?" The clerk answered, "They are 75 cents apiece, so 150 will cost you $2.25." What did the man buy?

This problem can be solved only if the solver realizes that the terms of the problem are not what they originally appear to be. In other words, the problem elements must be defined in a novel way. The "150" in the problem must be viewed as representing three numerals (as in house numbers) or three boxes (as in three boxes containing

50 nails each). Many of the problems found in the real-world are ill-structured and they are often more difficult to identify and define than are school-like problems or problems found on standardized tests (Hayes, 1981).

Cognitive development also influences one's ability to identify and define problems. As children increase in age and experience, they become better able to understand what is required in a problem situation (Flavell, 1977).

Representing the Problem

After a problem has been identified and defined, individuals must make a "mental map" of the elements, the relations among the elements, and the goals found in the externally presented problem. Information is mentally inserted, deleted, and interpreted from the original situation and held in memory (Hayes, 1981). These internal representations allow people to understand a problem and to think through its solution.

Kotovsky, Hayes, and Simon (1985) describe three advantages to creating mental representations of a problem. One advantage is that good representations allow the problem solver to organize blocks of planned moves or strategies as a single "chunk" of memory. In other words, good representations help reduce the memory demands found in many problems. Second, good representations allow the problem solver to organize the conditions and rules of a problem and to determine whether certain steps are allowable and productive. Finally, good representations allow the problem solver to keep track of where he or she is in terms of reaching a solution and to foresee potential obstacles to reaching the solution.

There is no single representation that is best for all problem situations. For some problems, such as geometric analogies, an attribute-value representation may be most efficient. For other problems, such as animal-name analogies, a spatial representation may be best (Sternberg & Gardner, 1983).

Just as no single representation is best for all situations, there is no single representation that is best for all individuals. Different people often represent the same problem in different ways. For example, younger children tend to organize information about concepts in terms of function, whereas older children tend to organize the same information taxonomically (Anglin, 1970; Nelson, 1977). Without sufficient knowledge about a class of concepts, taxonomic organization is not possible for the younger children. Cognitive abilities can also determine how a problem is mentally represented. Individuals who are high in verbal ability are likely to form verbal representations whenever possible, whereas individuals who are high in spatial ability are likely to form spatial representations (MacLeod, Hunt, & Mathews, 1978; Sternberg & Weil, 1980).

Domain-specific knowledge can also influence the content and effectiveness of the mental representations used in problem solving. Experts in a particular domain tend to have representations that are tied to abstract principles of the domain. In contrast, the mental representations of novices tend to be based on concrete surface features of the problem (Chi, Glaser, & Rees, 1982; Larkin, McDermott, Simon, & Simon, 1980). Also, novices spend less time than do experts in representing the problem and they are less able to add new evidence to their representations than are experts (Lesgold, 1988; Lesgold et al., 1988).

Frequently individuals change or develop their mental representations during the course of solving a problem (Hayes, 1981). Changes can occur as people gain a more complete understanding of the givens, goals, and restrictions in a problem or as they find some information that has been previously overlooked. For example, many insight or nonroutine problems are difficult to solve because the problem solver does not have a familiar representation and set of procedures that can be used (Greeno & Berger, 1987). According to Davidson and Sternberg (1984, 1986; Sternberg & Davidson, 1983), new mental representations are constructed through three related mental processes: selective encoding, selective combination, and selective comparison.

The Three-Process View of Representational Change

Selective Encoding

Selective encoding involves seeing in a stimulus, or set of stimuli, one or more relevant features that previously have been nonobvious. Selective encoding contributes to insight by restructuring one's mental representation so that information that was originally viewed as being irrelevant is now seen as relevant for problem solution. (Also, information that was originally seen as relevant may now be viewed as irrelevant and, therefore, eliminated from one's mental representation.)

There are many instances of selective encoding in real-world performances. Professors, for example, often have too much information to present to a class; an insightful professor focuses on the information that is relevant to the students' needs and abilities. Ignaz Semmelweis's discovery of the importance of asepsis is a famous example of a selective encoding insight. While on the staff of the general hospital in Vienna, Semmelweis noticed that more women on the poor ward were dying from infection during childbirth than were women on the rich ward. After encoding that doctors washed their hands less frequently while on the poor ward, he realized the relevance that this lack of cleanliness had for spreading puerperal fever. (Unfortunately, Semmelweis was ridiculed for his belief that obstetric attendants should cleanse their hands and he committed suicide before the relevance of his discovery was recognized.)

Selective Combination

Selective combination involves putting together elements of a problem situation in a way that previously has been nonobvious to the individual. This new way of combining the problem's elements results in a change in the solver's mental representation of the problem.

There are numerous examples of how selective combination insights operate in real-world situations. An insightful professor is able to fit facts together to form a coherent package for her students. Darwin's formulation of the theory of evolution seems to have involved an insight of selective combination. He had all of the facts for a long time: What Darwin finally discovered was how to put the facts together to form a coherent theory.

Selective Comparison

Selective comparison involves discovering a nonobvious relationship between new information and information acquired in the past. It is here that analogies, metaphors, and models are used to solve problems. The person having an insight suddenly realizes that new information is similar to old information in certain ways (and dissimilar to it in other ways), and then uses this information to form a mental representation based on the similarities.

One could cite any number of examples of selective comparison insights in operation. Our insightful professor might realize the ways in which new information to be presented is related to information that her students have already learned. By capitalizing on the relationship between new and old information, the professor can facilitate learning. Archimedes's theory of "specific gravity" is a famous example of a selective comparison insight. While trying to determine whether silver had been put into King Hiero's gold crown, Archimedes stepped into a bath. He noticed that the amount of water that was displaced was equal to the volume of his body that was under water. By drawing an analogy between his bath and the problem with the crown, Archimedes suddenly knew how to determine the purity of the crown. He could compute the crown's volume by placing it in water and measuring the amount of displaced water. The crown could then be weighed against an equal volume of gold. According to legend, his sudden discovery prompted Archimedes to leap from the bath and run naked through the streets shouting "Eureka" (I have found it).

In sum, these three processes form the basis for a theory of insightful thinking. To the extent that there is a commonality in the three processes, it appears to be in the importance of selection and relevance. In encoding, one is selecting elements from the often numerous possible elements that constitute the problem situation; the key is to select the relevant elements. In combination, an individual is selecting one of many possible ways in which elements of information can be integrated; the key is to select a relevant way of combining the elements in a given situation. In comparison, an individual is selecting one (or more) of numerous possible old elements of information to which to relate new information. There are any number of relations that might be drawn; the key is to select the relevant comparison or comparisons to make for one's purposes.

Not every instance of selective encoding, selective combination, or selective comparison leads to an insight. The products of these operations are referred to as "insights" when an individual suddenly realizes which relevant information to select for encoding, combining, and comparing. This realization results in a change in the problem solver's mental representation of the task. If individuals do not know an appropriate set of procedures for a problem, they must search through a space of alternative ways of approaching the problem. They can guide this search by (1) looking for and recognizing previously overlooked relevant information in the problem (selective encoding), (2) looking for and recognizing previously overlooked ways of combining information (selective combination), and (3) looking for and recognizing previously overlooked connections between prior knowledge and the problem situation (selective comparison). Successful search for, and selection of, this relevant information leads to a change in problem solvers' mental representations of the problem. In contrast, noninsightful applications of encoding, combination, and comparison do not involve nonobvious search nor do they lead to a sudden change in mental representations.

Hints and Representational Change

Some problem situations contain hints or clues about the problem's solution (Gick & Holyoak, 1980, 1983; Kaplan & Simon, 1990). When used successfully, hints seem to guide the problem solver in forming a new mental representation. For example, Kaplan and Simon (1990) asked subjects to solve the following problem:

You are given a checkerboard and 32 dominoes. Each domino covers exactly two adjacent squares on the board. Thus, the 32 dominoes can cover all 64 squares of the checkerboard. Now suppose two squares are cut off at diagonally opposite corners of the board. If possible, show how you would place 31 dominoes on the board so that all of the 62 remaining squares are covered. If you think it is impossible, give a proof of why.

Most individuals form an incomplete mental representation that consists of the numbers of squares (62) and dominoes (31). This representation leads them repeatedly to attempt to cover the board with the dominoes. When a hint is given to consider the color of the squares on the board, problem solvers quickly form a "parity" representation that includes the fact that each domino covers two squares of alternating color. After this new representation is formed, most problem solvers correctly realize that the board cannot be covered with dominoes when diagonally opposite squares are removed.

Many hints, however, are too general to help problem solvers change their mental representations. Hints such as "there is a trick way that does not involve trying to cover the board" (Kaplan & Simon, 1990) or "use the prior problem" (Gick & Holyoak, 1983) often lead problem solvers to abandon their old representations, but do not guide them to the correct mental representations that they need to solve the problems.

Planning How to Proceed

After a problem has been identified and mentally represented, the solver must decide which steps and resources to use in solving the problem. Planning often involves dividing a problem into subproblems and then devising a sequence for how the subproblems should be completed (Greeno, 1980; Hayes, 1981). There are three general characteristics of planning (Pea & Hawkins, 1987). First, individuals are more likely to engage in planning when the problem situation is novel and complex. Because people do not have well-known paths and strategies to follow in these situations, they must plan how to proceed. A second characteristic of planning is that it tends to be relatively abstract, rather than concrete and complete. As people proceed through a problem, they revise their plans based on how well the plans are working and on what opportunities for modification are available. A final characteristic of planning is that it has both costs and benefits. Plans take time and cognitive resources to develop but, in the long run, they can improve the efficiency of problem solving.

Implementing a plan involves the selection of a set of lower order, strategic processes to use on the problem. Selecting a nonoptimal set of processes can result in incorrect or inefficient problem-solving performance. These lower order processes must also be sequenced in a way that facilitates task performance, and a decision needs to be made about how exhaustively the processes will be executed. For example, younger children tend to process with early termination the same stimuli that older children tend to process exhaustively

(Brown & DeLoache, 1978; Sternberg & Nigro, 1980; Sternberg & Rifkin, 1979; Vurpillot, 1968). Overuse of an self-terminating strategy can result in a large number of errors (Sternberg, 1977; Sternberg & Rifkin, 1979). Overuse of an exhaustive strategy can result in an increased amount of time spent on the problem (Sternberg & Ketron, 1982).

Well-Structured Problems

Some problems have steps to solution that can be clearly identified by the problem solver. This type of problem generally requires multiple steps that change the initial state of the problem into the final state. In contrast to ill-defined problems, the solution does not follow rapidly once one or two crucial steps have been made. Instead, finding a solution depends on making the correct sequence of steps. For example, consider a typical missionary-cannibal problem:

Three missionaries and three cannibals are on the left bank of a river and they need to reach the right bank. Unfortunately, they have a boat that holds only two people. If the cannibals outnumber the missionaries on either bank, the cannibals will eat the missionaries. How can they all get to the other side of the river?

The solution to this problem is a sequence of 11 correctly applied transformations. The problem's difficulty lies in deciding which transformations to make, holding these transformations in memory, and applying them correctly.

Problem solvers often rely on heuristics, or short-cuts, when they solve missionaries and cannibals problem and others like it. There are four heuristics often used to find solutions to a problem (Greeno & Simon, 1988). These heuristics are applied in a problem space, which is the universe of all possible moves that can be applied to solve a problem. One heuristic is means-ends analysis. This heuristic involves trying to decrease the distance between one's current position in the problem space and where one wants to go in that space. An example of this heuristic applied to the missionaries and cannibals problem would be to try to get as many people on the far bank and as few people on the near bank as possible. Another heuristic, working forward, involves starting at the initial state of the problem and working toward the desired state. In contrast, the heuristic of working backward involves starting at the desired state and trying to work back to the initial state. A fourth heuristic, generate and test, involves generating alternative courses of action and evaluating whether each course will work. Heuristics can also be used to construct mental representations when a problem solver finds that a current representation is not working (Gick & McGarry, 1992; Kaplan & Simon, 1990).

Ill-structured Problems

There are at least two ways that an insight or nonroutine problem can be difficult for subjects in terms of planning (Kaplan & Davidson, 1993). One way has to do with stereotypy. In this case, the problem solver becomes fixated on a certain path to solution. A property of many insight problems is that, on the surface, they appear to be routine problems. However, routine procedures bring one to an obvious, but incorrect, solution. Even when problem solvers realize that they are approaching a problem incorrectly, they are not always able to break their fixation and develop a new plan for solution. In other words, fixation keeps individuals from changing their problem-solving sets, even when old procedures are not relevant to the present situation.

Consider the hatrack problem used by Maier (1930; Burke & Maier, 1965). In the hatrack problem, subjects are asked to build a structure, sufficiently stable to support a heavy coat, using only two boards and a C-clamp. The opening of the clamp is wide enough so that the two boards can be inserted and held together securely when the clamp is tightened. Participants are instructed to build the hatrack in the center of a small laboratory room. To solve this problem, subjects must include the floor and ceiling of the room in their mental representation of the problem. (The hatrack is built by clamping the boards together and wedging them between the floor and ceiling. The handle of the clamp serves as a hook for the coat.) Many subjects are not able to view the floor and ceiling of a room as part of the problem. Studies conducted by Luchins (1942; Luchins & Luchins, 1950), Duncker (1945), and others (Adamson, 1952; Adamson & Taylor, 1954; Birch & Rabinowitz, 1951) also illustrate how fixation on past procedures can interfere with the formation of new ones.

Another source of difficulty has to do with the inability to generate any new plans for solution of an insight problem. If a problem is sufficiently novel or complex, the solver may not know how to begin planning. Consider the following problem:

How can you cut a hole big enough to put your head through in a 3 inch by 5 inch postcard?

If problem solvers do not have the insight to cut a spiral out of the card, they often are not able to generate any plans or strategies for solving the problem (Davidson, in press).

Individuals with less expertise in solving a particular problem seem to spend relatively less time in global, "up front" planning for solution, and relatively more time in attempting to implement a solution than do experts. This pattern has been found across age levels and across different levels of expertise within age levels (see, e.g., Chi et al., 1982; Larkin et al., 1980; Sternberg, 1981; Sternberg & Rifkin, 1979). Less skilled problem solvers do not have the available knowledge and processing resources that are required for extended global planning.

Solution Evaluation: Knowing About What You Know

As individuals work on a problem, they must keep track of what they have already done, what they are currently doing, and what still needs to be done (Flavell, 1981). Solution evaluation includes an individual's control over the internal representations he or she has formed and still needs to form for understanding and solving a problem. Often, new strategies need to be formulated as a person realizes that the old ones are not working. Consider the following example:

Barbara asked me to bring her a pair of stockings from her bedroom. Unfortunately the bedroom is dark and the light is not working. I know there are black socks and brown socks in the drawer, mixed in the ratio of 4 to 5. What is the minimum number of stockings I will have to take out to make sure that I have two stockings of the same color?

Many children and adults begin solving this problem by using the ratio information. However, some individuals realize that their answers, such as 20 or 4/5, do not make sense. By evaluating their solutions, they know to try a new strategy (Davidson, in press).

In general, solutions for ill-structured problems are difficult to evaluate because the desired state is often not clearly defined. Metcalfe (1986a) found that although feelings of knowing an answer are predictive of memory performance, they do not predict performance on insight problems. In addition, high feelings of confidence (warmth) that one is converging on the solution to an insight problem seem to be negatively predictive of correct solution of these problems. In other words, subjects who felt they were gradually getting closer to solving the problems tended to arrive at incorrect solutions, whereas individuals who felt they were far from solving the problems and then suddenly felt they knew the answers tended to give correct solutions (Metcalfe, 1986b; Metcalfe & Weibe, 1987). Metcalfe concluded that insight problems are correctly solved by a subjectively catastrophic process rather than by accumulative processes. This view fits the Gestalt notion that insight involves a sudden realization of a problem's solution.

Individual Differences in the Use of Metacognitive Processes

The three-process view of representational change presented earlier in the chapter makes predictions about individual differences in problem solving ability and intelligence. According to the proposed theory, intelligence is in part a function of the three insight processes. Some individuals are better able to have insights than are other individuals; this difference is related to differences in intelligence. In other words, highly intelligent individuals are more likely spontaneously to apply the three insight processes to change their mental representations of problems than are individuals with average or below average intelligence.

The three-process view provided a good account of the data from experiments that involved testing both adults and children on problems requiring various mixtures of the three kinds of insights (Davidson & Sternberg, 1986; Sternberg & Davidson, 1983). Consider some examples of the problems that were used in these studies:

1. One day you decide to visit the zoo. While there, you see a group of giraffes and ostriches. Altogether they have 30 eyes and 44 legs. How many animals are there?

2. George wants to fry 3 eggs as quickly as possible. Unfortunately, his pan only holds two eggs and each egg takes 2 minutes a side to cook. What is the shortest amount of time in which George can fry his 3 eggs?

3. Heather and Lynn have three household tasks to perform.

a. Their floor must be vacuumed. They have only one vacuum and the task takes 30 minutes.

b. The lawn must be mowed. They have only one mower and this task also takes 30 minutes.

c. Their baby sister must be fed and bathed. This, too, takes 30 minutes.

How should Heather and Lynn divide the work so as to finish all three tasks in the shortest amount of time?

Of these particular problems, the first emphasizes selective encoding. The major key is realizing the relevance of the 30 eyes; giraffes and ostriches have the same number of eyes, but not the same number of legs. This problem can be solved by simply dividing the number of eyes by two. The second example emphasizes selective combination; if the pieces of information are put together correctly, the problem solver discovers that the eggs can be cooked in 6 minutes. Although the third example also requires selective combination, it is used here as an illustration of how selective comparison was measured. In some cases, subjects were taught how to solve sample problems, such as the egg problem used in the second example, that were similar to a few complex problems in the test booklet. Usually subjects could solve the test problems only if they saw a connection between these items and the related samples. For example, if the problem solver saw a relation between the second and third problems listed above, then he or she would realize that Heather and Lynn need to divide one of the tasks.

In the experiments conducted with adults from the New Haven area, subjects were given sets of problems that were similar to the examples discussed above. Subjects also completed an intelligence test and tests of inductive and deductive reasoning. Some of the more interesting results from this research were as follows:

1. Some subjects have considerable difficulty knowing when to apply each of the three kinds of insight processes; other subjects do not have this difficulty.

2. Some subjects' use of selective comparison can be facilitated by certain instruction sets, and impeded by others. In other words, some subjects need to be told which comparisons to make, while other subjects do not.

3. The ability to apply all three kinds of insight processes is fairly highly correlated with scores on a general intelligence test (roughly at the level of .6).

4. High IQ subjects are slower, not faster, than lower IQ subjects in analyzing the problems and applying the insights.

The studies with children examined each of the three insight processes in depth. These studies extended previous research in four ways. First, individuals in these studies were preselected so as to be of either high or average intelligence. Second, unlike most studies of insightful problem solving, the subjects in these studies were fourth, fifth, and sixth grade children rather than adults. Using a different population of subjects made it possible to test the generality of the theory. Third, convergent-discriminant validation of the mathematical insight problems was tested by comparing performance on these problems with performance on other problems, some of which tapped the same insight processes and others of which did not. Finally, each of the three types of insight processes was isolated in subjects' performance. The isolation of these processes was accomplished by manipulating the amount of information that was available to the subjects. In particular, subjects received insight problems with and without cueing of one of the three kinds of insights.

Results from these studies showed that highly intelligent children perform better than less intelligent children on mathematical and verbal insight problems. This is not a surprising finding since highly intelligent children perform better than less intelligent children on many tasks. However, the finding is worth noting because the theory of insight would have been completely unsupported if the results had been otherwise. The convergent-discriminant validity of the insight measures was established by showing that performance on the mathematical problems was highly correlated with performance on verbal insight problems, despite surface-structural differences between these two types of problems. The mathematical and verbal insight problems were also significantly correlated with a standard measure of intelligence. The next highest correlations were between the math insight problems and (1) short mysteries, which tapped some of the same insight processes, and (2) a test of inductive reasoning, which required subjects to think beyond the information given. The lowest correlation (although it was still significant) was between the insight problems and a test of deductive reasoning, which does not require subjects to think beyond the given information.

In addition to this pattern of convergent-discriminant validation, it was also found that the highly intelligent children spontaneously produced the three types of insights required to solve the problems; therefore, their performance improved very little when each type of insight was cued. In contrast, the children of average intelligence had difficulty producing the required insights and, therefore, did benefit from the cueing. An additional study with subjects of average intellectual ability was conducted to ensure that insight cueing, rather than other types of cueing, was most beneficial to increased performance on the insight problems. For example, cueing the math procedures on a selective encoding problem was not as effective as cueing the relevant information; informing subjects that they needed to use all of the information on selective combination problems was not as effective as cueing the relevant combinations (Davidson, 1991)

It was also found, in a later series of studies, that insight could be trained on the basis of the three processes and that the training effects were both transferable and durable. The training program included 14 hours of instruction, distributed over a 7-week period. A variety of procedures (e.g., group instruction, intra- and intergroup problem solving, and individual problem solving) were used to train gifted and nongifted children in executing the three processes. At the end of the program, the children were given a posttest that included mathematical and verbal insight problems (hypothesized to use the three insight processes) and deductive reasoning problems (hypothesized to require different processes). The nongifted children showed greater improvement on the insight problems than did the gifted children. Neither group showed improvement on the deductive-reasoning problems, which involved processes that were unrelated to the training program (Davidson, 1991; Sternberg & Davidson, 1983). Again, the gifted children were superior at constructing effective mental representations using selective encoding, selective combination, and selective comparison.

To summarize, selective encoding, selective combination, and selective comparison were found to play an important role in the solution of insight problems, and in individual differences in intelligent behavior. Highly intelligent individuals spontaneously generated and applied these three processes, whereas less intelligent individuals did not.

The Role of Situational Context in Problem Solving

Cognitive psychologists tend to focus on the mental processes and representations involved in problem solving and, as a result, they sometimes fail to consider the situational context in which these processes and representations are utilized. Neisser (1976) was among the first to emphasize the importance of connecting cognitive-psychological research to the real-world realities it is supposed to help us understand, but his plea fell upon a surprisingly large number of deaf ears. Indeed, the "contextual" movement became something of a fringe movement outside of mainstream cognitive and developmental psychology. Other psychologists, and especially cross-cultural ones such as Serpell (1976) and Michael Cole (see e.g., Cole, Gay, Glick, & Sharp, 1971), have also stressed the importance of context but, again, their ideas have not penetrated mainstream psychological research.

Given that most research on problem solving has been conducted in psychologists' laboratories, we need to address the question: Does situational context actually matter? There is now abundant evidence that it does. This evidence does not preclude laboratory experiments, or even argue that they should be deemphasized. Rather, it suggests we need at the very least to complement these experiments with real-world investigations of problem-solving behavior. From the present focus, the metacognitive processes that people bring to bear on problem solving may be different inside versus outside the laboratory.

For example, Ceci and Brofenbrenner (1985) studied children's monitoring of time in a home setting and in a laboratory setting. In particular, they looked at how children deal with time pressure in problem-solving tasks as a function of where they are doing the task. They found that the pattern of results was completely different in the two settings. Indeed, as far back as the early 1970s, Wason and Johnson-Laird (1972) showed in a review of studies of reasoning that people handle problems very differently if the content of these problems is familiar to them in their everyday lives versus if it is unfamiliar and especially abstract. For example, in syllogistic reasoning, people find syllogisms much easier if the content is familiar to them from their everyday lives than if it consists of nonsense words (Sternberg, 1985).

The situation in which problems are presented — whether through setting or content — can lead to vast differences in the conclusions one draws about people's metacognitive skills and problem-solving abilities. For example, Wagner (1978) found that performance on memory problems administered to people in Morocco could make the people look either quite intelligent or quite stupid, depending on the familiarity of the content. Give Oriental-rug dealers standard western types of abstract content to recall and their performance is poor. But give them Oriental-rug patterns and they put Westerners to shame. The rug dealers can effectively represent rug patterns, but not the symbols from our standard memory tests. Similarly, Wagner and Sternberg (1986) found that the same business executives who do not score particularly well on standard tests of intelligence may do very well on tests of practical intelligence, in particular, of tacit knowledge — what one needs to know to succeed in an environment that generally one is not explicitly taught and that may not even be verbalized. These business executives, for example, may be excellent at allocating their time and energy in a business situation, but not so excellent in allocating their time and energy in a standardized test situation.

A striking example of the effects of context was generated by Ceci and Liker (1986). They found that men who were particularly successful in their betting at race tracks, and who generated complicated mental strategies for predicting winners of the race, had an average IQ that was slightly below the population average. Again, we see that people who can effectively apply metacognitive skills and solve problems in their everyday lives are not necessarily those who most effectively apply metacognitive skills and solve the problems on standardized tests of intelligence.

Again, we do not wish to claim that the results of laboratory investigations are invalid. But we do believe that their generality is an open question until metacognition and problem solving are studied in natural contexts.

Summary

The four metacognitive processes described in this chapter apply to a wide range of problems. In general, problem identification, representation, planning how to proceed, and solution evaluation guide the active process of transforming the initial state of a problem into a desired state. Certain obstacles can interfere with the application of these metacognitive processes. These obstacles are related to characteristics of the problem and of the problem solver. When solving ill-structured problems, for example, individuals often have difficulty defining the givens and goals, constructing a mental representation of the problem, devising a plan or set of procedures for solving the problem, and evaluating their solutions. In contrast, all four metacognitive processes are easier to apply on well-structured problems. Knowledge, intelligence, and age are characteristics of individuals that can influence the effective use of metacognitive processes in problem solving.

When we think about problem solving, we tend to think about the results people get when they solve particular problems, or perhaps about the steps they take to reach a solution. We have argued in this chapter that many of the most important steps are not ones of problem solving, per se, but ones that direct and guide problem solving. For example, both the solution you reach and even the processes you use may be determined by how you define the problem. Moreover, whether you even perform any of the steps will depend on your realization that a problem exists.

Obviously, further research needs to be done on the role of metacognition in problem solving. In particular, context and interactions between the metacognitive processes need to be examined. How do the processes work on different types of problems? How can the use of the processes be enhanced, both in and out of natural settings? To the extent that we want to identify and develop good problem solvers, we need to focus as much on the metacognitive processes of problem solving as on the cognitive ones.

11

Metacognitive Development in Adulthood and Old Age

Christopher Hertzog and Roger A. Dixon

Gerontologists — those who study the aging process — have long been interested in the extent to which adults vary in processes related to intentional (Schneider & Pressley, 1989) or explicit memory (Craik & Jennings, 1992), particularly in terms of differences in strategies that influence acquisition and retention (Craik & Rabinowitz, 1984; Kausler, 1982). Interest in the construct of metacognition began shortly after Flavell and his colleagues introduced the concept into the literature on memory development during childhood (e.g., Flavell & Wellman, 1977). Perlmutter (1978) reported a pioneering study that, in many senses, set the stage for the entire field. Since that time, theoretical interest and empirical research on the topic of metacognition and adulthood have mushroomed (see reviews by Berry & West, 1993; Cavanaugh, 1989; Cavanaugh & Green, 1990; Dixon, 1989; Herrmann, 1990; Hertzog, Hultsch, & Dixon, 1990a; Hultsch & Dixon, 1990; Hultsch, Hertzog, Dixon, & Davidson, 1988; Lovelace, 1990; Perlmutter, Adams, Berry, Kaplan, Person, & Verdonik, 1987).

There are divergent views on the importance of metacognition in a general theory of cognitive development during adulthood. For some theorists, metacognition is a useful construct to the extent that it can explain age-related changes in such cognitive constructs as memory and problem solving. Recent reviews by Light (1991) and Salthouse (1991) argue that age changes in metacognition cannot account for all age changes in cognition. Salthouse argues for age changes in fundamental information processing mechanisms and structures as more plausible causal explanations of age changes in performance on complex cognitive tasks. Such treatments of metacognition represent it primarily as a rival to other explanatory constructs for age-related changes in cognition.

We accept the claim that age changes in metacognition cannot account for either the full range or the complete magnitude of age changes in cognitive task performance. For us, however, the inability of metacognitive variables to account for all age changes in cognition neither diminishes the potential importance of understanding metacognitive process nor justifies ignoring the potential influence of metacognitive variables in empirical studies of aging and cognition. We take a functional perspective (Bruce, 1991; Dixon & Hertzog, 1988), arguing that metacognition has adaptive significance for the developing organism, and plays a role in cognition as it is manifested in real-world behavior. As such it is one part of a full explanation of those changes. Metacognitive processes may, for example, play an important role in the extent to which older adults engage in compensatory behaviors designed to adapt to actual or perceived decline in information-processing capacity (Bäckman & Dixon, 1992).

Our chapter focuses on one particular domain of metacognition: metamemory. This focus helps narrow and define our task, while preserving attention to prototypical issues that undoubtedly generalize beyond memory to other aspects of cognition. We begin by discussing a theoretical perspective that encompasses multiple facets or dimensions of metamemory, including knowledge, beliefs, and monitoring. The latter facet receives the greatest emphasis in some accounts of metacognition (e.g., Nelson & Narens, 1990), but we argue that the other domains are required to attain a full understanding of metacognitive phenomena in adulthood. We then review, selectively, research on metamemory and adult development.

Dimensions of Metamemory

Metacognition is probably best conceptualized as a set of interrelated constructs pertaining to cognitions about cognition. One way of classifying this set is by the domain of cognition under consideration, such as memory, language production, and problem solving. Thus the term metamemory can be defined broadly as cognitions about memory (e.g., Wellman, 1983). A second way of defining the set of constructs subsumed under metacognition is to include, at any particular level of specificity in defining cognition, multiple types of cognitions. The metacognitions we refer to here can be generally classified as *stored* or *concurrent*. Stored metacognitions refer to information or representations held in permanent, long-term memory. We differentiate two types of such information: declarative knowledge and beliefs. Concurrent metacognitions are, in effect, the information generated by and associated with the act of cognizing. As such they are directly related to the control processes associated with monitoring the current status of the cognitive system (Nelson & Narens, 1990), and they may be associated with conscious awareness of the content and process of cognizing (Cavanaugh, 1989).

The term metamemory, then, is actually a label for multiple specific concepts related to memory (Cavanaugh & Green, 1990; Gilweski & Zelinski, 1986; Hertzog et al., 1990a; Hultsch et al., 1988; Lovelace, 1990). Three general categories of metamemory constructs include (1) declarative knowledge about memory tasks and memory processes — defined as knowledge about both how memory functions and the viability of strategic behaviors for tasks requiring memory processes; (2) memory monitoring — defined as awareness of the current state of one's memory system; and (3) self-referent beliefs about memory. The central construct in this category is memory self-efficacy — defined as one's sense of mastery or capability to use memory effectively in memory-demanding situations.

Earlier we and our colleagues (Hultsch et al., 1988) identified a fourth aspect of metamemory: memory-related affect. We defined it as a variety of emotional states that may be related to or generated by memory-demanding situations, including anxiety, depression, and fatigue. However, affect experienced in memory-demanding situations is not metamemory, per se, but rather an important class of proximal outcomes of metamemory (see below). On the other hand, representations of one's own tendency to react affectively to memory-demanding situations, as well as declarative knowledge about relationships between affective states and memory performance, are aspects of metamemory that can be subsumed under the categories of memory-related beliefs and knowledge, respectively.

A similar distinction should be maintained between cognitive behaviors (e.g., problem-solving strategies) and metacognitions associated with these behaviors. Knowledge about possible strategies, beliefs about their potential effectiveness in the current task situation, and monitoring the success of currently implemented strategies are all examples of metacognitions. They may well be important determinants of strategy selection and utilization (Schneider & Pressley, 1989). They are not, however, isomorphic with the ongoing utilization of the strategy itself.

Recognition of the multidimensional nature of metamemory is crucial for understanding the role metamemory plays in remembering, both in the laboratory and in everyday life. For example, declarative knowledge about the potential utility of memory strategies is necessary but not sufficient for effective strategy formation and utilization in memory-demanding situations. Other aspects of metamemory, including beliefs about one's ability to use a particular strategy effectively, also come into play. Likewise, a model of metamemory that assumes a memory-monitoring function, on the one hand, and a library of declarative knowledge regarding strategies on the other, probably will not suffice to explain strategy selection behavior as it occurs in naturalistic settings. Memory self-efficacy may determine whether an individual actively engages in a monitoring process. Individuals may be relatively "mindless" (Langer, 1989) because they do not believe that memory can be controlled by their own volitional behavior. Memory self-efficacy could also influence whether the contents of the monitoring process are used as a basis for deciding to switch strategies. If an individual experiencing failure in a memory task believes that such failure reflects a general inability of oneself to learn or remember (i.e., a reflection of a property of self, not of task and selected strategy for the task), then that individual is unlikely to infer that the outcome of memory monitoring ("I haven't learned it" or "I can't recall it") implies that one should select an alternative strategy, even if that strategy is familiar to the subject, is stored in memory, and would, if employed, be successful (Elliott & Lachman, 1989). Memory monitoring may trigger retrieval of beliefs about self-as-rememberer that constrain or guide behavior in ways not fully explained by a conceptualization of metamemory as knowledge and monitoring. Moreover, memory self-efficacy can help explain affect in memory-demanding situations, and as such has the potential for explaining some of the relationships observed between affect and memory task performance. Finally, it is difficult to conceptualize formation of experientially based knowledge and self-representations about memory without a monitoring process that allows one to form and store abstracted representations of memory successes and failures, linking those events to the internal states and behaviors that led to the memory outcomes.

Metamemory in Adult Populations

Metamemory: Knowledge, Self-Monitoring, and Strategic Behavior

Developmental psychologists have argued that poor memory performance in young children, or special groups such as the learning disabled, might be attributed to deficient metamemory and suboptimal use of memory strategies rather than to any inherent deficiencies in basic memory processes themselves (e.g., Borkowski, Carr, & Pressley, 1987; Brown, 1978; Schneider & Pressley, 1989).

Some gerontologists have also argued that deficient metamemory knowledge and awareness might result in inefficient memory task strategies by older persons, and, in turn, produce observed age differences in memory task performance (Lachman & Lachman, 1980; Perlmutter, 1978). Less spontaneous and effective use of appropriate mnemonic strategies by older persons, including organizational strategies at encoding and maintenance strategies prior to recall, have been reported (e.g., Hultsch, 1969; Murphy, Sanders, Gabriesheski, & Schmitt, 1981; Sanders, Murphy, Schmitt, & Walsh, 1980; Treat, Poon, Fozard, & Popkin, 1978).

Providing older subjects with information about strategies and their potential benefits does not necessarily lead to strategy utilization in the task environment. Rabinowitz (1989) showed that additional opportunities and encouragement to utilize strategies is, by itself, insufficient to guarantee optimal strategy utilization. Training that makes explicit the link between strategy and performance may be necessary for modifying strategic behavior by older adults. Older adults have been shown to improve their utilization of study time and rehearsal under explicit strategy instructions, with resulting benefits for memory performance (Murphy, Schmitt, Caruso, & Sanders, 1987; Schmitt, Murphy, & Sanders, 1981).

A metacognitive account of older adults' suboptimal strategy development and use would suggest either (1) age deficits in monitoring memory successes and failures or (2) age deficits in the formation of appropriate strategies, as a function of either inadequate initial task appraisal or failure to respond adaptively following performance monitoring. The first account might be termed a pure monitoring deficit.

The pure monitoring deficit hypothesis is not supported by the existing literature (Lovelace, 1990). Two studies have explicitly examined age differences in monitoring degree of learning during study of words in a memory task, and both suggest little age difference in the accuracy of monitoring that learning. Both studies use an immediate judgment of learning task (see Nelson & Narens, 1990). Lovelace and Marsh (1985) had groups of old and young subjects learn 60 high-frequency paired associates. After self-paced study of the pair, they gave a rating of the confidence that the pair would be recalled in a subsequent memory test. The memory task was a matching task, with the 60 pairs in columns in randomized order. Although there were age differences in matching, indicating age differences in memory for the associates, there were no age differences in the relationship between predicted and actual associative matches. Rabinowitz, Ackerman, Craik, and Hinchley (1982) combined the paired associate learning with an instructional condition that guided either an imagery strategy or an intentional learning strategy. Old and young subjects made an immediate judgment of learning after presentation of each pair of words. Again, there were age differences in memory performance. Ratings of likelihood of recall were related to actual recall, and equally so for both age groups. Ratings of recall likelihood did not reflect the differences in the instructional conditions. Ratings of likelihood of recall did not vary by instructional condition, but recall did, with better performance in the imagery condition.

The available evidence also suggests equivalent accuracy of feeling-of-knowing judgments in older and younger adults (Anooshian, Mammarella, & Hertel, 1989; Butterfield, Nelson, & Peck, 1988;

Lachman, Lachman, & Thronesbery, 1979). It appears that older adults can effectively monitor the contents of memory when asked to do so.

One should note, however, that the current literature is far from definitive regarding the existence of monitoring deficits, and negative outcomes in one paradigm thought to reflect memory monitoring may not generalize to other paradigms. For example, Anooshian et al. (1989) found age-equivalent relationships of feeling-of-knowing judgments to subsequent recognition performance. They also asked their subjects to predict the likelihood that they would recall the information if provided with different kinds of cues, and found age differences in the accuracy of these predictions, relative to the feeling-of-knowing judgments.

The timing of the judgment individuals are asked to make may also influence the accuracy of those judgments. Recently, Nelson and Dunlosky (1991) reported that young adults' delayed judgments of learning are much more accurate than their immediate judgments of learning (see also Dunlosky & Nelson, 1992). Delayed judgments may be more accurate because attempts to retrieve the word from memory after a delay is more diagnostic of the likelihood of successful retrieval during actual recall. Both Lovelace and Marsh (1985) and Rabinowitz et al. (1982) used immediate judgments of learning with explicitly provided cues. One possibility, then, is that older and younger adults are equally adept at making the immediate judgment, but that there would be age differences in the accuracy of delayed judgments. This could occur because the two kinds of judgments require monitoring of different aspects of the memory system (information held in working memory versus long-term [or secondary] memory).

Nevertheless, the pure monitoring deficit hypothesis has, to date, found little support in the literature. Using Craik and Rabinowitz's (1984) distinction of self-initiated versus automatic (or supported) memory processes, one can argue that monitoring during cognitive tasks can be thought of as a self-initiated, volitional memory control process (i.e., a controlled, not automatic process requiring conscious activation by the individual). Older adults may not accurately or adequately monitor memory in performance situations when such monitoring would be of assistance, even though they are, in principle, capable of doing so when monitoring is explicitly required by the experimental task (e.g., a judgment of learning).

Brigham and Pressley (1988) presented evidence that can be taken as support for the hypothesis of an inadequate link between memory monitoring and strategy utilization in older persons. They required old and young subjects to learn new, esoteric vocabulary words after exposure to two alternative mnemonic strategies: key word generation and semantic context generation. Subjects predicted performance levels before study, evaluated performance by postdicting performance after recall, and indicated which strategy they would choose if asked to learn a new vocabulary list. Young subjects were more likely to adjust their postdictions to reflect differences in strategy effectiveness, and were more likely to nominate the superior keyword method for subsequent use. Older persons were apparently less aware of the relative superiority of the keyword strategy, even after employing it.

Metamemory as a Belief System

Social cognitive theorists have emphasized the potential importance of schematic representations of self and context for understanding a wide variety of social and cognitive behaviors (Markus & Wurf, 1987; Sherman, Judd, & Park, 1989). Sehulster (1981) characterized perceptions of memory ability as components of a self-theory of memory, and argued that beliefs about one's memory ought to be viewed as a subset of the person's beliefs about self (see also Herrmann, 1982, 1990). The memory self-theory concept offers several theoretical benefits (Sehulster, 1981). It places metamemory within the larger framework of self-theories, rendering the larger social cognitive literature regarding self-conceptions and implicit theories relevant to the understanding of how beliefs about memory are formed and maintained (Cavanaugh, Feldman, & Hertzog, 1993). Second, the concept of belief explicitly raises the question the veridicality of beliefs about memory (Langer, 1989). Third, the concept of memory beliefs suggests that certain behaviors (e.g., the amount of risk one takes in situations perceived as demanding memory) may be more highly related to memory beliefs than actual memory ability.

Many gerontologists now accept the importance of differentiating knowledge about memory mechanisms and processes from beliefs about one's own memory abilities (e.g., Berry & West, 1993; Cavanaugh et al., 1993; Dixon & Hertzog, 1988; Hertzog et al., 1990a; Perlmutter et al., 1987). As noted earlier, a key construct is memory self-efficacy: the set of beliefs regarding one's own capability to use memory effectively.

Bandura (1989) treats memory self-efficacy as the specific set of beliefs operating in the memory task environment itself — for him a performance prediction is a relatively direct measure of self-efficacy (see also Berry & West, 1993). We have offered an alternative perspective on memory self-efficacy, conceptualizing it as a hierarchically organized set of beliefs about self-as-rememberer (Hertzog et al., 1990a). The hierarchical nature of the set reflects variation in generality from the most global (e.g., "I am losing my memory; I can't remember very well") to domain-specific (e.g., "I never forget a face, but I can't remember names") and context-specific (e.g., "I always forget where I'm parked, so I'd better write the area number down") to local, or concurrent ("I can remember this phone number, so I'll just dial it without writing it down").

Bandura (1989) views self-efficacy as a primary cause of poor cognitive task performance (see also Berry & West, 1993; Cavanaugh & Green, 1990). Self-efficacy beliefs can influence cognitive performance in several ways. First, self-efficacy beliefs can influence the construction of task strategies — that is, effective plans of action for attaining performance goals. Second, high self-efficacy beliefs lead to higher levels of effort and persistence in the face of initial failure (Bandura, 1986). Third, low self-efficacy beliefs can cause high levels of negative affect, especially anxiety, in the performance situation, which can lead to poor performance (Bandura, 1988).

Although Bandura (1986) acknowledges that self-efficacy and task performance are, inevitably, reciprocal causes of one another, his account emphasizes the primary importance of self-efficacy as a proximal cause of success and failure. We have argued that an alternative perspective on memory task performance and memory self-efficacy is equally plausible (Hertzog et al., 1990a). Individual differences in underlying memory abilities and skills could influence both performance and self-efficacy beliefs, with the latter being an outcome of a performance evaluation that is also influenced by a number of other processes (e.g., causal attributions for performance success and failure). Both accounts have theoretical justification and some empirical support (see below), and are extremely difficult in practice to disentangle.

Do Memory Self-Efficacy Beliefs Vary as a Function of Age?

One method for measuring memory beliefs has been the use of self-report questionnaires. There are a large number of questionnaires available for work with adults (for reviews, see Dixon, 1989; Gilewski & Zelinski, 1986; Herrmann, 1982). These questionnaires typically assess multiple facets of memory beliefs and practices. The construct of memory self-efficacy helps to explain much of the observed age differences in multidimensional metamemory questionnaire responses. The greatest age differences in metamemory are observed on measures of perceived change in memory ability during adulthood (Hultsch, Hertzog, & Dixon, 1987; Perlmutter, 1978). It also appears that measures of current memory complaints and perceived memory ability show age differences, with lower perceived memory capacity and a greater degree of memory complaints by older persons (Dixon & Hultsch, 1983b; Hultsch et al., 1987; Zelinski, Gilewski, & Anthony-Bergstone, 1990), although some studies have failed to find age differences in current memory complaints (e.g., Chaffin & Herrmann, 1983). It appears that questionnaire measures of perceived frequency of forgetting may be less likely to show age differences than scales measuring perceived memory ability (Hultsch et al., 1987).

The Metamemory in Adulthood (MIA; see Dixon, Hultsch, & Hertzog, 1988) questionnaire contains eight subscales that capture multiple dimensions of metamemory (see table 11.1 for a summary of the scales and some sample items). Three of the scales seem closely related to the concept of memory self-efficacy (Capacity — measuring perceived ability; Change — measuring perceived change in memory ability; and Locus — measuring perceived control over one's memory). A fourth MIA subscale, Anxiety, measures self-rated anxiety when required to use memory, which may be a proximal outcome of self-efficacy beliefs. Hertzog, Hultsch, and Dixon (1989) showed

Table 11.1.
The dimensions of the Metamemory in Adulthood (MIA) instrument[a]

Dimension	Description	Sample item
1. Strategy (18[b])	Knowledge and use of information about one's remembering abilities such that performance in given instances is potentially improved (+ = high use)	Do you write appointments on a calendar to help you remember them?
2. Task (15)	Knowledge of basic memory processes, especially as evidenced by how most people perform (+ = high knowledge)	For most people, facts that are interesting are easier to remember than facts that are not
3. Capacity (17)	Perception of memory capacities as evidenced by predictive report of performance on given tasks (+ = high capacity)	I am good at remembering names
4. Change (18)	Perception of memory abilities as generally stable or subject to long-term decline (+ = stability)	The older I get the harder it is to remember things clearly
5. Anxiety (14)	Feelings of stress related to memory performance (+ = high anxiety)	I do not get flustered when I am put on the spot to remember new things
6. Achievement (16)	Perceived importance of having a good memory and performing well on memory tasks (+ = high achievement)	It is very important that I am very accurate when remembering names of people
7. Locus (9)	Perceived personal control over remembering abilities (+ = internality)	Even if I work on it my memory ability will go downhill

[a]Based on Dixon and Hultsch (1983b).
[b]Number of total items.

that these scales from the MIA and several scales from the Memory Functioning Questionnaire (Zelinski et al., 1990) converged to measure a factor they identified as Memory Self-Efficacy (MSE). Cavanaugh and Poon (1989) also found convergence between these MIA scales and measures of frequency of forgetting from another metamemory questionnaire. Several studies have found that there are reliable age differences on the MIA scales related to MSE (Cavanaugh & Poon, 1989; Dixon & Hultsch, 1983b, Hultsch et al., 1987; Loewen, Shaw, & Craik, 1992). MSE may account, then, for the bulk of age differences in scales measuring aspects of metamemory.

The MIA also measures the knowledge component of metamemory, in the form of the Task scale. Age differences on Task have been found (e.g., Dixon & Hultsch, 1983b), but not as consistently. The MIA Strategy scale measures self-reported usage of internal mnemonics and external memory aids, and can be divided into Internal and External subscales (Dixon & Hultsch, 1983b). Age differences in self-reported strategy use are usually not found, although Loewen et al. (1992) found that older persons may report greater use of external aids and lower use of mnemonic strategies.

The literature on questionnaire measures of metamemory in adult populations supports the notion that memory self-efficacy beliefs are often inaccurate. One common method for evaluating this hypothesis is to examine correlations of memory self-efficacy scales and memory task performance, although there are some valid reasons to be concerned about this operational definition of the accuracy of MSE (Rabbitt & Abson, 1990). These correlations typically range between 0 and 0.3 in both normal and memory-impaired adult populations (e.g., Cavanaugh & Poon, 1989; Hertzog et al., 1990b; O'Hara, Hinrichs, Kohout, Wallace, & Lemke, 1986; Rabbitt & Abson, 1990; Sunderland, Harris, & Baddeley, 1983; Sunderland, Watts, Baddeley, & Harris, 1986; Zelinski et al., 1990). The magnitude of the MSE/memory performance correlations may be influenced by a number of factors, including type of memory task and correspondence between domain of self-reported memory and memory tasks. Larrabee, West, and Crook (1991) correlated tasks simulating everyday memory demands (e.g., dialing a newly learned phone number) with self-reported frequency of forgetting in the same task in every-

Metacognition in Adulthood and Old Age

day life. They found relatively small associations between self-reports and performance.

As noted by Herrmann (1982), the lack of strong relationships between questionnaire measures and memory performance might be attributed to low reliability and construct validity of metamemory questionnaires (see also Dixon, 1989; Gilewski & Zelinski, 1986). This does not appear to be the case. Most recent work suggests adequate internal consistency for metamemory scales. In addition to the evidence for strong convergent validity across different questionnaires (Cavanaugh & Poon, 1989; Hertzog et al., 1989), the available evidence suggests that metamemory questionnaires also have adequate discriminant validity. Metamemory scales do show some significant correlations with measures of personality, depression, affective states, and general measures of self-efficacy and locus of control (Broadbent, Cooper, Fitzgerald, & Parkes, 1982; Cavanaugh & Murphy, 1986; Hertzog et al., 1990a; Niederehe & Yoder, 1989; Rabbitt & Abson, 1990; Zelinski et al., 1990). The correlations typically found are sufficiently small to support the argument that MSE and other metamemory factors are related to, but distinct from, constructs such as extraversion, neuroticism, depressive affect, and general self-efficacy beliefs. It appears that questionnaires may give relatively valid reflections of memory beliefs, but that individual differences in MSE beliefs are not necessarily valid reflections of relative memory ability, at least as measured by experimental tasks (see also Herrmann, 1990).

The relationship of self-reports of memory problems or capacities and depression has been a special focus in the literature, perhaps because of its obvious implications for accurate psychological assessment. Is a person complaining of memory loss memory-impaired or dysphoric? Some studies have suggested that memory complaints are more likely to be related to depressive affect than actual memory functioning (Popkin, Gallagher, Thompson, & Moore, 1982; West, Boatwright, & Schleser, 1984; Zarit, Cole, & Guider, 1981). In and of itself this pattern of results does not necessarily imply that memory complaints are merely a manifestation of depression. Beliefs could cause depression, not the other way around. A belief that one's memory is declining, and that the decline is beyond one's control, can be depressing! Recent work suggests that, although negative affect such as depression and anxiety do correlate with memory complaints, the magnitude of the relationship can explain neither age differences in perceived memory ability nor the modest correlations of memory beliefs and memory performance (Hertzog et al., 1990a; Zelinski et al., 1990).

A crucial issue for understanding memory self-efficacy beliefs is, where do they come from? Are they are derived from inferences about actual memory-related experiences, possibly mediated by performance monitoring? Or do they represent an internalization of stereotypes about the effects of aging on memory? There is little question that such generalized beliefs about memory develop early in life (e.g., Crawford, Herrmann, Holdsworth, Randall, & Robbins, 1989; Wellman, 1983). Older persons and younger persons alike typically believe that memory declines in adulthood (Erber, 1989; Ryan, 1992).

A key to understanding the development of memory self-efficacy may be the implicit theories people have about cognition and memory. Dweck and Leggett (1988) argued that children tend to view cognition as depending on either relatively fixed ability traits or skills that can be improved through learning. In principle, these implicit assumptions about the nature of cognition will have direct impact on whether one believes that memory functioning is, in principle, malleable and controllable. Furthermore, differences in implicit theories about memory may result in differences regarding the expected effects of aging on memory (Langer, 1981; Perlmutter et al., 1987; Person & Wellman, 1988; Ryan, 1992). To the extent that one believes that memory is a biologically fixed ability, and that aging is inevitably associated with a biologically determined decline in functioning, one is likely to assume that one's own memory must decline. In other words, one may internalize the stereotype of decline (Elliott & Lachman, 1989; Langer, 1981). Uncritical adoption of the stereotype of decline could lead individuals to believe their memory has declined, irrespective of any age-related changes in actual frequency of memory successes or failures. Moreover, beliefs of inevitable memory decline may make incidents of forgetting more salient, and bias older adults to attribute memory failures to age-related loss of effective functioning.

It is therefore reasonable to ask about the extent to which memory self-efficacy beliefs identified by metamemory questionnaires are influenced by biased interpretations of everyday events. Beliefs can be conceptualized as schemas stored in memory, with individuals varying in the extent to which schemas are chronically accessible (see Cavanaugh et al., 1993). The robust relationship of age to perceived change in memory might merely reflect the increasing availability as individuals grow older of the belief that aging leads to memory decline. The increasing availability might be further reinforced by the likelihood that an incident of forgetting will trigger an attribution of declining capacity due to aging, given the chronic accessibility of that belief.

Mnemonic training studies may require intervention to change memory self-efficacy beliefs as well as beliefs about strategy use, in order to achieve changes in use of memory-enhancing behaviors in everyday life (Elliott & Lachman, 1989).

Memory Self-Efficacy and Performance Anxiety

Age differences in memory performance are almost undoubtedly not an artifact of age differences in test anxiety (Kausler, 1990). Nevertheless, older persons' performance on memory tasks are, in at least some studies, negatively influenced by test anxiety (e.g., Eisdorfer, 1968; Whitbourne, 1976). Thus anxious affect may have an adverse impact on the performance of some older adults, and whether it does may be a function of a complex set of eliciting conditions.

Under what conditions are individuals likely to experience anxiety in performance situations? Bandura (1986, 1988) argued that anxiety is a direct outcome of individuals' low self-efficacy beliefs. If one believes that one is likely to fail in a performance situation, then one experiences anxious affect, phobic desires to avoid the failure experience, and self-protective cognitions. High self-efficacy beliefs limit the experience of concurrent negative affect (depression and anxiety), whereas low self-efficacy beliefs lead to increased levels of performance anxiety in the testing situation. Anxiety in the performance situation may then influence the extent to which individuals effectively monitor their performance. To the extent that individuals are preoccupied with their affective state, or are dealing with the consequences of negative ideation associated with anxiety regarding failure, they may be less likely to attend to the implications of goal/ performance discrepancies for potential modifications of task strategies (Zimmerman & Schunk, 1989).

Self-reported anxiety about memory performance has been found to be related to text recall in elderly samples (Dixon and Hultsch, 1983a). Davidson, Dixon, and Hultsch (1991) reported evidence that domain-specific anxiety about memory (1) is more highly related to free recall of words than measures of state anxiety, and (2) may be a better predictor of actual memory task performance in older adults than in middle-aged and younger adults.

Memory self-efficacy and memory-related anxiety may therefore help to explain why studies have often failed to observe strong relationships between measures of trait anxiety and memory performance in older adults (Kausler, 1990). The degree of anxiety experienced in cognitive performance settings may vary widely across individuals, depending on which aspects of the cognitively related belief system are activated as individuals proceed through the experimental task. Moreover, the domain-specific construct of anxiety about cognitive performance, *not trait anxiety*, may be the proximal determinant of performance anxiety as experienced in the situation (Hertzog, 1992). Most older individuals rate themselves as being relatively calm and as generally lacking anxious affect. Nevertheless, they may have volunteered for the study partly out of concern about recent experiences of memory failure, and the possibility that these failures may indicate declining memory. This concern could trigger anxious affect, but only when the subject directly anticipates or actually begins performing on the memory task.

Given the preceding arguments, it would seem that adequate explication of anxiety/performance relationships in older adults must account for individual differences in belief systems that both mediate and moderate the relationships between age, anxiety, and performance.

Predicting Memory Performance: A Metacognitive Account

Memory predictions have often been conceptualized as an index of knowledge about one's own memory (Cavanaugh & Perlmutter, 1982; Schneider & Pressley, 1989). The implicit logic is often as follows: the more accurate the prediction, the better one's knowledge about one's own memory and how it functions.

There is a complex literature on age differences in prediction accuracy. One major factor influencing these patterns is whether the predictions are *global* or *aggregated* estimates of subsequent task performance (e.g., the total number of words to be correctly recalled in a free recall task) or *item-by-item judgments* of likelihood of subsequent recall (e.g., ratings of likelihood of remembering a target word given the cue it was paired with during study). As already noted, there appear to be minimal age differences in the accuracy of such item-by-item judgments.

Several studies have suggested that old subjects are less accurate in their global or aggregated performance predictions than younger adults (Brigham & Pressley, 1988; Bruce, Coyne, & Botwinick, 1982; Coyne, 1985; Lachman & Jelialian 1984). In contrast, other studies have found relatively accurate memory task predictions by older adults (Camp, Markley, & Kramer, 1983; Lachman, Steinberg, & Trotter, 1987; Perlmutter, 1978). Studies using multiple experimental tasks have found that accuracy scores vary as a function of the task (Devolder, Brigham, & Pressley, 1990; Rabbitt & Abson, 1991).

Evidence suggests that older persons are equally adept at improving prediction accuracy in multiple trial memory tasks (Hertzog et al., 1990b) and that their performance postdictions (that is, aggregated postperformance evaluations of performance) are more accurate than their prior predictions (Devolder et al., 1990). The upgrading in prediction accuracy and the superiority of postdictions to predictions both suggest little age-related change in the ability to accurately monitor task performance.

The complex patterns of results regarding prediction accuracy raise the larger question of how aggregated performance predictions should be conceptualized. Different psychologists have treated them as operational definitions of alternative, related, but differentiable constructs: (1) reflections of knowledge about one's memory and how to approach a memory task (Schneider & Pressley, 1989), (2) task-specific memory self-efficacy judgments (Berry et al., 1989), or (3) measures of on-line awareness of the operations and contents of memory (Cavanaugh & Green, 1990).

If performance predictions are treated as operational definitions of knowledge about memory task characteristics, then one can inquire about the accuracy of the knowledge adults have about variables that influence memory. Shaw and Craik (1989) and Rabinowitz et al. (1982) demonstrated that neither young nor old subjects vary predicted item recall to accurately reflect the influence of experimentally manipulated variables on subsequent recall. Brigham and Pressley (1988) found that both young and old adults failed to show a preference for the keyword strategy after being introduced to it, but prior to actually using it to study vocabulary items. As noted by Lovelace (1990), one reasonable account of the results in the literature is that predictions are more sensitive to manipulations of materials (e.g., concreteness of words) than to manipulations of processing demands (e.g., orienting tasks). Nevertheless, the frequent failure of individuals to adjust predictions to be sensitive to experimental conditions suggests that experimental psychologists may make unwarranted assumptions about the extent of knowledge people have about memory functioning, as well as the degree to which individuals can evaluate the memory processing demands of tasks with which they have little or no prior experience.

An alternative perspective on predictions argues that predictions are in fact a complex amalgam of all three classes of variables listed above: knowledge, self-efficacy, and on-line monitoring (Hertzog et al., 1990a). According to this view, a performance prediction is a constructed judgment, dependent on a set of representations of task, task context, and self-as-remember in the particular task context. Metamemorial knowledge, in this sense, can be partitioned into a set of representations of the task and a set of representations of the self. Hertzog et al. (1990b) argued that a prediction implicitly requires some kind of appraisal of the demands or requirements of the task. This appraisal is then combined with self-efficacy beliefs to form a task-specific prediction of performance. The importance of task appraisal as a determinant of prediction accuracy has only recently been emphasized in the literature (see also Lovelace, 1990; McDonald-Miszczak, Hunter, & Hultsch, 1993).

Hertzog et al. (1990b) provided some support for the argument that performance predictions are influenced by more general MSE. The design included three trials of free recall of categorizable nouns (word recall) and narrative texts. Subjects alternated between the two tasks, with a different list of nouns (or a different text) used for each trial. Initial performance predictions were moderately correlated with MSE, and MSE correlated approximately .3 with actual recall.

The pattern of correlations of predictions with recall is of special interest. Table 11.2 provides these correlations from the Hertzog et al. (1990b) study. The initial prediction, for trial 1 word recall, correlated about .3 with actual word recall. However, task experience increased the prediction/performance correlations substantially. The pattern of correlations suggested a lagged effect of performance on subsequent predictions, because predictions were more highly correlated with recall on the preceding trial than for the immediately following recall. Indeed, a structural equation model showed that when paths from performance to prediction were modeled, there was no indication of a direct effect of a prediction on the immediately following performance. These results suggested that increasing prediction accuracy was primarily a function of learning about task and self from actual performance (see Hertzog et al., 1990a).

Hertzog, Saylor, Fleece, and Dixon (1993) recently reported a set of experiments that adds to the picture of performance predictions

Table 11.2
Correlations of recall predictions with recall performance

	Word recall		
	Trail 1	Trial 2	Trial 3
Trial 1	.24	.58	.62
Trial 2	.24	.52	.71
Trial 3	.29	.52	.62
	Text recall		
	Trial 1	Trial 2	Trial 3
Trial 1	.44	.54	.51
Trial 2	.50	.54	.54
Trial 3	.58	.58	.58

Adapted from Hertzog et al. (1990b, table 5)

as complex constructed judgments. The study replicated and extended the effects reported in Hertzog et al. (1990b). Three of the four experiments used the same categorized word lists used in the previous study. All of the experiments included recall predictions and recall postdictions.

Postdictions were almost perfectly accurate in the word recall task when written recall was obtained — the method used by Hertzog et al. (1990b). However, consistent with Devolder et al. (1990), postdiction accuracy varied by task and by method of recall. Postdictions in an oral recall condition correlated roughly .7 with performance. Postdictions for recognition memory of words correlated roughly .6 with performance. In all cases, postdictions were more accurate than initial predictions, and there were no age differences in the upgrading of accuracy. The results support the hypothesis that improvement in predictions across multiple recall trials is mediated by accurate evaluations of performance.

The Hertzog et al. (1993) study also found that prediction accuracy improves even before a recall is made. It used a phased prediction paradigm, in which subjects (1) predicted performance after a brief description of the task, (2) actually studied the materials, and then (3) predicted performance again immediately prior to recall. Two experiments showed that the second prediction, after study, correlated more highly with subsequent recall than the initial prediction. However, there was, to our surprise, an age difference in the magnitude of this upgrading. Table 11.3 reports correlations for the trial 1 predictions and postdictions with written free recall, aggregated over the two experiments, for young and old subjects. As can be seen, younger persons show a greater magnitude of upgrading from the first to the second prediction, but correlations of postdictions with performance are essentially equal.

Hertzog et al. (1993) also found an interesting disassociation of correlations of predictions and performance from two different measures of prediction accuracy (signed and unsigned differences between predicted and actual performance) for the free recall task. Unlike the correlations, there were significant age differences in prediction accuracy. Older subjects were more accurate than younger adults on both prediction accuracy measures. In addition, neither of these measures showed upgrading in accuracy from the first to the

Table 11.3
Correlations of phased predictions and postdictions with free recall across two recall trials for young and old adults

	Young	Old
Trial 1		
Prediction 1	.15	.13
Prediction 2	.49	.30
Postdiction	.94	.92
Trial 2		
Prediction 1	.35	.45
Prediction 2	.53	.53
Postdiction	.95	.92

Correlations are weighted averages (using r to z transformations) of correlations from experiments 2 and 3 from Hertzog et al. (1993). Based upon $N = 261$ in each age group.

second prediction that can be observed in the correlations of table 11.3. On the recognition memory task, all subjects underpredicted the number of hits (correct recognitions), with a mean difference of more than 10 hits in both young and old groups. Performance postdictions correlated more highly with performance than did performance predictions, and the postdiction accuracies (as measured by simple and absolute difference scores) improved significantly relative to prediction accuracies. But in all cases the postdictions also underestimated performance.

The most plausible explanation is that subjects did not appreciate that chance performance in a Yes/No decision is 50% correct, and hence that they should have expected to get 32 out of 64 words correct by chance alone. If so, then faulty task appraisal may be implicated as a major influence on difference score measures of prediction accuracy. Correlations of predictions and performance measures would be less susceptible to this effect because of the standardization of both prediction and performance measures.

The disassociation of prediction accuracy measures from prediction/performance correlations for word recall suggests that the same influence may be operating in that task as well. It is interesting to note that subjects in all age groups used 15 words as the modal prediction in the word recall task, possibly because it was the midpoint of the the range of performance on a 30-word list. This behavior was observed both when the benchmark of 15 words was explicitly provided as a mean performance level by the experimenter and when no prior information was provided. This finding sheds a different light on the age differences in prediction accuracy. We found that younger subjects were less accurate than older persons, on average. Some might argue that this effect suggests that that older persons are more knowledgeable about themselves or about the memory task. An alternative hypothesis is that, in an absence of task experience, individuals will interpret the midpoint of the prediction scale as a neutral, best guess response. If so, then by accident of experimental design (including factors such as list length, difficulty of the word list, study time) the average performance of older persons for the lists used in our studies was closer to the intrinsically preferred prediction of 15 than was the average performance of younger persons. This hypothesis is consistent with other work showing that the predictions of both young and old subjects are relatively insensitive to experimental manipulations that affect task difficulty (Shaw & Craik, 1989). If correct, it calls into serious question assumptions that prediction accuracy measures are good operational definitions of the accuracy of knowledge about either self or task.

The results from the phased prediction paradigm support the inference that memory monitoring can also influence predictions that are made after study of the word lists. The influence of memory-monitoring ability on predictions apparently differs as a function of age. However, as noted above, studies measuring immediate judgments of learning suggest little or no age deficits in on-line monitoring of the memory system (see Lovelace, 1990).

One possible explanation of this apparent discrepancy involves potential limitations in the immediate judgment of learning used to infer equivalent on-line monitoring (see above). It is possible, for example, that age differences would emerge in delayed judgments of learning (Dunlosky & Nelson, 1992) just as they do in the (necessarily) delayed global prediction after study obtained by Hertzog et al. (1993).

It is probably the case, however, that the global prediction made after study is not based on an exhaustive search of the contents of long-term memory across all items in the memory set, followed by aggregation into a total number of predicted words recalled. It seems more likely that the judgment is based on rapid access to information about the availability of words in memory, possibly even without retrieval of specific items (see Reder & Ritter, 1992). If so, there may be age differences in the nature of the information accessed, or in the way in which that information is used to construct the aggregated prediction. As noted earlier, older adults may not spontaneously monitor memory to the same degree without explicit instructions or implicit task demands that initiate the monitoring.

In any event, it is clear that a definitive explanation of the age difference in the prediction after study will require research that frames the prediction process in a more complex conceptual framework than has been common in the literature, and that considers the influence of a host of variables. In retrospect, assumptions that predictions are a relatively clean measure of either knowledge, self-efficacy beliefs, or awareness of memory performance seem far too simplistic. Creating a general model that synthesizes the multiple influences on prediction behavior, and using it to test age differences in metamemorial constructs, is an exciting task for the future.

Summary and Conclusions

We have presented a perspective on metacognition and metamemory that begins with the premise that metacognition is a multidimensional construct domain. Although most experimental psychologists emphasize the facets of knowledge and monitoring, work in the adult developmental area has started to place equal or greater emphasis on another facet of metacognition: beliefs about cognition, particular self-relevant beliefs, and the functional role they play in the utilization of metacognitive knowledge and monitoring capabilities. We have summarized evidence that increasing age is accompanied by changes in memory self-efficacy, and by increasing adoption of the belief that one's own capabilities have declined as a function of aging. For a given individual, these beliefs may be inaccurate, and, indeed, correlations of memory self-efficacy and memory task performance in adult samples are typically quite modest in magnitude. One cannot reasonably attribute the limited degree of correlation to poor psychometric properties of scales measuring memory-related beliefs. Instead, it appears that these beliefs have limited predictive validity for between-person differences in memory performance. Nevertheless, they can have profound impact on the psychological well-being of older adults, and can also influence older adults' effective levels of functioning in cognitively demanding situations.

Older adults are sometimes found to be deficient in the use of optimal task strategies and may not recognize the potential utility of strategies they have not independently selected. These results occur despite (admittedly limited) evidence of age-equivalence in memory monitoring abilities. As yet we do not understand the factors that cause deficient spontaneous use of intentional strategies for organizing encoding and retrieval of information by older adults. One exciting avenue for future research is determining whether memory self-efficacy and related beliefs may represent a moderator variable that influences both the affective response and the task-related behaviors of older adults.

The multidimensional view of metamemory has important implications for the construct validity of some measures that have been common in the metamemory literature, especially performance predictions. Certainly these implications extend beyond the developmental literature to the area of metamemory, in general. Our own work has emphasized that performance predictions are complex, constructed judgments potentially relying on self-efficacy beliefs, task appraisal, prior task experience, and other factors. Under some, but not all, conditions, predictions may reflect the outcome of a memory monitoring process. However, psychologists are ill-advised to presume that predictions are relatively pure measures of memory monitoring, knowing about remembering, or any other single aspect of metamemory. The challenge to all of us is to develop theoretical models and empirical paradigms that do justice to the complexity of the phenomena we categorize under the rather broad umbrella of metacognition.

Acknowledgments

Empirical research by the authors and their colleagues summarized in this chapter was supported in part by a grant from the National Institute on Aging to C. Hertzog (R01 AG06162) and a grant from the Natural Sciences and Engineering Research Council of Canada to R. A. Dixon.

12

The Neuropsychology of Metacognition

Arthur P. Shimamura

Knowing about one's own cognitions forms the basis for most metacognitive abilities. These abilities include knowledge about one's perceptions, memories, decisions, and actions. The neuropsychology of metacognition involves the study of impairments in aspects of "knowing" that occur as a result of brain injury or disease. In many instances, metacognitive dysfunction involves a problem in the experience or feeling of conscious awareness. That is, to know about one's cognitions is to be consciously aware of their operations. In the past decade, progress in the neuropsychology of metacognition has advanced considerably by interest in conceptual bridges between cognitive and biological approaches. This progress is exemplified by new fields of study, such as *cognitive neuroscience* and *cognitive neuropsychology*.

Disruptions of metacognition can take many forms, depending on the aspect of knowledge that is inaccessible or unavailable to conscious awareness. In fact, many of these disruptions can be characterized as cognition without awareness — such as *vision without awareness* or *memory without awareness*. Such neuropsychological findings provide important clues to the understanding of cognitive function. They suggest that many cognitive functions can operate without conscious control or awareness. Such findings also provide information concerning the neural systems that support cognitive function. That is, certain cognitive functions appear to be organized in a componential fashion — involving specific neural circuits and operating in parallel with other functions. Based on this componential view, it is likely that different metacognitive impairment will be mediated by different neural circuits, depending on the form or type of cognitive function that is disrupted.

This chapter examines examples of neurological disorders that cause impairment in metacognition. Although many examples could be presented, this chapter focuses only on several representative forms of metacognitive dysfunction. Generally, these disorders affect the ability to know about or have awareness of one's own cognitive performance. For each dysfunction, attempts will be made to describe the behavioral anomaly, the cognitive component believed to be disrupted, and the neural system that is affected.

Blindsight

When an individual incurs damage to the primary visual area of the cerebral cortex — identified as *area 17* in the occipital lobe — he or she will exhibit blindness in certain portions of the visual field. If the damage is contained within a circumscribed area in one cerebral hemisphere, a *scotoma* or blind spot will be apparent in the visual field. If the damage involves much or all of area 17 in one cerebral hemisphere, a *hemianopia* will occur in which the individual is functionally blind across an entire half field of vision. *Blindsight* is the ability to exhibit some visual capacity within a scotoma or a hemianopic field, despite the absence of any conscious experience of visual perception (Weiskrantz, 1986). For example, patients with blindsight can detect the "presence" of a stimulus in the blind region, though they acknowledge no visual perception in that region and often claim that their responses were based on mere guesses.

Weiskrantz, Warrington, Sanders, and Marshall (1974) provided the first extensive case study of blindsight in their investigations of a patient identified as D.B. D.B. underwent surgery in 1973 at the age of 34 years to remove an arteriovenous malformation in the region of the right occipital pole (Weiskrantz et al., 1974; see also Weiskrantz, 1986, 1989). Following surgery, D.B. exhibited a left-field hemianopia, with some sparing of vision in the upper left quadrant. Vision in the right visual field was normal. Although D.B. was functionally blind for information presented in his left visual field, careful analyses of vision revealed some residual capacity. For example, D.B.

could point accurately to spots of light presented at various target positions in the hemianopic field (figure 12.1). This ability was extraordinary, considering the fact that D.B. claimed to be basing his performance on guesses. D.B. could also "make guesses" based on orientation or shape information. That is, he could determine whether an *X* or an *O* was presented or whether a horizontal or a vertical line was presented in his blind field, though he had no experience of seeing shapes. In general, his performance was better for larger stimuli than for smaller ones. Also, performance in the blind field was not as good as his performance in the normal field. Nevertheless, these findings indicate that some visual capacity was available even when *conscious awareness* of perception was not. Indeed, when D.B. was shown a videotape of himself performing remarkably well to targets presented in his *blind* field he was "openly astonished" (Weiskrantz et al., 1974).

Subsequent studies of D.B. and other patients with similar cortical lesions indicate an array of residual visual capacity in hemianopic fields and scotomas. Tests of D.B. indicate that he was able to perform well on tests of detection, localization, color, movement, and orientation (Weiskrantz et al., 1974; Weiskrantz, 1986). Tests of other patients generally have confirmed findings of residual capacity in detection, localization, and color (Barbur, Ruddock, & Watefield, 1980; Perenin, 1978; Perenin & Jeannerod, 1978; Stoerig, 1987; Zihl, 1980). The residual capacity to discriminate orientation or form is less clear in other blindsight patients (Barbur et al., 1980; Perenin, 1978). These other cases involved patients with vascular lesions of the posterior cerebral artery, patients with traumatic head injuries, and hemidecorticate patients who, as a result of early neurological disorders, have had one cerebral hemisphere entirely removed during childhood. In all cases, blindsight is demonstrated by good performance on visual tests of detection or localization within a scotoma or hemianopic field, despite the lack of subjective experience that performance is based on anything more than "guesses" or gross hunches.

D.B.'s ability to discriminate orientation and form appears to be rather unique among blindsight patients. As mentioned before, D.B. was able to distinguish Xs from Os and horizontal lines from vertical lines. When pressed to describe the basis for these judgments, D.B.

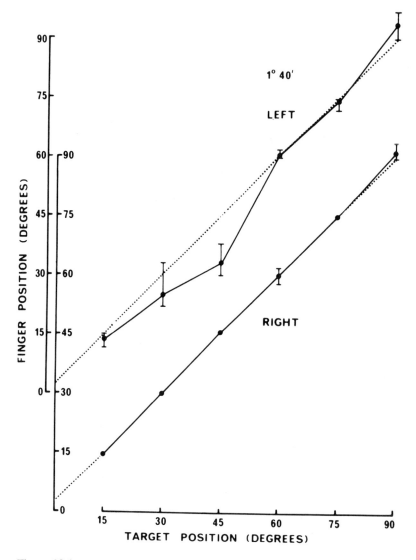

Figure 12.1
Finger reaching ability in blindsight patient D.B. Solid lines refer to finger reaching performance as a function of target position away from central fixation for left ("blind" field) and right field presentations (bars refer to ranges). Dotted lines refer to perfect finger location. Left and right graphs are displaced vertically by 30° for ease of graphic presentation. Reprinted from Weiskrantz et al. (1974).

said he had the feeling of stimuli being "smooth" (Os) or "jagged" (Xs) or pointing one way or another (Weiskrantz et al., 1974). In fact, D.B.'s form discriminations may have been based on orientation information, because he could not discriminate squares from rectangles but could discriminate squares from diamonds (Weiskrantz, 1986). Hemidecorticate patients do not exhibit residual capacity to discriminate changes in orientation, though they do exhibit residual capacity to detect and locate stimuli in their hemianopic field (Perenin, 1978; Perenin & Jeannerod, 1978). Also, a blindsight case who exhibited a hemianopia following a traumatic head injury could not discriminate changes in orientation or form (Barbur et al., 1980). Perhaps the distinction between D.B.'s performance and those of other patients was the result of the rather circumscribed lesion in D.B. compared to other patients. The surgical lesion in D.B. was probably limited to the occipital pole, whereas other patients had larger lesions, sometimes involving the whole cerebral hemisphere.

What is the neural mechanism that underlies the residual visual capacity in patients with blindsight? Attempts have been made to reject gross artifacts, such as decisions based on stray light impinging on the normal visual field or gross problems in response decision criteria — that is, claiming to be "blind" or "just guessing" when vision is actually good (see Perenin & Jeannerod, 1978; Weiskrantz, 1986). For example, visually impaired patients do not exhibit blindsight if they have retinal pathology or pathology of optic nerve fibers. If gross artifacts cannot explain blindsight, then what other routes are available when the primary visual area of the neocortex is damaged?

Two likely neural mechanisms have been proposed to explain blindsight (for review, see Cowey & Stoerig, 1991; Weiskrantz, 1986). First, about 10–20% of optic nerve fibers project directly to midbrain structures such as the superior colliculus and pulvinar. The other fibers project to area 17 via the lateral geniculate nucleus of the thalamus. It has been suggested that midbrain structures may provide rudimentary visual capacity. To demonstrate the importance of the superior colliculus in visual processing, Mohler and Wurtz (1977) developed an animal analogue of blindsight. They showed that lesions of the occipital lobe in monkeys produce a scotoma. However, when these animals were trained to detect stimuli in the region of the scotoma, visual sensitivity within that area returned, and ultimately the scotoma disappeared. When subsequent lesions of the superior colliculus were made in these same animals, the scotoma reappeared and residual vision could not be reinstated with further training.

Recent evidence for the contribution of midbrain structures in human visual processing comes from a paradigm used to assess visual attention (Posner, Rafal, Choate, & Vaughan, 1985; Rafal, Smith, Krantz, Cohen, & Brennan, 1990). In this paradigm, each trial begins with subjects fixating their gaze on a square in the center of the visual field. Attention is then directed to a left or right square by a brief brightening of the peripheral square (300 millisecond duration). Attention is then redirected to the center by a brightening of the center square. During these shifts of attention, subjects are asked to maintain fixation on the center square. Finally, one of the peripheral squares is targeted by presenting a filled circle in the location, and subjects are asked to execute an eye fixation to the targeted location or make a left or right keypress response to indicate the targeted location. In this paradigm, normal individuals exhibit slower response latencies on trials in which the targeted location was just recently cued compared to trials in which the opposite location was previously cued. This phenomenon has been termed *inhibition of return* and appears to be related to attentional mechanisms that bias the visual system against fixations to recently attended spatial locations. Interestingly, inhibition of return is abolished in patients with midbrain lesions resulting from progressive supranuclear palsy (Posner et al., 1985).

Further evidence for the contribution of midbrain structures in the phenomenon of inhibition of return was obtained in a study of patients with hemianopias due to cortical lesions (Rafal et al., 1990). In that study, visual input to the hemianopic field would presumably affect midbrain structures but not cortical structures. Indeed, in such conditions, patients still exhibited an inhibition of return response. The study capitalized on the finding that midbrain projections from the optic fibers have more crossed connections than ipsilateral connections. Thus, under monocular conditions stimuli presented on the nasal portion of the retina would activate midbrain structures more than stimuli presented on the temporal portion of the retina.

In patients with cortical hemianopias, inhibition of return occurred when patients were asked to execute saccadic eye movements to stimuli presented in the intact visual field when cues were presented in the nasal portion of the retina of the "blind" visual field. That is, even when information was not available to the neocortex, it influenced (inhibited) eye movement responses. This finding suggests that midbrain structures can contribute to performance even though cortical structures are damaged.

An alternative view of blindsight is that residual visual function is mediated by "extrastriate" cortical regions. These extrastriate regions (e.g., areas 18 and 19) are adjacent to the primary visual area and have been associated with secondary or associative visual functions. These functions may be facilitated or controlled in part by activity in midbrain structures, because there exist direct projections from the pulvinar to these secondary visual areas (see Cowey & Stoerig, 1991). Projections between the pulvinar and superior colliculus would enable collicular activity to influence cortical processing in these secondary areas. There also appears to be evidence for an alternative route to extrastriate areas via direct projections from the lateral geniculate nucleus of the thalamus (see Cowey & Stoerig, 1991). Finally, to the extent that residual neuronal activity is maintained in the primary visual area, this activity may be sufficient for the processing of visual information to occur in secondary visual cortex. One evidence against the role of extrastriate areas in blindsight is the finding that hemidecorticate patients — that is, patients with one entire hemisphere removed — have been shown to exhibit blindsight (Perenin, 1978; Perenin & Jeannerod, 1978). However, it should be noted that in these patients surgery was conducted during childhood, and these patients may represent a special case of extensive neural organization or plasticity during development.

The hypothesis that extrastriate cortical activity mediates visual capacity in blindsight patients is supported by a recent finding by Fendrich, Wessinger, and Gazzaniga (1992). In that study, a patient exhibited signs of blindsight in a scotoma. However, embedded within the scotoma was an island of residual vision that could not be detected by standard tests of vision. To observe these islands of vision, the researchers used a Purkinje eye tracking device, which is a computer-controlled instrument that stabilizes images onto the retina even when eye movements are made. Fendrich et al. (1992) suggest that these areas of preserved sight within a scotoma may activate the primary cortex enough to route visual information to extrastriate areas. These islands of preserved sight have been confirmed by magnetic resonance imaging data that revealed preserved tissue in the primary visual cortex in this patient.

The biological basis of blindsight has not been completely resolved. It is likely that several alternative processing routes could lead to residual visual capacity. For example, midbrain structures could mediate rudimentary ocular responses, such as eye fixations to "blind" areas in the visual field. Also, the phenomenon of inhibition of return may be associated with visual processing in midbrain structures. Perhaps other responses, such as "guessing" where a stimulus occurred or "feeling" that a stimulus is smooth or angular, are mediated by residual cortical activity via alternative routes to secondary visual areas. Despite incomplete resolution of the biological basis of blindsight, the phenomenon has provided important clues to components of visual perception. Specifically, it suggests that conscious awareness is not a necessary concomitant of vision. Indeed, there may be a extensive mental activity of which we have little conscious awareness.

Visual Agnosia

Visual agnosia refers to a rare disorder that specifically disrupts the ability to recognize visually presented objects (for review, see Farah, 1990; Rubens, 1979). The disorder cannot be explained by blindness or other general impairment of visual sensation. The deficit in recognition is, however, restricted to the visual modality. For example, an agnosic patient will not be able recognize a comb placed on a table but will be able to recognize the comb tactually when it is placed in the patient's hand. One particular form of visual agnosia, *associative visual agnosia* or *object agnosia,* is most representative of a metacognitive failure in *knowing*. Patients with associative visual agnosia exhibit preserved sensory capabilities, such as the ability to draw objects from memory or copy drawings of objects (figure 12.2). Yet, they cannot recognize what they have drawn! Such remarkable cases led Teuber (1968) to describe the quality of visual agnosia as "a normal percept that has somehow been stripped of its meaning."

Figure 12.2
Drawings by the associative visual agnosic patient studied by Rubens and Benson (1971). Shown for each object are the sample presented to the patient and the patient's own drawing. Note that despite good copies of the objects, the patient was unable to recognize them. Reprinted from Rubens and Benson (1971).

One particularly interesting case study of associative visual agnosia was studied by Rubens and Benson (1971). The patient was a 47-year-old physician who had a past medical history of hypertension and alcoholism. Visual agnosia was present after an episode of unconsciousness due to severe hypotension apparently caused by the ingestion of sedative drugs and alcohol. Subsequent neuropsychological tests revealed a right hemianopia with sparing of central fixation (i.e., macular sparing). In fact, visual acuity at central fixation was 20/30 with corrective lenses. The outstanding impairment was a severe deficit in the ability to recognize visual presentations of objects, faces, colors, and words. The patient could write sentences and copy drawings of objects, but he could not read what he had written nor name what he had drawn. He described a pipe as "some type of utensil, I'm not sure" and a stethoscope as "a long cord with a round thing at the end." Eight months following his injury, the patient's ability to recognize common objects was good, yet typically his judgments were laborious and uncertain. Recognition of drawings of objects and recognition of faces were still impaired.

Other cases of associative visual agnosia have provided further detail concerning the cognitive impairment related to this disorder. The impairment is often accompanied by a visual field hemianopia, indicating some damage to the primary visual area. However, the presence of an hemianopia itself cannot explain agnosia because in many other cases, a hemianopia can occur without the presence of visual agnosia. Thus, visual agnosia may be related to damage to occipital areas adjacent to primary visual areas (e.g., extrastriate areas). In terms of behavioral symptoms, object agnosia is often associated with problems in the ability to recognize colors, faces, and written material, though each of these deficits is to some degree dissociable from object agnosia. For example, object agnosia can be severely impaired though the ability to read is preserved (Albert, Reches, & Silverberg, 1975). Also, impairment in face recognition can persist despite recovery in the ability to recognize common objects (Rubens & Benson, 1971). Thus, each of these associated disorders of knowing has its own area of investigation and nomenclature — achromatopsia (color discrimination and recognition impairment), prosopagnosia (face recognition impairment), and alexia (reading impairment).

Clearly, associative visual agnosia represents a breakdown *between* visual sensation and semantic knowledge. In most cases, both visual acuity and access to knowledge via other sensory modalities are preserved. Less clear is the locus of this breakdown in the association of visual sensations to semantic knowledge. Some have viewed the disorder as a disconnection between primary visual areas and temporal lobe areas associated with language processing (Geschwind, 1965; Benson, Segarra, & Albert, 1973). Support for this view comes from a postmortem analysis by Benson et al. (1974) of the brain of the agnosic patient studied by Rubens and Benson (1971). The study revealed bilateral lesions involving mesial areas of the occipital lobes. In addition, necrosis was observed in the splenium, the white matter fibers of the corpus callosum that connect the two occipital lobes. The left lesion was larger than the right and extended as far as 1 cm from the posterior tip of occipital lobe. Such a lesion would account for the right-field hemianopia. Benson et al. (1974) speculate that the right hemisphere lesion and the lesion of the splenium could have prevented visual information from the good visual field from gaining access to language areas in the left, language-dominant hemisphere. Yet, one problem with the visual-verbal disconnection hypothesis is that it does not account for the failure of agnosic patients to identify objects in a nonverbal manner. That is, agnosia appears to involve a disruption between visual and semantic processing rather than a disruption between visual and language processing.

An alternative explanation suggests that associative visual agnosia is caused by a specific dysfunction in a process that integrates visual sensations into the perception of recognizable objects. Humphreys and Riddoch (1987) offer a model of object perception and data from an agnosic patient (case H.J.A.) that tends to support this view. In the model, visual information is analyzed by processing components that evaluate visual features (e.g., local geometric features and global shapes). The outcome of this analysis is integrated and compared with knowledge about object forms or representations (i.e., structural form analysis). Form analysis is presumed to be based strictly on knowledge of visual forms rather than semantic knowledge. Based on this model, case H.J.A. appeared to exhibit an impairment in the ability to evaluate or integrate visual feature information. For example, he could not discriminate drawings of real objects from drawings of meaningless forms. Moreover, some residual recognition of features was available by laborious viewing of the stimulus (e.g., "an animal with horns and a tail"). Nevertheless, the patient was still unable to integrate this information into a recognizable object. He also exhibited many of the classic symptoms of associative visual agnosia — he exhibited normal visual acuity but could not recognize objects, colors, or faces. His reading was poor and restricted to letter-by-letter analysis. Computed tomography scans revealed bilateral occipital lesions due to a stroke in the posterior cerebral artery.

In summary, visual agnosia reflects a metacognitive impairment in higher order visual processes associated with object recognition. This impairment may be related to a failure to associate visual information with semantic or verbal knowledge or it may be related to a failure to integrate percepts into a recognizable form. In many cases, recovery of function is observed during the months following brain injury. Following recovery, more specific disorders of recognition may still be present, such as prosopagnosia or alexia. The transient nature of object agnosia has suggested to some that it is due to degraded visual perception or diffuse cognitive deficits rather than to any specific deficit in object perception (Bay, 1953; Bender & Feldman, 1972). However, more recent neuropathological and neuroimaging data suggest a specific impairment associated with damage to mesial occipital and temporal areas (see Benson et al., 1974; Farah, 1990).

Organic Amnesia and Implicit Memory

In 1953, H.M. at the age of 27 years underwent surgery for relief of severe epileptic seizures (see Milner, et al., 1968). The surgery involved bilateral excision of the medial temporal region, which reportedly included removal of the amygdala, anterior two-thirds of the hippocampus, and some neocortical tissue surrounding the amygdala and hippocampus (figure 12.3). Following surgery, H.M.'s seizure activity was attenuated, but he exhibited a severe impairment in new learning capacity (i.e., *anterograde amnesia*). Indeed, he was hardly able to remember any facts or events encountered after his operation. For example, he could not recall words that had been presented to him only minutes before nor could he recollect any recent personal experiences (e.g., whether or not he had eaten lunch

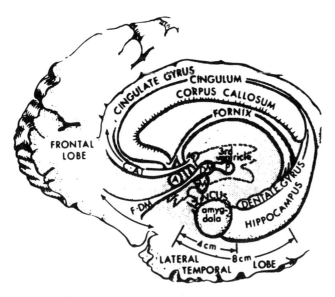

Figure 12.3
Schematic drawing of the brain area damaged in organic amnesia. Shown are structures in the medial temporal region (e.g., hippocampus, amygdala) and in the diencephalic midline (e.g., dorsomedial [DM] thalamic nucleus, the anterior [AT] thalamic nucleus, and the mammillary nucleus [M]). Figure reprinted from Squire (1984).

recently). H.M. is still alive and has reflected on his impairment as always "waking from a dream."

The deficit in memory that is associated with damage to the medial temporal region is often termed *organic amnesia* (for review, see Mayes, 1988; Shimamura, 1989; Squire, 1986). Patients with organic amnesia fail to remember facts and events encountered since the onset of amnesia; yet, they perform normally on tests of perception, object recognition, language, and intelligence. *Retrograde amnesia* — that is, memory loss for information encountered before the onset of amnesia — can also occur in these patients. For example, H.M. exhibited some memory loss for events and people encountered just before his operation. Yet, premorbid memories were not grossly affected, as indicated by the fact that he performed well on a memory test for faces of celebrities who became famous prior to 1950 (Marslen-Wilson & Teuber, 1975).

Other neurological disorders can produce an amnesic syndrome similar to that seen in H.M. For example, tumors, viral infections, and vascular disorders such as ischemia (i.e., loss of blood flow to the brain) can damage the medial temporal region and cause organic amnesia. In these disorders, as in the case of H.M., anterograde amnesia is the outstanding impairment. Certain disorders, such as Alzheimer's disease and head injuries, affect the medial temporal region as well as many other brain areas. In these cases of more widespread brain injury, memory in addition to other cognitive impairments (e.g., language, attention, intelligence) are typically observed.

Another area of the brain, the *diencephalic midline,* can also produce organic amnesia (figure 12.3). This area includes various midline thalamic nuclei (e.g., dorsomedial nucleus) as well as the mammilliary nuclei. These nuclei receive and send projections to various areas in the brain, including the medial temporal region. The best-studied etiology of amnesia resulting from damage to the diencephalic midline is *Korsakoff's syndrome,* which can develop after many years of chronic alcohol abuse and nutritional deficiency (for review, see Butters, 1984; Butters & Cermak, 1980). Pathological studies of Korsakoff's syndrome have identified bilateral tissue damage along the diencephalic midline, typically involving the dorsomedial thalamic nuclei, the mammillary nuclei, and other adjacent nuclei (Mayes, Meudell, Mann, & Pickering, 1988; Mair, Warrington, & Weiskrantz, 1979; Victor, Adams, & Collins, 1989). Cortical atrophy and cerebellar damage are also observed in patients with Korsakoff's syndrome. Neuroimaging data in living patients confirm these pathological findings and indicate that memory impairment is correlated with the extent of brain damage in the diencephalic midline and in the frontal neocortex (Shimamura, Jernigan, & Squire, 1988; Squire, Amaral, & Press, 1990).

Although organic amnesia severely affects normal daily living, certain aspects of new learning capacity are not impaired (for review, see Schacter, 1987; Shimamura, 1986). These findings of preserved memory capacity suggested a distinction between conscious recollections of memory and unconscious or automatic recollections that appear to "pop into mind." In other words, in certain instances amnesic patients have been shown to exhibit "memory without awareness." Entirely normal memory performance has been observed in tests involving skill learning. For example, H.M. acquired a perceptual-motor skill in which he was able to trace the outline of a star while viewing the star in a mirror (Milner et al., 1968). The task is difficult at first but then becomes easier with practice. Both amnesic patients and control subjects exhibit learning in this perceptual-motor task. Cohen and Squire (1980) observed preserved skill learning by amnesic patients on a mirror-reading task in which subjects were asked to read mirror-reversed words. In addition, these patients retained the mirror-reading skill even when they were tested 1 month after learning. Nevertheless, these patients failed to recognize the words used in the task, and some patients did not even have conscious recollection of having engaged in the task before.

Priming is another form of preserved memory capacity. It refers to a facilitation or bias in performance as a result of recently encountered information (see Schacter, 1987; Shimamura, 1986, 1993). Aspects of preserved priming ability in amnesic patients were first studied empirically by Warrington and Weiskrantz (1968, 1982). Amnesic patients were presented pictures in a degraded form and asked to identify them. If the subject could not identify the stimulus, a succession of less degraded versions of the stimuli was shown until identification was successful. Later, when amnesic patients were asked to identify the same degraded pictures, they were able to identify the stimuli more quickly. This priming effect occurred despite failure to discriminate previously presented stimuli from new ones in a recognition memory test. Graf, Squire, and Mandler (1984) used a word completion task to study priming effects. In this task, words were presented (e.g., MOTEL) to the subject and later cued by three-letter word stems (e.g., MOT). Subjects are asked to say the first word that came to mind for each word stem. In both amnesic patients and control subjects, the tendency to use previously presented words in the word completion test was increased by two or three times over baseline levels. In this test, words appeared to "pop" into mind, and amnesic patients exhibited this effect to the same level as control subjects. However, when subjects were asked to use the same word stems as aids to recollect consciously the words from the study session, the control subjects exhibited better performance than amnesic patients.

A variety of test paradigms have since been used to demonstrate preserved priming in amnesia. For example, in one test subjects were presented words (e.g., BABY) and later asked to "free associate" to related words (e.g., CHILD). Amnesic patients exhibited a normal bias to use recently presented words in this word association task (Shimamura & Squire, 1984). This finding suggests that semantic associations can also be used to prime information in memory. Other findings suggest that the processing of novel nonverbal stimuli can be facilitated or primed (see Schacter, 1990). Also, the process of reading can be facilitated by multiple presentations of the same sentences (Musen, Shimamura, & Squire, 1990). In these cases, facilitation occurs in amnesic patients, despite conscious recollection that the stimulus had been presented recently (figure 12.4).

Preserved memory functions in amnesic patients suggest that some memory aspects of new learning occur outside the domain of conscious recollection. Apparently, these functions can operate independently of the brain regions that are damaged in organic amnesia. As reviewed by Squire (1986), various taxonomies have been used to

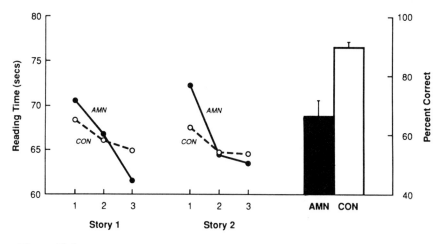

Figure 12.4
Time required to read aloud two different stories, each presented three times in succession. Amnesic patients (AMN) exhibited normal reading speeds compared to control subjects (CON), despite impaired recognition memory for the story content (right bar graphs). Figure from Musen et al. (1990).

distinguish the memory forms that are impaired in amnesia from those that are not impaired. These taxonomies include the distinction between aspects of memory impaired in amnesia, such as *declarative, explicit,* or *cognitive mediational* memory and memory spared in amnesia, such as *procedural, implicit,* or *habit* memory. In all of these distinctions, one primary criterion is that amnesic patients appear to exhibit impairment in the ability to recollect memories in a conscious manner. Thus, the term "memory without awareness" (Jacoby & Witherspoon, 1982) appears to capture the forms of memory preserved in amnesia.

Several theories have been proposed to account for the dissociation between memory with awareness and memory without awareness. For example, it has been suggested that the establishment of conscious memories involves a storage or consolidation process that depends critically on interactions between the hippocampus and areas in neocortex (Squire, Shimamura, & Amaral, 1989). The medial temporal region receives projections from many neocortical areas and these projections may provide a link or association between two geographically separate areas in neocortex. That is, such memories may require the integration and reorganization of neocortical connections that cannot be established easily by cortical-cortical connections. Rapid associations in the hippocampus may provide a quick way to link associations, such as a name with a face or an experience with a time and place. Memory without awareness or implicit memory may be restricted to activity in localized regions of the neocortex and perhaps subcortical areas (e.g., basal ganglia). Thus, implicit memories may be more encapsulated and not require extensive cortical modification or reorganization. Other theoretical interpretations of organic amnesia include those proposed by Mishkin (1982), Tulving, and Schacter (1990), and Warrington and Weiskrantz (1982).

There are intriguing parallels between the phenomenon of implicit memory and blindsight. First, implicit memory suggests memory without conscious awareness, whereas blindsight suggests perception without conscious awareness. That is, both indicate a level of processing that can influence behavior but is not accessible to conscious experience. Second, both phenomena suggest a supplementary or alternative component of cognitive function that is independent of a primary route of information processing. Third, the neural systems that support these alternative routes are available even when there is damage to the brain areas involved in the primary route of information processing. Finally, these primary or typical routes of information processing that support conscious awareness may be a phylogenetically recent phenomena in evolution. For example, visual impairment following cortical lesions is not as dramatic in monkeys as it is in humans. Also, hippocampal-cortical connections become more extensive in humans than in other mammals. One possibility is that conscious processing evolved to support greater participation or integration of cortical activity than is required for nonconscious processes, such as blindsight and implicit memory.

Disorders of Metamemory

Metamemory refers to knowledge about one's memory capabilities and knowledge about strategies that can aid memory. The term was first used to characterize memory development in children (Brown, 1978; Flavell & Wellman, 1977). In children, one can observe the development of processes that aid or influence memory performance, such as improved learning strategies during study or more sophisticated search strategies during memory retrieval. In neuropsychological studies, one can observe the breakdown of metamemory processes. For example, Hirst (1982) reported that patients with Korsakoff's syndrome exhibit poor knowledge of mnemonic strategies, such as strategies to help remember a friend's birthday party. Indeed, it was reported that the knowledge of memory strategies exhibited by patients with Korsakoff's syndrome was below that of fifth-grade children. Other amnesic patients, such as patients with medial temporal lobe lesions, did not exhibit poor metamemory.

Another aspect of metamemory impaired in patients with Korsakoff's syndrome is the feeling-of-knowing phenomenon (Shimamura & Squire, 1986). This phenomenon refers to the "feeling" of knowing some information without being able to recall it. It is related to the "tip-of-the-tongue" phenomenon in which partial information is available (e.g., the first syllable of the to-be-remembered information) but full knowledge is still inaccessible. Hart (1965a) first investigated the feeling-of-knowing phenomenon in normal individuals. Subjects were asked to recall general information questions, such as

"Who painted "Afternoon at La Grand Jatte?" If the answer was not available (e.g., Seurat), subjects were asked to predict whether they would be able to recognize the correct answer if it were presented with some other false alternatives. Hart (1965a) showed that accurate feeling-of-knowing predictions could be made, despite initial failure to recall the answers to the questions. Since the first study by Hart (1965a), numerous investigations of the feeling-of-knowing phenomenon have been performed (for review, see Nelson & Narens, 1990).

In a neuropsychological investigation of feeling-of-knowing accuracy, Shimamura and Squire (1986) presented general information questions to patients with Korsakoff's syndrome and to other amnesic patients (e.g., patients with medial temporal lobe lesions, non-Korsakoff patients with lesions in the diencephalic midline). If the answer to a question could not be recalled, subjects were asked to rate their ability to recognize the answer on a seven-point scale (1 = high feeling of knowing, 7 = pure guess). Also, each subject was asked to rank nonrecalled questions from the question judged to have the highest feeling of knowing to the one judged to have the lowest feeling of knowing. To validate the feeling-of-knowing ratings, subjects were then given a seven-alternative, forced-choice recognition memory test, which was then correlated with feeling-of-knowing ratings. If feeling of knowing judgments were accurate, questions ranked high in feeling of knowing would more likely be recognized than questions ranked low in feeling of knowing.

The findings indicated that patients with Korsakoff's syndrome but not other amnesic patients exhibited an impairment in feeling-of-knowing accuracy. This metacognitive deficit indicated a failure to be aware of what the patient knew or did not know. The deficit was observed in patients with Korsakoff's syndrome, despite the fact that these patients performed as well as the other amnesic patients in their ability to recognize the correct answer from other choices (recognition performance = 47%, chance = 14%). That is, patients with Korsakoff's syndrome exhibited fact knowledge but could not evaluate that knowledge to determine whether they had a "feeling of knowing." These findings corroborate findings reported by Hirst (1982), who suggested that patients with Korsakoff's syndrome but not other amnesic patients exhibit impairment in metamemory. Thus, metamemory impairment is not an obligatory deficit in amnesic patients. That is, one can be amnesic and yet still be aware of the disorder and still have knowledge about strategies that improve memory.

The particular deficit of metamemory observed in patients with Korsakoff's syndrome suggests that such patients exhibit more widespread memory impairment than is observed in other amnesic patients. Indeed, other findings suggest that Korsakoff's syndrome produces deficits that are not observed in other amnesic patients, such as deficits in encoding, attention, and memory for temporal order (see Butters & Cermak, 1980; Oscar-Berman, 1980; Shimamura, 1989). As mentioned earlier, general cortical atrophy is observed in neuroimaging data of patients with Korsakoff's syndrome (Shimamura et al., 1988; Squire et al., 1990). Also, other patients with widespread cortical damage, such as patients with Alzheimer's disease, can exhibit impaired metamemory (McGlynn & Kaszniak, 1991).

One possibility is that frontal lobe damage mediates disorders of metamemory. There is evidence for the role of the frontal lobe in the mediation of the extracognitive disorders associated with Korsakoff's syndrome (Squire, 1982). Moreover, patients with lesions restricted to the frontal lobes exhibit deficits in attention, encoding, and memory for temporal order, but they are not amnesic (for review see Milner, Petrides, & Smith, 1985; Shimamura, Janowsky, & Squire, 1991). Metacognitive deficits also have been observed in patients with frontal lobe lesions. For example, Shallice and Evans (1978) observed deficits in the ability to make metacognitive assessments used to make inferences. Specifically, patients with frontal lobe lesions had difficulty making reasonable responses to questions such as "How tall is the average English woman?" or "How long is the average man's necktie?" Answers to such questions are not directly available but require estimates based on reasoning and inferences. Other findings indicate that patients with frontal lobe lesions have difficulty estimating the price of everyday objects (Smith & Milner, 1984). These deficits suggest impairment in the organization and retrieval of semantic knowledge. Such deficits led Baddeley (1986) to describe the cognitive deficits associated with frontal lobe lesions as a "dysexecutive" disorder related to problems in working memory.

Feeling-of-knowing judgments also appear to be impaired in patients with frontal lobe lesion (Janowsky, Shimamura, & Squire, 1989). For example, patients with frontal lobe lesions were impaired in the ability to judge what they had learned. In this task, patients with frontal lobe lesions and control subjects were given sentences to learn ("Mary's garden was full of marigolds"). Following a retention interval of 5 minutes or 1–3 days, subjects were given the sentences with the last word missing ("Mary's garden was full of _____") and asked to recall the last word. If recall memory was not available, subjects were asked to rate their feeling of knowing. These ratings were then correlated with performance on a subsequent recognition memory test. A long retention interval was included in this task to allow a match in item recall ability between patients with frontal lobe lesions and amnesic patients (Korsakoff and non-Korsakoff patients). That is, memory for the words in patients with frontal lobe lesions tested after a 1- to 3-day delay was comparable to that of amnesic patients tested after a 5-minute delay. The critical question was the accuracy of feeling-of-knowing judgments in patients with frontal lobe lesions when the level of item memory was matched across groups.

Figure 12.5 displays feeling-of-knowing performance for patients with frontal lobe lesions (F) and control subjects (F-CON). Patients with frontal lobe lesions exhibited poor feeling-of-knowing accuracy when memory was tested after a 1- to 3-day delay but not after a 5-minute delay. That is, when item memory was not readily available, estimates about what had been learned were impaired in patients with frontal lobe lesions. Shown also are data from patients with Korsakoff's syndrome (KOR) and other amnesic patients (AMN) following a 5-minute delay. Patients with Korsakoff's syndrome exhibited an impairment in this test compared to other amnesic patients. As intended, the level of item recall memory was matched in all subject groups. Despite equivalent levels of item memory, only patients with frontal lobe lesions and patients with Korsakoff's syndrome exhibited impaired metamemory. It should be noted that metamemory impairment was not always observed in patients with frontal lobe lesions, and thus their impairment was not as pervasive as that observed in patients with Korsakoff's syndrome. For example, patients with frontal lobe lesions did not exhibit impaired feeling-

274

A. P. Shimamura

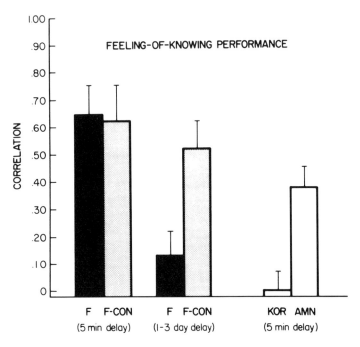

Figure 12.5
Feeling-of-knowing performance by patients with frontal lobe lesions (F), control subjects (F-CON), patients with Korsakoff's syndrome (KOR), and five other patients wtih amnesia (AMN). Feeling-of-knowing accuracy was calculated by correlating feeling-of-knowing ranking with subsequent recognition performance. Patients with frontal lobe lesions and patients with Korsakoff's syndrome exhibited impaired feeling-of-knowing accuracy (bars show standard error of the mean). Reprinted from Janowsky et al. (1989).

feeling-of-knowing accuracy following the 5-minute retention interval nor did they exhibit impaired feeling of knowing for general information questions (Janowsky et al., 1989).

Deficits in metamemory appear to be related to failed judgments or decisions. This interpretation is consistent with other disorders associated with frontal lobe pathology. Indeed, patients with frontal lobe lesions do not exhibit impairment in perception or memory. Instead, they exhibit impairment in the evaluation or integration of perceptions and memories. This impairment may be associated with the on-line handling of information (Baddeley, 1986). In a related view, Metcalfe (1993) suggests that metamemory is related to problems in monitoring information which can lead to problems in discriminating familiar information from new information. Thus, the metacognitive impairment associated with frontal lobe pathology may be related to a failure to make appropriate judgments or decisions based on perceptual and semantic knowledge.

Concluding Remarks

Several other forms of metacognitive impairment can occur following brain injury (see Schacter, 1987; Weiskrantz, 1988). For example, so-called "split-brain" patients exhibit metacognitive deficits because communication between the two cerebral hemispheres is prevented as a result of a surgical lesion of the corpus callosum (see Gazzaniga, Bogen, & Sperry, 1965; Sergent, 1987). Split-brain patients perform as if knowledge is isolated within a cerebral hemisphere. Thus, the left hand can recognize by touch an object that was presented in the left visual field, but it is not aware of objects presented in the right visual field. This deficit occurs because tactile perception of the left hand and visual perception of the left visual field are both mediated by the right hemisphere. Another metacognitive impairment occurs in patients with unilateral parietal lobe lesions who exhibit a *neglect syndrome* (Bisiach, Perani, Vallar, & Berti, 1986; Mesulam, 1981). Such patients do not perceive or attend to one side of the body. In severe cases, they fail to dress themselves on the neglected side and even fail to acknowledge the presence of body parts on the neglected side. Finally, there is a general class of deficits associated with *anosognosia* or a failure in awareness of deficits (see McGlynn & Schacter, 1989; Prigatano & Schacter, 1991). In such cases, patients appear oblivious to seemingly obvious deficits, such as hemiplegia or hemianopia.

The four examples of metacognitive impairment described in detail in this chapter — blindsight, agnosia, amnesia, and metamemory impairment — were chosen because they represent failures of *knowing* at various levels of cognitive processing. Moreover, these examples provide evidence that brain injury can affect specific aspects of knowing rather than causing a global impairment in knowing. Thus, blindsight affects conscious knowledge of primary visual sensations, and visual agnosia affects secondary or associative processes related to object recognition. These disorders are related to different aspects of visual processing. Organic amnesia affects conscious recollection of facts and events and occurs following damage to the medial temporal lobe or the diencephalic midline. Metamemory disorders are related to problems in judgment or decision making and can occur following frontal lobe lesions. Consequently, these four examples of metacognitive impairment are mediated by different neural systems and affect knowing at different levels of analysis — perception, object recognition, conscious memory, and decision making.

One remarkable observation from studies of the neuropsychology of metacognition is that certain cognitive functions can operate without conscious knowledge. Thus, patients with blindsight can locate objects in apparently "blind" visual fields; patients with visual agnosia can perceive well enough to provide adequate drawings of objects; patients with amnesia can learn new perceptual-motor skills; and, finally, patients with metamemory disorders can demonstrate memory capabilities but cannot make accurate decisions about what they know and what they do not know. Based on these investigations of metacognition, it is possible — though probably not prudent — to speculate about the biology of conscious awareness. Such investigations suggest that conscious awareness is not embodied as a single neural function or operation. Instead, it may require a convergence of information from many components. It is likely that the cerebral cortex is necessary for this convergence to occur. Yet, despite the remarkable experience of conscious awareness, neuropsychological investigations suggest that a variety of cognitive components can operate without our knowledge. Awareness of this fact may significantly temper our own confidence about the way we think and behave.

References

Adamson, R. E. (1952). Functional fixedness as related to problem solving: A repetition of three experiments. *Journal of Experimental Psychology*, *44*, 288–291.

Adamson, R. E., & Taylor, D. W. (1954). Functional fixedness as related to elapsed time and set. *Journal of Experimental Psychology*, *47*, 122–216.

Albert, M. L., Reches, A., & Siverberg, R. (1975). Associative visual agnosia without alexia. *Neurology*, *25*, 322–326.

Anderson, J. A. (1977). Neural models with cognitive implications. In D. LaBerge & S. Samuels (Eds.), *Basic processes in reading* (pp. 27–90). Hillsdale, NJ: Erlbaum.

Anderson, J. R. (1985). *Cognitive psychology and its implications* (2nd ed.) New York: W.H. Freeman.

Anderson, M. C., & Bjork, R. A. (1993). Mechanisms of inhibition in long-term memory: A new taxonomy. In D. Dagenbach & T. Carr (Eds.), *Inhibition in attention, memory, and language*. New York: Academic Press, in press.

Andrews, D. H. (1988). Relationships among simulators, training devices, and learning: A behavioral view. *Educational Technology, January*, 48–54.

Anglin, J. M. (1970). *The growth of word meaning*. Cambridge, MA: MIT Press.

Anooshian, L. J., Mammarella, S. L., & Hertel, P. T. (1989). Adult age differences in knowledge of retrieval processes. *International Journal of Aging and Human Development*, *29*, 39–52.

Atkinson, R. C., & Shiffrin, R. M. (1968). Human memory: A proposed system and its control processes. In K. W. Spence & J. T. Spence (Eds.), *The psychology of learning and motivation: Advances in research and theory*. New York: Academic Press.

278

References

Bäckman, L., & Dixon, R. A. (1992). Psychological compensation: A theoretical framework. *Psychological Bulletin, 112,* 259–283.

Baddeley, A. (1986). *Working memory.* Oxford, UK: Oxford University Press.

Baddeley, A. D., & Longman, D. J. A. (1978). The influence of length and frequency of training session on the rate of learning to type. *Ergonomics, 21,* 627–635.

Bahrick, H. P. (1970). A two-phase model for prompted recall. *Psychological Review, 77,* 213–219.

Bahrick, H. P. (1979). Maintenance of knowledge: Questions about memory we forgot to ask. *Journal of Experimental Psychology: General, 108,* 296–308.

Bahrick, H. P. (1984). Semantic memory content in permastore — fifty years of memory for Spanish learned in school. *Journal of Experimental Psychology: General, 113,* 1–29.

Balfour, S.P. (1992). *Do meaning-related blockers induce TOT states?* Unpublished master's thesis, Texas A&M University.

Balota, D. A., & Chumbly, J. I. (1984). Are lexical decisions a good measure of lexical access? The role of word frequency in the neglected decision stage. *Journal of Experimental Psychology: Human Perception and Performance, 10,* 340–357.

Bandura, A. (1986). *Social foundation of thought & action: A social cognitive theory.* Englewood Cliffs, NJ: Prentice-Hall.

Bandura, A. (1988). Self-efficacy conception of anxiety. *Anxiety Research, 1,* 77–98.

Bandura, A. (1989). Regulation of cognitive processes through perceived self-efficacy. *Developmental Psychology, 25,* 729–735.

Barbur, J. L., Ruddock, K. H., & Waterfield, V. A. (1980). Human visual responses in the absence of the geniculo-striate projection. *Brain, 102,* 905–928.

Bartlett, F. C. (1932). *Remembering: A study in experimental and social psychology.* New York: Macmillan.

Bateson, G. (1972). *Steps toward an ecology of mind.* New York: Ballantine.

Battig, W. E. (1966). Facilitation and interference. In E. A. Bilodeau (Ed.), *Acquisition of skill* (pp. 215–244). New York: Academic Press.

Battig, W. F. (1979). The flexibility of human memory. In L. S. Cermak & F. I. M. Craik (Eds.), *Levels of processing in human memory* (pp. 23–44).Hillsdale, NJ: Erlbaum.

References

Bay, E. (1953). Disturbances of visual perception and their examination. *Brain*, *76*, 515–530.

Begg, I., Duft, S., Lalonde, P., Melnick, R., & Sanvito, J. (1989). Memory predictions are based on ease of processing. *Journal of Memory and Language*, *28*, 610–632.

Bekerian, D. A., & Bowers, J. M. (1983). Eyewitness testimony: Were we misled? *Journal of Experimental Psychology: Learning, Memory, and Cognition*, *9*, 139–145.

Belli, R. F. (1989). Influences of misleading postevent information: Misinformation interference and acceptance. *Journal of Experimental Psychology: General*, *118*, 72–85.

Bender, M. B., & Feldman, M. (1972). The so-called "visual agnosias." *Brain*, *95*, 173–186.

Benson, D. F., Segarra, J., & Albert, M. L. (1973). Visual agnosia-prosopagnosia: A clinicopathologic correlation. *Archives of Neurology*, *30*, 307–310.

Berlyne, D. E. (1960). *Conflict, arousal, and curiosity*. New York: McGraw Hill.

Berry, J. M., & West, R. L. (1993). Cognitive self-efficacy across the life-span: An integrative review. *International Journal of Behavioral Development*, in press.

Berry, J. M., West, R. L., & Dennehy, D. M. (1989). Reliability and validity of the Memory Self-Efficacy Questionnaire (MSEQ). *Developmental Psychology*, *25*, 701–713.

Birch, H. G., & Rabinowitz, H. S. (1951). The negative effect of previous experience on productive thinking. *Journal of Experimental Psychology*, *41*, 121–125.

Bisiach, E., Perani, D., Vallar, G., & Berti, A. (1986). Unilateral neglect: Personal and extra-personal. *Neuropsychologia*, *24*, 759–767.

Bjork, R. A. (1975). Retrieval as a memory modifier. In R. Solso (Ed.), *Information processing and cognition: The Loyola Symposium* (pp. 123–144). Hillsdale, NJ: Erlbaum.

Bjork, R. A., & Bjork, E. L. (1992). A new theory of disuse and an old theory of stimulation fluctuation. In A. F. Healy, S. M. Kosslyn, & R. M. Shiffrin (Eds.), *From learning processes to cognitive processes: Essays in honor of William K. Estes*, (Vol. 2) (pp. 35–67). Hillsdale, NJ: Erlbaum.

Blake, M. (1973). Prediction of recognition when recall fails: Exploring the feeling-of-knowing phenomenon. *Journal of Verbal Learning and Verbal Behavior*, *12*, 311–319.

Boneau, C. A. (1990). Psychological literacy: A first approximation. *American Psychologist*, *45*, 891–900.

Borkowski, J. G., Carr, M., & Pressley, M. (1987). "Spontaneous" strategy use: Perspectives from metacognitive theory. *Intelligence, 11,* 61–75.

Bothwell, R. K., Brigham, J. C., & Pigott, M. A. (1987). An exploratory study of personality differences in eyewitness memory. *Journal of Social Behavior and Personality, 2,* 335–343.

Bothwell, R. K., Deffenbacher, K. A., & Brigham, J. C. (1987). Correlation of eyewitness accuracy and confidence: Optimality hypothesis revisited. *Journal of Applied Psychology, 72,* 691–695.

Bower, G. H. (1967). A multicomponent theory of memory trace. In K.W. Spence (Ed.), *The psychology of learning.* New York: Academic Press.

Bower, G. H. (1971). Adaptation-level coding of stimuli and serial position effects. In M. H. Appley (Ed.), *Adaptation-level theory* (pp. 175–201). New York: Academic Press.

Bower, G. H. (1972). Stimulus sampling theory of encoding variability. In A. W. Melton & E. Martin, (Eds.), *Coding processes in human memory* (pp. 85–123). Washington, D. C.: Winston.

Bradley, J. V. (1981). Overconfidence in ignorant experts. *Bulletin of the Psychonomic Society, 17,* 82–84.

Bransford, J. D., Franks, J. J., Morris, C. D., & Stein, B. S. (1979). Some general constraints on learning and memory research. In L. S. Cermak & F. I. M. Craik (Eds.), *Levels of processing in human memory* (pp. 331–354). Hillsdale, NJ: Erlbaum.

Brennen, T., Baguley, T., Bright, J., & Bruce, V. (1990). Resolving semantically induced tip-of-the-tongue states for proper nouns. *Memory & Cognition, 18,* 339–347.

Brigham, J. C., Maas, A., Snyder, L. D., & Spaulding, K. (1982). Accuracy of eyewitness identifications in a field setting. *Journal of Personality and Social Psychology, 42,* 673–681.

Brigham, J. C. N., & Pressley, M. (1988). Cognitive monitoring and strategy choice in younger and older adults. *Psychology and Aging, 3,* 249–257.

Broadbent, D. E. (1977). Levels, hierarchies, and the locus of control. *Quarterly Journal of Experimental Psychology, 29,* 181–201.

Broadbent, D. E., Cooper, P. F., FitzGerald, P., & Parkes, K. R. (1982). The Cognitive Failures Questionnaire (CFQ) and its correlates. *British Journal of Clinical Psychology, 21,* 1–16.

Brown, A. L. (1978). Knowing when, where, and how to remember: A problem of metacognition. In R. Glaser (Ed.), *Advances in instructional psychology* (pp. 367–406). Hillsdale, NJ: Erlbaum.

Brown, A. L., & DeLoache, J. S. (1978). Skills, plans, and self-regulation. In R. Siegler (Ed.), *Children's thinking: What develops?* Hillsdale, NJ: Erlbaum.

Brown, A. L., & Lawton, S. C. (1977). The feeling of knowing experience in educable retarded children, *Developmental Psychology, 13*, 364–370.

Brown, A. S. (1991). A review of the tip of the tongue experience. *Psychological Bulletin, 109*(2), 204–223.

Brown, R., & McNeill, D. (1966). The "tip-of-the-tongue" phenomenon. *Journal of Verbal Learning and Verbal Behavior, 5*, 325–337.

Bruce, D. R. (1991). Mechanistic and functional explanations of memory. *American Psychologist, 46*, 46–48.

Bruce, P. R., Coyne, A. C., & Botwinick, J. (1982). Adult age differences in metamemory. *Journal of Gerontology, 37*, 354–357.

Burke, D., MacKay, D. G., Worthley, J. S., & Wade, E. (1991). On the tip of the tongue: What causes word finding failures in young and older adults? *Journal of Memory and Language, 30*, 542–579.

Burke, R. J., & Maier, N. R. F. (1965). Attempts to predict success on an insight problem. *Psychological Reports, 17*, 303–310.

Butterfield, E. C., & Belmont, J. M. (1977). Assessing and improving the executive cognitive functions of mentally retarded people. In I. Bialer & M. Sternlicht (Eds.), *Psychology of mental retardation: Issues and approaches* (pp. 277–318). New York: Psychological Dimensions.

Butterfield, E. C., Nelson, T. O., & Peck, V. (1988). Developmental aspects of the feeling of knowing. *Developmental Psychology, 24*, 654–663.

Butterfield, E. C., Wambold, C., & Belmont, J. M. (1973). On the theory and practice of improving short-term memory. *American Journal of Mental Deficiency, 77*, 654–669.

Butters, N. (1984). Alcoholic Korsakoff's syndrome: An update. *Seminars in Neurology, 4*, 226–244.

Butters, N., & Cermak, L. S. (1980). *Alcoholic Korsakoff's syndrome: An information processing approach.* New York: Academic Press.

Camp, C. J., Markley, R. P., & Kramer, J. J. (1983). Spontaneous use of mnemonics by elderly individuals. *Educational Gerontology, 9*, 57–71.

References

Campione, J. C., & Brown, A. L. (1977). Memory and metamemory development in educable retarded children. In R. V. Kail, Jr., & J. W. Hagen (Eds.), *Perspectives on the development of memory and cognition.* Hillsdale, NJ: Erlbaum.

Campione, J. C., & Brown, A. L. (1979). Toward a theory of intelligence: Contributions from research with retarded children. In R.J. Sternberg & D.K. Detterman (Eds.), *Human intelligence: Perspectives on its theory and measurement.* Norwood, NJ: Ablex.

Carlson, R. A. (1992). Starting with consciousness. *American Journal of Psychology, 105,* 598–604.

Carmichael, L. C., Hogan, H. P., & Walters, A. A. (1932). An experimental study of the effect of language on the reproduction of visually perceived form. *Journal of Experimental Psychology, 15,* 73–86.

Carroll, M., & Nelson, T. O. (1993). Overlearning has a greater influence on the feeling of knowing in within-subject designs than in between-subject desings. *American Journal of Psychology,* in press.

Carroll, M., & Simington, A. (1986). The effects of degree of learning, meaning, and individual differences on the feeling-of-knowing. *Acta Psychologica, 61,* 3–16.

Carson, L. M., & Wiegand, R. L. (1979). Motor schema formation and retention in young children: A test of Schmidt's schema theory. *Journal of Motor Behavior, 11,* 247–251.

Catalano, J. F., & Kleiner, B. M. (1984). Distant transfer in coincident timing as a function of variability of practice. *Perceptual and Motor Skills, 58,* 851–856.

Cavanaugh, J. C. (1989). The importance of awareness in memory aging. In L W. Poon, D. C. Rubin, & B. A. Wilson (Eds.), *Everyday cognition in adulthood and late life* (pp. 416–436). Cambridge: Cambridge University Press.

Cavanaugh, J. C., Feldman, J. M., & Hertzog, C. (1993). *Metamemory as process: A reconceptualization of what memory questionnaires assess.* Unpublished Manuscript.

Cavanaugh, J. C., & Green, E. E. (1990). I believe, therefore I can: Self-efficacy beliefs in memory aging. In E. A. Lovelace (Ed.), *Aging and cognition: Mental processes, self-awareness, and interventions* (pp. 189–230). Amsterdam: Elsevier.

Cavanaugh, J. C., & Murphy, N. Z. (1986). Personality and metamemory correlates of memory performance in younger and older adults. *Educational Gerontology, 12,* 385–394.

Cavanaugh, J. C., & Perlmutter, M. (1982). Metamemory: A critical examination. *Child Development, 53,* 11–28.

References

Cavanaugh, J. C. & Poon, L. W. (1989). Metamemorial predictors of memory performance in young and old adults. *Psychology and Aging, 4,* 365–368.

Ceci, S. J., & Brofenbrenner, U. (1985). Don't forget to take the cupcakes out of the oven: Strategic time-monitoring, prospective memory and context. *Child Development, 56,* 175–190.

Ceci, S. J., & Liker, J. (1986). Academic and nonacademic intelligence: An experimental separation. In R. J. Sternberg & R. K. Wagner (Eds.), *Practical intelligence* (pp. 119–142). New York: Cambridge University Press.

Cermak, L. S., Butters, N., & Morienes, J. (1974). Some analyses of the verbal encoding deficits of alcoholic Korsakoff patients. *Brain and Language, 1,* 141-150.

Chaffin, R., & Herrmann, D. J. (1983). Self-reports of memory ability by old and young adults. *Human Learning, 2,* 17–28.

Chase, W. G., & Simon, H. A. (1973). The mind's eye in chess. In W. G. Chase (Ed.), *Visual information processing.* New York: Academic Press.

Chi, M. T. H., Glaser, R., & Rees, E. (1982). Expertise in problem solving. In R.J. Sternberg (Ed.), *Advances in the psychology of human intelligence* (Vol. 1). Hillsdale, NJ: Erlbaum.

Christina, R. W., & Bjork, R. A. (1991). Optimizing long-term retention and transfer. In D. Druckman & R. A. Bjork (Eds.), *In the mind's eye: Enhancing human performance* (pp. 23–56). Washington, DC: National Academy Press.

Cohen, N. J., & Squire, L. R. (1980). Preserved learning and retention of pattern analyzing skill in amnesia: Association of knowing how and knowing that. *Science, 210,* 207–209.

Cole, M., Gay, J., Glick, J., & Sharp, D. W. (1971). *The cultural context of learning and thinking.* New York: Basic Books.

Conant, R. C., & Ashby, W. R. (1970). Every good regulator of a system must be a model of that system. *International Journal of Systems Science, 1,* 89–97.

Connor, L. T., Balota, D. A., & Neely, J. H. (1992). On the relation between feeling of knowing and lexical decision: Persistent subthreshold activation or topic familiarity? *Journal of Experimental Psychology: Learning, Memory, and Cognition, 18,* 544–554.

Costermans, J., Lories, G., & Ansay, C. (1992). Confidence level and feeling of knowing in question answering: The weight of inferential processes. *Journal of Experimental Psychology: Learning, Memory and Cognition, 18,* 142–150.

References

Courchesne, E., Hillyard, S. A., & Galambos, R. (1975). Stimulus novelty, task relevance, and the visual evoked potential in man. *Electroencephalography and Clinical Neurophysiology, 39,* 131–142.

Cowey, A., & Stoerig, P. (1991). The neurobiology of blindsight. *Trends in Neuroscience, 14,* 140–145.

Coyne, A. C. (1985). Adult age, presentation time, and memory performance. *Experimental Aging Research, 11,* 147–149.

Craik, F. I. M., & Jennings, J. M. (1992). Human memory. In F. I. M. Craik & T. A. Salthouse (Eds.), *The handbook of aging and cognition* (pp. 51–110). Hillsdale, NJ: Erlbaum.

Craik, F. I. M., & Lockhart, R. S. (1972). Levels of processing: A framework for memory research. *Journal of Verbal Learning and Verbal Behavior, 11,* 671–684.

Craik, F. I. M., & Rabinowitz, J. M. (1984). Age differences in the acquisition and use of verbal information: A tutorial review. In H. Bouma & D. G. Bouwhuis (Eds.), *Attention and performance X* (pp. 471–499). Hillsdale, NJ: Erlbaum.

Crawford, M., Herrmann, D. J., Holdsworth, M. J., Randall, E. P., & Robbins, D. (1989). Gender and beliefs about memory. *British Journal of Psychology, 80,* 391–401.

Cuddy, L. J., & Jacoby, L. L. (1982). When forgetting helps memory: Analysis of repetition effects. *Journal of Verbal Learning and Verbal Behavior, 21,* 451–467.

Cultice, J. C., Somerville, S. C., & Wellman, H. M. (1983). Preschoolers memory monitoring: Feeling of knowing judgments, *Child Development, 54,* 1480–1486.

Cummins, R. (1983). *The nature of psychological explanation.* Cambridge, MA: MIT Press.

Cutler, B. L., Penrod, S. D., & Stuve, T. E. (1988). Juror decision making in eyewitness identification cases. *Law and Human Behavior, 12,* 41–55.

Damasio, A. R. (1985). The frontal lobes. In K. M. Hielman & E. Valenstein (Eds.), *Clinical neuropsychology.* New York: Oxford University Press.

Davidson, H. A., Dixon, R. A., & Hultsch, D. F. (1991). Memory anxiety and memory performance in adulthood. *Applied Cognitive Psychology, 5,* 423–434.

Davidson, J. E. (1991). Insights about giftedness: The role of problem solving abilities. In N. Colangelo, S. G. Assouline, & D. L. Ambroson (Eds.), *Talent development: Proceedings from the 1991 Henry B. and Jocelyn Wallace National Research Symposium on Talent Development.* Unionville, NY: Trillium Press.

Davidson, J. E. (in press). Searching for insight. To appear is R. J. Sternberg & J. E. Davidson (Eds.), *The Nature of Insight.* Cambridge, MA: MIT Press.

References

Davidson, J. E, & Sternberg, R. J. (1984). The role of insight in intellectual giftedness. *Gifted Child Quarterly, 28,* 58–64.

Davidson, J. E., & Sternberg, R. J. (1986). What is insight? *Educational Horizons, 64,* 177–179.

Deffenbacher, K. A. (1980). Eyewitness accuracy and confidence: Can we infer anything about their relationship? *Law and Human Behavior, 4,* 243–260.

Deffenbacher, K. A. (1991). A maturing of research on the behaviour of eye-witnesses. *Applied Cognitive Psychology, 5,* 377–402.

Dempster, F. N. (1990). The spacing effect: A case study in the failure to apply the results of psychological research. *American Psychologist, 43,* 627–634.

Devolder, P. A., Brigham, M. C., & Pressley, M. (1990). Memory performance awareness in younger and older adults. *Psychology and Aging, 5,* 291–303.

Dixon, R. A. (1989). Questionnaire research on metamemory and aging: Issues of structure & function. In L. W. Poon, D. C. Rubin, & B. A. Wilson (Eds.), *Everyday cognition in adulthood and old age* (pp. 394–415). New York: Cambridge University Press.

Dixon, R. A., & Hertzog, C. (1988). A functional approach to memory and metamemory development in adulthood. In F. E. Weinert & M. Perlmutter (Eds.), *Memory development: Universal changes and individual differences* (pp. 293–330). Hillsdale, NJ: Erlbaum.

Dixon, R. A., & Hultsch, D. F. (1983a). Metamemory and memory for text relationships in adulthood: A cross-validation study. *Journal of Gerontology, 38,* 689–694.

Dixon, R. A., & Hultsch, D. F. (1983b). Structure and development of metamemory in adulthood. *Journal of Gerontology, 38,* 682–688.

Dixon, R. A., Hultsch, D. F., & Hertzog, C. (1988). The Metamemory In Adulthood (MIA) questionnaire. *Psychopharmacology Bulletin, 24,* 671–688.

Donchin, E., & Fabiani, M. (1993) The use of event-related brain potentials in the study of memory: Is P300 a measure of event distinctiveness? In J. R. Jennings & M. G. H. Coles (Eds.), *Handbook of cognitive psychophysiology: Central and autonomic system approaches.* Chichester, UK: Wiley, in press.

Dristas, W. J., & Hamilton, V. L. (1977). *Evidence about evidence: Effect of presuppositions, item salience, stress, and perceiver set on accident recall.* Unpublished manuscript, University of Michigan.

Duncker, K. (1945). On problem solving. *Psychological Monographs, 58:5, Whole. No. 270.*

References

Dunlosky, J., & Nelson, T. O. (1992). Importance of the kind of cue for judgments of learning (JOL) and the delayed-JOL effect. *Memory & Cognition, 20,* 374–380.

Dweck, C. S., & Leggett, E. L. (1988). A social-cognitive approach to motivation and personality. *Psychological Review, 95,* 256–273.

Eagle, M. (1967). The effect of learning strategies upon free recall. *American Journal of Psychology, 80,* 421–425.

Ebbinghaus, H. (1964). *Memory: A contribution to experimental psychology.* New York: Dover. (Originally published in 1885.)

Eisdorfer, C. (1968). Arousal and performance: Experiments in verbal learning and a tentative theory. In G. A. Talland (Ed.), *Human aging and behavior: Recent advances in research and theory* (pp. 189–216). New York: Academic Press.

Elliott, E., & Lachman, M. E. (1989). Enhancing memory by modifying control beliefs, attributions, and performance goals in the elderly. In P. S. Fry (Ed.), *Psychological perspectives on helplessness and control in the elderly* (pp. 339–367). Amsterdam: Elsevier.

Elman, J. (1990). Finding structure in time. *Cognitive Science, 14,* 179–212.

Epstein, W., Glenberg, A. M., & Bradley, M. (1984). Coactivation and comprehension: Contribution of text variables to the illusion of knowing. *Memory & Cognition, 12,* 355–360.

Erber, J. T. (1989). Young and older adults' appraisal of memory failures in young and older adult target persons. *Journal of Gerontology: Psychological Sciences, 44,* 170–175.

Erdry, E. (1990). *Access to partial information concerning an unrecallable target.* Unpublished M.A. thesis, University of Haifa.

Ericsson, K. A., & Simon, H. A. (1980). Verbal reports as data. *Psychological Review, 87,* 215–251.

Ericsson, K. A., & Simon, H. A. (1984). *Protocol analysis: Verbal reports as data.* Cambridge, MA: MIT Press.

Estes, W. K. (1955). Statistical theory of distributional phenomena in learning. *Psychological Review, 62,* 369–377.

Estes, W. K. (1972). An associative basis for coding and organization in memory. In A. W. Melton & E. Martin (Eds.), *Coding processes in human memory* (pp. 161–190). New York: Wiley.

Estes, W. K. (1975). The state of the field: General problems and issues of theory and metatheory. In W. K. Estes (Ed.), *Handbook of learning and cognitive processes* (Vol. 1). Hillsdale, NJ: Erlbaum.

Eysenck, M. W. (1979). The feeling of knowing a word's meaning. *British Journal of Psychology, 70,* 243–251.

Fabiani, M., Karris, D., & Donchin, E. (1986). P300 and recall in an incidental memory paradigm. *Psychophysiology, 23,* 298–308.

Fabiani, M., Karis, D., & Donchin, E. (1990). Effects of mnemonic strategy manipulation in a von Restorff paradigm. *Electroencephalography and Clinical Neurophysiology, 75,* 22–35.

Farah, M. J. (1990). *Visual agnosia.* Cambridge, MA: MIT Press.

Farr, M. J. (1987). *The long-term retention of knowledge and skills: A cognitive and instructional perspective.* New York: Springer-Verlag.

Fendrich, R., Wessinger, C. M., & Gazzaniga, M. S. (1992). Residual vision in a scotoma: Implications for blindsight. *Science, 258,* 1489–1491.

Finley, G. E., & Sharp, T. (1989). Name retrieval by the elderly in the tip-of-the-tongue paradigm: Demonstrable success in overcoming initial failure. *Educational Gerontology, 15,* 259–265.

Fischhoff, B. (1975). Hindsight is not equal to foresight: The effects of outcome knowledge on judgment under uncertainty. *Journal of Experimental Psychology: Human Perception and Performance, 1,* 288–299.

Fischhoff, B., Slovic, P., & Lichtenstein, S. (1977). Knowing with certainty: The appropriateness of extreme confidence. *Journal of Experimental Psychology: Human Perception and Performance, 3,* 552–564.

Flanagan, O. (1992). *Consciousness reconsidered.* Cambridge, MA: MIT Press.

Flavell, J. H. (1977). *Cognitive development.* Englewood Cliffs, NJ: Prentice-Hall.

Flavell, J. H. (1979). Metacognition and cognitive monitoring: A new area of cognitive-developmental inquiry. *American Psychologist, 34,* 906–911.

Flavell, J. H. (1981). Cognitive monitoring. In W. P. Dickson (Ed.), *Children's oral communication skills.* New York: Academic Press.

Flavell, J. H., & Wellman, H. M. (1977). Metamemory. In R. V. Kail & J. W. Hagen (Eds.), *Perspectives on the development of memory and cognition.* Hillsdale, NJ: Erlbaum.

Fodor, J. A. (1983). *The modularity of mind.* Cambridge, MA: MIT Press.

288

References

Foley, M. A., & Johnson, M. K. (1985). Confusions between memories for performed and imagined actions: A developmental comparison. *Child Development, 56,* 1145–1155.

Foley, M. A., Johnson, M. K., & Raye, C. L. (1983). Age related changes in confusion between memories for thoughts and memories for speech. *Child Development, 54,* 51–60.

Freedman, J. L., & Landauer, T. K. (1966). Retrieval of long-term memory: "Tip of the tongue" phenomenon. *Psychonomic Science, 4,* 309–310.

Fuster, J.M. (1980). *The prefrontal cortex: Anatomy, physiology, and neuropsychology of the frontal lobe.* New York: Raven Press.

Gardiner, J. M., Craik, F. I. M., & Birtwistle, J. (1972). Retrieval cues and release from proactive inhibition. *Journal of Verbal Learning and Verbal Behavior, 11,* 778–783.

Gardiner, J. M., Craik, F. I. M., & Bleasdale, F. A. (1973). Retrieval difficulty and subsequent recall. *Memory & Cognition, 1,* 213–216.

Gates, A. I. (1917). *Archives of Psychology #40.*

Gazzaniga, M. S., Bogen, J. E., & Sperry, R. W. (1965). Observations on visual perception after disconnexion of the cerebral hemispheres in man. *Brain, 88,* 221–236.

Geiselman, R. E., Fisher, R. P., MacKinnon, D. P., & Holland, H. L. (1985). Eyewitness memory enhancement in the police interview: Cognitive retrieval mnemonics versus hypnosis. *Journal of Applied Psychology, 70,* 401–412.

Gentner, D., & Gentner, D. R. (1975). Flowing waters or teeming crowns: Mental models of electricity. In D. Gentner & A. L. Stevens (Eds.), *Mental models.* Hillsdale, NJ: Erlbaum.

Geschwind, N. (1965). Disconnexion syndromes in animals and man. Part II. *Brain, 88,* 585–645.

Gick, M. L., & Holyoak, K. J. (1980). Analogical problem solving. *Cognitive Psychology, 12,* 306–355.

Gick, M. L., & Holyoak, K. J. (1983). Schema induction and analogical transfer. *Cognitive Psychology, 15,* 1–38.

Gick, M. L., & McGarry, S. J. (1992). Learning from mistakes: Inducing analogous solution failures to a source problem produces later successes in analogical transfer. *Journal of Experimental Psychology: Learning, Memory, and Cognition, 18,* 623–639.

Gilewski, M. J., & Zelinski, E. M. (1986). Questionnaire assessment of memory complaints. In L. W. Poon (Ed.), *Handbook for clinical memory assessment of older adults* (pp. 93–107). Washington, DC: American Psychological Association.

Glenberg, A. M. (1992). Distributed practice effects. In L. R. Squire (Ed.), *Encyclopedia of learning and memory.* (pp. 138–142). New York: Macmillan.

Glenberg, A. M., & Epstein, W. (1985). Calibration of comprehension. *Journal of Experimental Psychology: Learning, Memory, and Cognition, 11,* 702–718.

Glenberg, A. M., & Epstein, W. (1987). Inexpert calibration of comprehension. *Memory & Cognition, 15,* 84–93.

Glenberg, A. M., Sanocki, T., Epstein, W., & Morris, C. (1987). Enhancing calibration of comprehension. *Journal of Experimental Psychology: General, 116,* 119–136.

Glenberg, A. M.,Wilkinson, A. C., & Epstein, W. (1982). The illusion of knowing: Failure in the self-assessment of comprehension. *Memory & Cognition, 10,* 597–602.

Glucksberg, S., & McCloskey, M. (1981). Decisions about ignorance: Knowing that you don't know. *Journal of Experimental Psychology: Human Learning and Memory, 7,* 311–325.

Goldman-Rakic, P. S., & Friedman, H. R. (1991). The circuitry of working memory revealed by anatomy and metabolic imaging. In H. S. Levin, H. M. Eisenberg, & A. L. Benton (Eds.), *Frontal lobe function and dysfunction* (pp. 72–91). New York: Oxford Univeristry Press.

Graf, E. A., & Payne, D. (1992). *Assessing the scope of the delayed-JOL effect: Is it evident in the prediction of the self-paced allocation of study?* Honors Thesis, State University of New York at Binghamton.

Graf, P., Squire, L. R., & Mandler, G. (1984). The information that amnesic patients do not forget. *Journal of Experimental Psychology: Learning, Memory, and Cognition, 10,* 164–178.

Greeno, J. (1980). Trends in the theory of knowledge for problem solving. In D.T. Tuma & F. Reif (Eds.), *Problem solving and education: Issues in teaching and research.* Hillsdale, NJ: Erlbaum.

Greeno, J. G., & Berger, D. (1987). A model of functional knowledge and insight. *Technical Report.* GK-1, Office of Naval Research.

Greeno, J. G., & Bjork, R. A. (1973). Mathematical learning theory and the new mental forestry. In P. H. Mussen & M. R. Rosenzweig (Eds.), *Annual review of psychology* (pp. 81–116). Palo Alto: Annual Reviews.

Greeno, J. G., & Simon, H. A. (1988). Problem solving and reasoning. In R. C. Atkinson, R. J. Hernstein, G. Lindzey, & R. D. Luce (Eds.) *Steven's handbook of experimental psychology* (rev. ed.). New York: Wiley.

Greeno, J. G., Smith, D. R., & Moore, J. L. (1993). Transfer of situated learning. In D. K. Detterman & R. J. Sternberg (Eds.). *Transfer on Trial: Intelligence, cognition, and instruction* (pp. 99–167). Norwood, NJ: Ablex.

Gruneberg, M. M., & Monks, J. (1974). Feeling of knowing and cued recall. *Acta Psychologica, 38,* 257–265.

Gruneberg, M. M., Monks, J. , & Sykes, R. N. (1977). Some methodological problems with feeling of knowing studies. *Acta Psychologica, 41,* 365–371.

Gruneberg, M. M., Morris, P., & Sykes, R. N. (1991). The obituary on everyday memory and its practical applications is premature. *American Psychologist, 46,* 74–76.

Gruneberg, M. M., Smith, R. L., & Winfrow, P. (1973). An investigation into response blockaging. *Acta Psychologica, 37,* 187–196.

Gruneberg, M. M., & Sykes, R. N. (1978). Knowledge and retention: The feeling of knowing and reminiscence. In M. M. Gruneberg, P. E. Morris, & R. N. Sykes (Eds.), *Practical aspects of memory* (pp. 189–196). New York: Academic Press.

Hall, J. W. (1992). Unmixing effects of spacing on free recall. *Journal of Experimental Psychology: Learning, Memory, and Cognition, 18,* 608–614.

Hall, K. G., Domingues, E., & Cavazos, R. (1992). *The effects of contextual interference on extra batting practice.* Unpublished paper.

Hart, J. T. (1965a). Memory and the feeling-of-knowing experience. *Journal of Educational Psychology, 56,* 208–216.

Hart, J. T. (1965b). *Recall, recognition, and the memory monitoring process.* Doctoral dissertation, Stanford University. (University Microfilms No. 66–2565.)

Hart, J. T. (1967a). Memory and the memory-monitoring process. *Journal of Verbal Learning and Verbal Behavior, 6,* 685–691.

Hart, J. T. (1967b). Second-try recall, recognition, and the memory-monitoring process. *Journal of Educational Psychology, 58,* 193–197.

Hashtroudi, S., Johnson, M. K., & Chrosniak, L. (1989). Aging and source monitoring. *Psychology and Aging, 4,* 106–112.

Hayes, J. R. (1981). *The complete problem solver.* Hillsdale, NJ: Erlbaum.

Herrmann, D. J. (1982). Know thy memory: The use of questionnaires to assess and study memory. *Psychological Bulletin, 92,* 434–452.

Herrmann, D. J. (1990). Self perceptions of memory performance. In K. W. Schaie (Ed.), *Self directedness and efficacy: Causes and effects throughout the life course* (pp 199–211). Hillsdale, NJ: Erlbaum.

Hertzog, C. (1992). Improving memory: The possible roles of metamemory. In D. J. Herrmann, H. Weingartner, A. Searleman, & C. McEvoy (Eds.), *Memory improvement: Implications for memory theory* (pp. 61–78). New York: Springer.

Hertzog, C., Dixon, R. A., & Hultsch, D. F. (1990a). Metamemory in adulthood: Differentiating knowledge, belief, and behavior. In T. M. Hess (Ed.), *Aging and cognition: Knowledge organization and utilization* (pp. 161–212). Amsterdam: Elsevier.

Hertzog, C., Dixon, R. A., & Hultsch, D. F. (1990b). Relationships between metamemory, memory predictions, and memory task performance in adults. *Psychology and Aging, 5,* 215–227.

Hertzog, C., Hultsch, D. F., & Dixon, R. A. (1989). Evidence for the convergent validity of two self-report metamemory questionnaires. *Developmental Psychology, 25,* 687–700.

Hertzog, C., Saylor, L. L., Fleece, A. M., & Dixon, R. A. (1993). *Aging, memory, and metamemory: Relations between predicted, actual, and perceived task performance.* Unpublished Manuscript.

Higbee, K. L. (1988). *Your memory: How it works and how to improve it.* New York: Prentice-Hall.

Hillyard, S. A., & Picton, T. W. (1987). Electrophysiology of cognition. In F. Plum (Ed.), *Handbook of Physiology: Higher functions of the nervous system. Section 1: The nervous system V. Higher functions of the brain, Part 2* (pp. 519–584). Bethesda, MD: American Physiological Society.

Hinton, G. E. (1989). Deterministic Boltzmann learning performs steepest descent in weight-space. *Neural Computation, 1,* 143–150.

Hintzman, D. L. (1974). Theoretical implications of the spacing effect. In R. L. Solso (Ed.) *Theories in cognitive psychology: The Loyola Symposium.* Hillsdale, NJ: Erlbaum.

Hirst, W. (1982). The amnesic syndrome: Descriptions and explanations. *Psychological Bulletin, 91,* 435–460.

Hoffding, H. (1891). *Outlines of psychology* (M. E. Lowndes, Trans.). London: Macmillan.

Hogan, R. M., & Kintsch, W. (1971). Differential effects of study and test trials on long-term recognition and recall. *Journal of Verbal Learning and Verbal Behavior, 10,* 562–567.

Homa, D., & Cultice, J. (1984). Role of feedback, category size, and stimulus distortion on the acquisition and utilization of ill-defined categories. *Journal of Experimental Psychology: Learning, Memory, and Cognition, 10,* 83–94.

Hultsch, D. F. (1969). Adult age differences in the organization of free recall. *Developmental Psychology, 1,* 673–678.

Hultsch, D. F., & Dixon, R. A. (1990). Learning and memory in aging. In J. E. Birren & K. W. Schaie (Eds.), *Handbook of the psychology of aging* (3rd Ed., pp. 258–274). New York: Academic Press.

Hultsch, D. F., Hertzog, C., & Dixon, R. A. (1987). Age differences in metamemory: Resolving the inconsistencies. *Canadian Journal of Psychology, 41,* 193–208.

Hultsch, D. F., Hertzog, C., Dixon, R. A., & Davidson, H. (1988). Memory self-knowledge and self-efficacy in the aged. In M. L. Howe & C. J. Brainerd (Eds.), *Cognitive developmental in adulthood: Progress in cognitive development research* (pp. 65–92). New York: Springer.

Humphreys, G. W., & Riddoch, M. J. (1987). *Visual object processing: A cognitive neuropsychological approach.* London: Erlbaum.

Izawa, C. (1970). Optimal potentiating effects and forgetting-prevention effects of tests in paired-associate learning. *Journal of Experimental Psychology, 83,* 340–344.

Jacoby, L. L., Bjork, R. A., & Kelley, C. M. (1993). Illusions of comprehension and competence. In D. Druckman and R. A. Bjork (Eds.), *Learning, remembering, believing: Enhancing team and individual performance.* Washington, DC: National Academy Press, in press.

Jacoby, L. L., & Brooks, L. R. (1984). Nonanalytic cognition: Memory, perception, and concept learning. In G. Bower (Ed.), *The Psychology of learning and motivation: Advances in research and theory* (Vol. 18). New York: Academic Press.

Jacoby, L. L., & Kelley, C. M. (1987). Unconscious influences of memory for a prior event. *Personality and Social Psychology Bulletin, 13,* 314–336.

Jacoby, L. L., & Kelley, C. M. (1991). Unconscious influences of memory: Dissociations and automaticity. In D. Milner & M. Rugg (Eds.), *The neuropsychology of consciousness* (pp. 210–233). London: Academic Press.

Jacoby, L. L., Kelley, C. M., & Dywan, J. (1989). Memory attributions. In H. L. Roediger & F. I. M. Craik (Eds.), *Varieties of memory and consciousness: Essays in honour of Endel Tulving* (pp. 391–422). Hillsdale, NJ: Erlbaum.

Jacoby, L. L., Lindsay, S. D., & Toth, T. J. (1992). Unconsious influences revealed: Attention, awareness, and control. *American Psychologist, 47,* 802–809.

Jacoby, L. L., & Witherspoon, D. (1982). Remembering without awareness. *Canadian Journal of Psychology, 32*, 300–324.

James, W. (1890). *Principles of psychology*. New York: Holt.

Jameson, K. A. , Narens, L., Goldfarb, K., & Nelson, T. O. (1990). The influence of near-threshold priming on metamemory and recall. *Acta Psychologica, 73*, 55–68.

Janowsky, J. S., Shimamura, A. P., Kritchevsky, M., & Squire, L. R. (1989). Cognitive impairment following frontal lobe damage and its relevance to human amnesia. *Behavioral Neuroscience, 103*, 548–560.

Janowsky, J. S., Shimamura, A. P., & Squire, L. R. (1989). Memory and metamemory: Comparisons between frontal lobe lesions and amnesic patients. *Psychobiology, 17*, 3–11.

Jeffrey, W. E. (1976). Habituation as a mechanism of perceptual development. In T. J. Tighe & R. N. Leaton (Eds.), *Habituaiton* (pp. 279–296). Hillsdale, NJ: Erlbaum.

Johnson, M. K. (1988). Reality monitoring: An experimental phenomenological approach. *Journal of Experimental Psychology: General, 117*, 390–394.

Johnson, M. K., Foley, M. A., Suengas, A. G., & Raye, C. L. (1988). Phenomenal characteristics of memories for perceived and imagined autobiographical events. *Journal of Experimental Psychology: General, 117*, 371–376.

Johnson, M. K., & Hirst, W. (1991). Processing subsystems of memory. In R. G. Lister & H. J. Weingartner (Eds.), *Perspectives on cognitive neuroscience*. New York: Oxford University Press.

Johnson, M. K., & Raye, C. L. (1981). Reality monitoring. *Psychological Review, 88*, 67–85.

Johnson, M. K., Raye, C. L., Foley, H. J., & Foley, M. A. (1981). Cognitive operations and decision bias in reality monitoring. *American Journal of Psychology, 94*, 37–64.

Johnson, M. K., Raye, C. L., Foley, M. A., & Kim, J. K. (1982). Pictures and images: Spatial and temporal information compared. *Bulletin of the Psychonomic Society, 19*, 23–26.

Johnson-Laird, P. N. (1983). A computational analysis of consciousness. *Cognition and Brain Theory, 6*(4), 499–508.

Jones, G. V. (1989). Back to Woodworth: Role of interlopers in the tip-of-the-tongue phenomenon. *Memory & Cognition, 17*, 69–76.

Jones, G. V., & Langford, S. (1987). Phonological blocking in the tip of the tongue state. *Cognition, 26,* 115–122.

Jouandet, M., & Gazzaniga, M. S. (1979). The frontal lobes. In M. S. Gazzaniga (Ed.), *Handbook of Behavioural Neurobiology* (Vol 2). New York: Plenum Press.

Kaplan, C. A., & Davidson, J. E. (1993). Incubation effects in problem solving. Manuscript submitted for publication.

Kaplan, C. A., & Simon, H. A. (1990). In search of insight. *Cognitive Psychology, 22,* 374–419.

Karis, D., Fabiani, M., & Donchin, E. (1984). "P300" and memory: Individual differences in the von Restorff effect. *Cognitive Psychology, 16,* 177–216.

Kausler, D. H. (1982). *Experimental psychology and human aging.* New York: Wiley.

Kausler, D. H. (1990). Motivation, human aging, and cognitive performance. In J. E. Birren & K. W. Schaie (Eds.), *Handbook of the psychology of aging* (3rd Ed., pp. 171–182).

Kelley, C. M., & Lindsay, D. S. (1993). Remembering mistaken for knowing: Ease of retrieval as a basis for confidence in answers to general knowledge questions. *Journal of Memory and Language, 32,* 1–24.

Kerr, R., & Booth, B. (1978). Specific and varied practice of a motor skill. *Perceptual and Motor Skills, 46,* 395–401.

Kinsbourne, M., & Wood, F. (1975). Short-term memory processes and the amnesic syndrome. In D. Deutsch & A. J. Deutsch (Eds.), *Short-term memory.* New York: Academic Press.

Klinke, R. , Fruhstrorfer, H., & Finkenzellar, P. (1968). Evoked responses as a function of external and stored information. *Electroencephalography and Clinical Neurophysiology, 25,* 119–122.

Knight, R. T. (1991). Evoked potential studies of attention capacity in human frontal lobe lesions. In H. S. Levin, H. M. Eisenberg, & A. L. Benton (Eds.), *Frontal lobe function and dysfunction* (pp. 139–153). New York: Oxford University Press.

Kohler, W. (1969). *The task of gestalt psychology.* Princeton, NJ: Princeton University Press.

Kohn, S. E., Wingfield, A., Menn, L., Goodglass, H., Gleason, J. B., & Hyde, M. (1987). Lexical retrieval: The tip-of-the-tongue phenomenon. *Applied Psycholinguistics, 8,* 245–266.

Kohonen, T. (1982). Self-organized formation of topologically correct feature maps. *Biological Cybernetics, 43,* 56–69.

References

Kolers, P. A., & Palef, S. R. (1976). Knowing not. *Memory & Cognition, 4,* 553–558.

Konorski , J. (1967). *Integrative activity of the brain.* Chicago: Univeristy of Chicago Press.

Koriat, A. (1976). Another look at the relationship between phonetic symbolism and the feeling of knowing. *Memory & Cognition, 4,* 244–248.

Koriat, A. (1993). How do we know that we know? The accessibility account of the feeling of knowing. *Psychological Review,* in press.

Koriat, A., & Goldsmith, M. (1993). Metaphors for memory assessment: Comparing quantity-oriented and accuracy-oriented approaches. Manuscipt under submission.

Koriat, A., Lichtenstein, S., & Fischhoff, B. (1980). Reasons for confidence. *Journal of Experimental Psychology: Human Learning and Memory, 6,* 107–118.

Koriat, A., & Lieblich, I. (1974). What does a person in a "TOT" state know that a person in a "don't know" state doesn't know. *Memory & Cognition, 2,* 647–655.

Koriat, A., & Lieblich, I. (1975). Examination of the letter serial position effect in the "TOT" and the "Don't Know" states. *Bulletin of the Psychonomic Society, 6,* 539–541.

Koriat, A., & Lieblich, I. (1977). A study of memory pointers. *Acta Psychologica, 41,* 151–164.

Kotovsky, K., Hayes, J. R., & Simon, H. A. (1985). Why are some problems hard? Evidence from the tower of Hanoi. *Cognitive Psychology, 17,* 248–294.

Kozlowski, L. T. (1977). Effects of distorted auditory and of rhyming cues on retrieval of tip-of-the-tongue words by poets and nonpoets. *Memory & Cognition, 5,* 477–481.

Krinsky, R., & Nelson, T. O. (1985). The feeling of knowing for different types of retrieval failure. *Acta Psychologica, 58,* 141–158.

Kuhn, T. S. (1962). *The structure of scientific revolutions.* Chicago: University of Chicago Press.

Kutas, M., McCarthy, G., & Donchin, E. (1977). Augmenting mental chronometry: The P300 as a measure of stimulus evaluation time. *Science, 197,* 792–795.

Lachman, J. L., & Lachman, R. (1980). Age and actualization of world knowledge. In L. W. Poon, J. L. Fozard, L. S. Cermak, D. Arenberg, & L. W. Thompson (Eds.), *New directions in memory and aging* (pp. 285–311). Hillsdale, NJ: Erlbaum.

References

Lachman, J. L., Lachman, R., & Thronesbury, C. (1979). Metamemory through the adult life span. *Developmental Psychology*, *15*, 543–551.

Lachman, M. E., & Jelalian, E. (1984). Self-efficacy and attributions for intellectual performance in young and elderly adults. *Journal of Gerontology*, *39*, 557–582.

Lachman, M. E., Steinberg, E. S., & Trotter, S. D. (1987). Effects of control beliefs and attributions on memory self-assessments and performance. *Psychology and Aging*, *2*, 266–271.

Landauer, T. K., & Bjork, R. A. (1978). Optimum rehearsal patterns and name learning. In M. M. Gruneberg, P. E. Morris, & R. N. Sykes (Eds.), *Practical aspects of memory* (pp. 625–632). London: Academic Press.

Langer, E. (1981). Old age: An artifact? In J. McGaugh & S. Kiesler (Eds.), *Aging: Biology and behavior* (pp. 255–282). New York: Academic Press.

Langer, E. (1989). *Mindfulness*. Reading, MA: Addison-Wesley.

Langley, D. J., & Zelaznik, H. N. (1984). The acquisition of time properties associated with a sequential motor skill. *Journal of Motor Behavior*, *16*, 275–301.

Larkin, J. H., McDermott, J., Simon, D. P., & Simon, H. A. (1980). Expert and novice performance in solving physics problems. *Science*, *208*, 1335–1342.

Larrabee, G. J., West, R. L., & Crook, T. H. (1991). The association of memory complaint with computer-simulated everyday memory performance. *Journal of Clinical and Experimental Neuropsychology*, *13*, 466–478.

Lave, J., & Wenger, E. (1991). *Situated learning: Legitimate peripheral participation*. Cambridge, England: Cambridge University Press.

Lee, T. D., & Genovese, E. D. (1988). Distribution of practice in motor skill acquisition: Learning and performance effects reconsidered. *Research Quarterly for Exercise and Sport*, *59*, 277–287.

Lee, T. D., & Magill, R. A. (1983). The locus of contextual interference in motor-skill acquisition. *Journal of Experimental Psychology: Learning, Memory, and Cognition*, *9*, 730–746.

Lee, V. A., Narens, L., & Nelson, T. O. (1993). Subthreshold priming and the judgment of learning. Manuscript under submission.

Lefebvre, V. A. (1977). *The structure of awareness*. Beverly Hills: Sage.

Lefebvre, V. A. (1992). *A psychological theory of bipolarity and reflexivity*. Lewiston: The Edwin Mellen Press.

Leonesio, R. J., & Nelson, T. O. (1990). Do different metamemory judgments tap the same underlying aspects of memory. *Journal of Experimental Psychology: Learning, Memory, and Cognition, 16*, 464–470.

Lesgold, A. (1988). Problem solving. In R. J. Sternberg & E. E. Smith (Eds.), *The psychology of human thought* (pp. 188–213). New York: Cambridge University Press.

Lesgold, A., Runinson, H., Feltovich, P., Glaser, R., Klopfer, D., & Wang, Y. (1988). Expertise in a complex skill: Diagnosing x-ray pictures. In M.T.H. Chi, R. Glaser, & M. Farr (Eds.), *The nature of expertise*. Hillsdale, NJ: Erlbaum.

Levine, D. S., & Prueitt, P. S. (1989). Modeling some effects of frontal lobe damage — Novelty and perseveration. *Neural Networks, 2*, 103–116.

Lewandowsky, S., & Murdock, B. B. (1989). Memory for serial order. *Psychological Review, 96*, 25–57.

Lichtenstein, S., & Fischhoff, B. (1977). Do those who know more also know more of how much they know? The calibration of probability judgments. *Journal of Experimental Psychology: Learning, Memory, and Cognition, 16*, 464–470.

Lichtenstein, S., Fischhoff, B., & Phillips, L. D. (1977). Calibration of probabilities: The state of the art. In H. Jungermann & G. deZeeuw (Eds.), *Decision making and change in human affairs*. Amsterdam: D. Reidel.

Light, L. L. (1991). Memory and aging: Four hypotheses in search of data. *Annual Review of Psychology, 42*, 333–376.

Lindsay, D. S. (1990). Misleading suggestions can impair eyewitness' ability to remember event details. *Journal of Experimental Psychology: Learning, Memory, and Cognition, 16*, 1077–1083.

Lindsay, D. S., & Johnson, M. K. (1987). Reality monitoring and suggestibility: Children's ability to discriminate among memories from different sources. In S. J. Ceci, M. P. Toglia, & D. F. Ross (Eds.), *Children's eyewitness memory*. New York: Springer-Verlag.

Lindsay, D. S., & Johnson, M. K. (1989). The eyewitness suggestibility effect and memory for source. *Memory & Cognition, 17*, 349–358.

Lindsay, R. C. L., Wells, G. L., & Rumpel, C. (1981). Can people detect eyewitness identification accuracy within and across situations? *Journal of Applied Psychology, 66*, 79–89.

Linton, M. (1982). Transformation in memory in everyday life. In U. Neisser (Ed.), *Memory observed*. San Francisco: W. H. Freeman.

Loewen, E. R., Shaw, R. J., & Craik, F. I. M. (1992). Age differences in components of metamemory. *Experimental Aging Research, 16*, 43–48.

References

Loftus, E. F. (1975). Leading questions and the eyewitness report. *Cognitive Psychology, 7,* 560–572.

Loftus, E. F., Donders, K., & Hoffman, H. G., & Schooler, J. W. (1989). Creating new memories that are quickly accessed and confidently held. *Memory & Cognition, 17,* 607–616.

Loftus, E. F., & Greene, E. (1980). Warning: Even memory for faces can be contagious. *Law and Human Behavior, 4,* 323–334.

Loftus, E. F., & Hoffman, H. G. (1989). Misinformation and memory: The creation of new memories. *Journal of Experimental Psychology: General, 118,* 100–104.

Loftus, E. F., & Ketcham, K. (1991). *Witness for the defense: The accused, the eyewitness, and the expert who puts memory on trial.* New York: St. Martin's Press.

Loftus, E. F., Miller, D. G., & Burns, H. J. (1978). Semantic integration of verbal information into a visual memory. *Journal of Experimental Psychology: Human Learning and Memory, 4,* 19–31.

Loftus, E. F., Schooler, J. W., & Wagenaar, W. A. (1985). The fate of memory: Comment on McCloskey and Zaragoza. *Journal of Experimental Psychology: General, 114,* 375–380.

Logan, G. D., & Cowan, W. B. (1984). On the ability to inhibit thought and action: A theory of an act of control. *Psychological Review, 91,* 295–327.

Lovelace, E. A. (1987). Attributes that come to mind in the TOT state. *Bulletin of the Psychonomic Society, 25,* 370–372.

Lovelace, E. A. (1990). Aging and metacognitions concerning memory function. In E. A. Lovelace (Ed.), *Aging and cognition: Mental processes, self awareness, and interventions* (pp. 157–188). Amsterdam: North Holland.

Lovelace, E. A., & Marsh, G. R. (1985). Prediction and evaluation of memory performance by young and old adults. *Journal of Gerontology, 40,* 192–197.

Luchins, A. S. (1942). *The mentality of apes* (2nd ed.) New York: Harcourt Brace.

Luchins, A. S., & Luchins, E. S. (1950). New experimental attempts at preventing mechanization in problem solving. *Journal of General Psychology, 42,* 279–297.

Lupker, S. J., Harbluk, J. L., & Patrick, A. S. (1991). Memory for things forgotten. *Journal of Experimental Psychology: Learning, Memory, and Cognition, 17,* 897–907.

Luria, A. R. (1966). *Higher cortical function in man.* New York: Plenum Press.

MacLeod, C. M., Hunt, E. B., & Mathews, N. N. (1978). Individual differences in the verification of sentence-picture relationships. *Journal of Verbal Learning and Verbal Behavior, 17,* 493–508.

Madigan, S. (1969). Intraserial repetition and coding processes in free recall. *Journal of Verbal Learning and Verbal Behavior, 8,* 828–835.

Maier, N. R. F. (1930). Reasoning in humans: I. On direction. *Journal of comparative psychology, 12,* 115–143.

Mair, W. G. P., Warrington, E. K., & Weiskrantz, L. (1979). Memory disorder in Korsakoff's psychosis: A neuropathological and neuropsychological investigation of two cases. *Brain, 102,* 749–783.

Maki, R. H., & Berry, S. L. (1984). Metacomprehension of text material. *Journal of Experimental Psychology: Learning, Memory, and Cognition, 10,* 663–679.

Mannes, S. M., & Kintsch, W. (1987). Knowledge organization and text organization. *Cognition and Instruction, 4,* 91–115.

Marcel, A. (1983). Conscious and unconscious perception: Experiments on visual masking and word recognition. *Cognitive Psychology, 15,* 197–237.

Markus, H., & Wurf, E. (1987). The dynamic self-concept: A social psychological perspective. *Annual Review of Psychology, 38,* 299–338.

Marslen-Wilson, W. D., & Teuber, H. (1975). Memory for remote events in anterograde amnesia: Recognition of public figures from news photographs. *Neuropsychologia, 13,* 353–364.

Marx, M. H. (1963). *Theories in contemporary psychology.* New York: Macmillan.

Mayes, A. R. (1988). *Human organic memory disorders.* Cambridge, UK: Cambridge University Press.

Mayes, A. R., Meudell, P. R., Mann, D., & Pickering, A. (1988). Location of lesions in Korsakoff's syndrome: Neuropsychological and neuropathological data on two patients. *Cortex, 24,* 367–388.

Maylor, E.A. (1990). Recognizing and naming faces: Aging, memory retrieval, and the tip of the tongue state. *Journal of Gerontology, 45,* 215–226.

Mazzoni, G., & Cornoldi, C. (1993). Strategies in study time allocation: Why is study time sometimes not effective? *Journal of Experimental Psychology: General, 122,* 47–60.

McClelland, J. L., & Rumelhart, D. E. (1986). *Parallel distributed processing* (Vol. 1). Cambridge, MA: MIT Press.

McCloskey, M., & Zaragoza, M. S. (1985). Misleading postevent information and memory for events: Arguments and evidence against memory impairment hypotheses. *Journal of Experimental Psychology: General, 114,* 1–16.

McDonald-Miszczak, L., Hunter, M. A., & Hultsch, D. F. (1992). *Adult age differences in predicting memory performance: The effects of task appraisal.* Unpublished manuscript.

McGlynn, S. M., & Kaszniak, A. W. (1991). When metacognition fails: Impaired awareness of deficit in Alzheimer's disease. *Journal of Cognitive Neuroscience, 3,* 183–198.

McGlynn, S. M., & Schacter, D. L. (1989). Unawareness of deficits in neuropsychological syndromes. *Journal of Clinical and Experimental Neuropsychology, 11,* 143–205.

McKellar, P. (1957). *Imagination and thinking.* New York: Basic Books.

Melton, A. W. (1967). Repetition and retrieval from memory. *Science, 158,* 532.

Mesulam, M. M. (1981). A cortical network for directed attention and unilateral neglect. *Annals of Neurology, 10,* 309–325.

Metcalfe, J. (1986a). Feeling of knowing in memory and problem solving. *Journal of Experimental Psychology: Learning, Memory, and Cognition, 12,* 288–294.

Metcalfe, J. (1986b). Premonitions of insight predict impending error. *Journal of Experimental Psychology: Learning, Memory, and Cognition, 12,* 623–634.

Metcalfe, J. (1990). Composite holographic associative recall model (CHARM) and blended memories in eyewitness testimony. *Journal of Experimental Psychology: General, 119,* 145–160.

Metcalfe, J. (1991). Recognition failure and the composite memory trace in CHARM. *Psychological Review, 98,* 529–553.

Metcalfe, J. (1993). Novelty monitoring, metacognition and control in a composite holographic associative recall model: Implications for Korsakoff amnesia. *Psychological Review, 100,* 3–22.

Metcalfe, J. (1993). Monitoring and gain control in an episodic memory model: Relation to P300 event-related potentials. In A. Collins, M. Conway, S. Gathercole, & P. Morris (Eds.), *Theories of memory.* Hillsdale, NJ: Erlbaum.

Metcalfe Eich, J. (1982). A composite holographic associative recall model. *Psychological Review, 89,* 627–661.

Metcalfe Eich, J. (1985). Levels of processing, encoding specificity, elaboration, and CHARM. *Psychological Review, 92,* 1–38.

Metcalfe, J., Cottrell, G. W., & Mencl, W. E. (1993). Cognitive binding: A computational-modeling analysis of a distinction between implicit and explicit memory. *Journal of Cognitive Neuroscience, 4,* 289–298.

References

Metcalfe, J., Schwartz, B. L., & Joaquim, S. G. (1993). The cue familiarity heuristic in metacognition. *Journal of Experimental Psychology: Learning, Memory, and Cognition, 19,* 851–861.

Metcalfe, J., & Wiebe, D. (1987). Intuition in insight and non-insight problem solving. *Memory & Cognition, 15,* 238–246.

Meyer, A. S., & Bock, K. (1992). The tip-of-the-tongue phenomenon: Inhibition or facilitation of word retrieval? *Memory & Cognition, 20,* 17–26.

Miller, G. A., Galanter, E., & Pribram, K. H. (1960). *Plans and the structure of behavior.* New York: Holt.

Milner, B., Corkin, S., & Teuber, H. (1968). Further analysis of the hippocampal amnesic syndrome: 14-year follow-up study of H. M. *Neuropsychologia, 6,* 215–234.

Milner, B., Petrides, M., & Smith, M. L. (1985). Frontal lobes and the temporal organization of memory. *Human Neurobiology, 4,* 137–142.

Minsky, M. (1985). *Society of mind.* New York: Simon & Shuster.

Mishkin, M. (1982). A memory system in the monkey. In D. E. Broadbent & L. Weiskrantz (Eds.). *The neuropsychology of cognitive function* (pp. 85–95). London: The Royal Society.

Mishkin, M., Malamut, B., & Bachevalier, J. (1984). Memories and habits: Two neural systems. In J. L. McGaugh, G. Lynch, & N. Weinberger (Eds.), *The neurobiology of learning and memory* (pp. 65–77). New York: Guilford Press.

Miyamoto, J.M. (1991). Personal correspondence. June 18, 1991.

Mohler, C. W., & Wurtz, R. H. (1977). Role of striate cortex and superior colliculus in visual guidance of saccadic eye movements in monkeys. *Journal of Neurophysiology, 40,* 74–94.

Morris, C. C. (1990). Retrieval processes underlying confidence in comprehension judgments. *Journal of Experimental Psychology: Learning, Memory, and Cognition, 16,* 223–232.

Morris, C. D., Bransford, J. D., & Franks, J. J. (1977). Levels of processing versus transfer appropriate processing. *Journal of Verbal Learning and Verbal Behavior, 16,* 519–533.

Morris, P. (1987). *Modelling cognition.* New York: Wiley.

Moscovitch, M. (1982). Multiple dissociations of function in amnesia. In L. S. Cermak (Ed.), *Human memory and amnesia.* Hillsdale, NJ: Erlbaum.

Moscovitch, M. (1989). Confabulation and the frontal systems: Strategic versus associative retrieval in neuropsychological theories of memory. In H. L. Roediger, III, & F. I. M. Craik (Eds.), *Varieties of memory and consciousness, Essays in honour of Endel Tulving* (pp. 133–160). Hillsdale, NJ: Erlbaum.

Munsterberg, H. (1908). *On the witness stand: Essays on psychology and crime.* New York: Clark Boardman.

Murdock, B. B., Jr. (1960). The distinctiveness of stimuli. *Psychological Review, 67,* 16–31.

Murdock, B. B., Jr. (1974). *Human memory: Theory and data.* Potomac, MD: Erlbaum.

Murdock, B. B., Jr. (1982). A theory for the storage and retrieval of item and associative information. *Psychological Review, 89,* 609–626.

Murdock, B. B., Jr. (1990). Learning in a distributed memory model. In C. Izawa (Ed.), *Current issues in cognitive processes: The Tulane Floweree Symposium on Cognition.* Hillsdale, NJ: Erlbaum.

Murdock, B. B., Jr., & Babick, A. J. (1961). The effect of repetition on the retention of individual words. *American Journal of Psychology, 74,* 596–601.

Murphy, M. D., Sanders, R. E., Gabriesheski, A. S., & Schmitt, F. A. (1981). Metamemory in the aged. *Journal of Gerontology, 36,* 185–193.

Murphy, M. D., Schmitt, F. A., Caruso, M. J., & Sanders, R. E. (1987). Metamemory in older adults: The role of monitoring in serial recall. *Psychology and Aging, 2,* 331–339.

Musen, G., Shimamura, A. P., & Squire, L. R. (1990). Intact text-specific reading skill in amnesia. *Journal of Experimental Psychology: Learning, Memory, and Cognition, 16,* 1068–1076.

Neisser, U. (1976). *Cognition and reality: Principles and implications of cognitive psychology.* San Francisco: W. H. Freeman.

Neisser, U. (1982). *Memory observed.* San Francisco: W. H. Freeman.

Nelson, D. L., & McEvoy, C. L. (1979). Encoding context and set size. *Journal of Experimental Psychology: Human Learning, and Memory, 5,* 279–314.

Nelson, K. (1977). The syntagmatic-paradigmatic shift revisited: A review of research and theory. *Psychological Bulletin, 84,* 93–116.

Nelson, T. O. (1984). A comparison of current measures of the accuracy of feeling-of-knowing predictions. *Psychological Bulletin, 95,* 109–133.

Nelson, T. O. (1988). Predictive accuracy of the feeling of knowing across different criterion tasks and across different subject populations and individuals. In M. M. Gruneberg, P. Morris, & R. N. Sykes (Eds.), *Practical aspects of memory* (Vol. 2). New York: Wiley.

Nelson, T. O. (1992). *Metacognition: Core readings.* Boston: Allyn & Bacon.

Nelson, T. O. (1993). Judgments of learning and the allocation of study time. *Journal of Experimental Psychology: General, 122,* 269–273.

Nelson, T. O., & Dunlosky, J. (1991). When people's judgments of learning (JOLs) are extremely accurate at predicting subsequent recall: The "delayed-JOL effect." *Psychological Science, 2,* 267–270.

Nelson, T. O., & Dunlosky, J. (1992). How shall we explain the delayed-judgment-of-learning effect? *Psychological Science, 3,* 317–318.

Nelson, T. O., Dunlosky, J., & Narens, L. (1992). *Allocation of study time after delayed judgments of learning.* Unpublished experiment. (Summarized in Nelson, 1993.)

Nelson, T. O., Dunlosky, J., White, D. M., Steinberg, J., Townes, B. D., & Anderson, D. (1990). Cognition and metacognition at extreme altitude on Mount Everest. *Journal of Experimental Psychology: General, 119,* 367–374.

Nelson, T. O., Gerler, D., & Narens, L. (1984). Accuracy of feeling of knowing judgments for predicting perceptual identification and relearning. *Journal of Experimental Psychology: General, 113,* 282–300.

Nelson, T. O., Gerler, D., & Narens, L. (1992). Accuracy and feeling-of-knowing judgments for predicting perceptual identification and relearning. In T. O. Nelson (Ed.), *Metacognition: Core readings* (pp. 142–150). Boston: Allyn & Bacon.

Nelson, T. O., & Leonesio, R. J. (1988). Allocation of self-paced study time and the 'labor-in-vain effect.' *Journal of Experimental Psychology: Learning, Memory, and Cognition, 14,* 476–486.

Nelson, T. O., Leonesio, R. J., Landwehr, R. S., & Narens, L. (1986). A comparison of three predictors of an individual's memory performance: The individual's feeling of knowing versus the normative feeling of knowing versus base-rate item difficulty. *Journal of Experimental Psychology: Learning, Memory, and Cognition, 12,* 279–287.

Nelson, T. O., Leonesio, R. J., Shimamura, A. P., Landwehr, R. S., & Narens, L. (1982). Overlearning and the feeling of knowing. *Journal of Experimental Psychology: Learning, Memory, and Cognition, 8,* 279–288.

Nelson, T. O., McSpadden, M., Fromme, K., & Marlatt, G. A. (1986). Effects of alcohol intoxication on metamemory and on retrieval from long-term memory. *Journal of Experimental Psychology: General, 115,* 247–254.

Nelson, T. O., & Narens, L. (1980a). Norms of 300 general-information questions: Accuracy of recall, latency of recall, and feeling-of-knowing ratings. *Journal of Verbal Learning and Verbal Behavior, 19,* 338–368.

Nelson, T. O., & Narens, L. (1980b). A new technique for investigating the feeling of knowing. *Acta Psychologica, 46,* 69–90.

Nelson, T. O., & Narens, L. (1990). Metamemory: A theoretical framework and new findings. In G. Bower (Ed.), *The psychology of learning and motivation* (Vol. 26). New York: Academic Press.

Newell, A., & Simon, H.A. (1972). *Human problem solving.* Englewood Cliffs, NJ: Prentice-Hall.

Niederehe, G., & Yoder, C. (1989). Metamemory perceptions in depressions of young and older adults. *The Journal of Nervous and Mental Disease, 177,* 4–14.

Nisbett, R. E., & Wilson, T. D. (1977). Telling more than we can know: Verbal reports on mental processes. *Psychological Review, 84,* 231–259.

Nowlan, S. J., & Hinton, G. E. (1991). Evaluation of adaptive mixtures of competing experts. *Advances in Neural Information Processing systems, 3,* 774–780.

O'Hara, M. W., Hinrichs, Kohout, F. J., Wallace, R. B., and Lemke, J. H. (1986). Memory complaint and memory performance in the depressed elderly. *Psychology and Aging, 1,* 208–214.

O'Rourke, T. E., Penrod, S. D., Cutler, B. L., & Stuve, T. E. (1989). The external validity of eyewitness identification research: Generalizing across age groups. *Law and Human Behavior, 13,* 385–395.

Oscar-Berman, M. (1980). The neuropsychological consequences of long-term chronic alcoholism. *American Scientist, 68,* 410–419.

Paivio, A., & Yuille, J. C. (1969). Changes in associative strategies and paired-associate learning over trials as a function of word attributes and type of learning set. *Journal of Experimental Psychology, 79,* 458–463.

Parducci, A., & Sarris, V. (1984). *Perspectives in psychological experimentation: Toward the year 2000.* Hillsdale, NJ: Erlbaum.

Patrick, J. (1992). *Training: Research and practice.* San Diego, CA: Academic Press.

Pea, R. D., & Hawkins. (1987). Children's planning process in a chore-scheduling task. In S. L. Friedman, E. K. Scholnick, & R. R. Cocking (Eds.), *Blueprints for thinking: The role of planning in psychological development*. New York: Cambridge University Press.

Perenin, M. T. (1978). Visual function within the hemianopic field following early cerebral hemidecortication in man. II. Pattern discrimination. *Neuropsychologia, 16,* 698–708.

Perenin, M. T., & Jeannerod, M. (1978). Visual function within the hemianopic field following early cerebral hemidecortication in man. I. Spatial localization. *Neuropsychologia, 16,* 1–13.

Perlmutter, M. (1978). What is memory aging the aging of? *Developmental Psychology, 14,* 330–345.

Perlmutter, M., Adams, C., Berry, J., Kaplan, M., Person, D., & Verdonik, F. (1987). Aging and memory. In K. W. Schaie (Ed.), *Annual review of gerontology and geriatrics* (Vol. 7, pp. 57–92). New York: Springer.

Person, D. C., & Wellman, H. M. (1988). *Older adults' theories of memory difficulties.* Unpublished Manuscript.

Picton, T. W. (1992). The P300 wave of the human event-related potential. *Journal of Clinical Neurophysiology, 9,* 456–479.

Popkin, S. J., Gallagher, D., Thompson, L. W., & Moore, M. (1982). Memory complaint and performance in normal and depressed older adults. *Experimental Aging Research, 8,* 141–145.

Posner, M. I., Rafal, R. D., Choate, L., & Vaughan, J. (1985). Inihibition of return: Neural basis and function. *Cognitive Neuropsychology, 2,* 211–228.

Postman, L. (1975). Verbal learning and memory. *Annual Review of Psychology, 26,* 291–335.

Prevey, M. L., Delaney, R. C., Mattson, R. H., & Tice, D. M. (1991). Feeling-of-knowing in temporal lobe epilepsy: Monitoring knowledge inaccessible to conscious recall. *Cortex, 27,* p. 81–92.

Prigatano, G. P. (1991). The relationship of frontal lobe damage to diminished awareness: Studies in rehabilitation. In H. S. Levin, H. M. Eisenberg, & A. L. Benton (Eds.), *Frontal lobe function and dysfunction* (pp. 381–400). New York: Oxford University Press.

Prigatano, G. P., & Schacter, D. L. (Eds.). (1991). *Awareness of deficit after brain injury: Clinical and theoretical issues.* New York : Oxford University Press.

Rabbitt, P., & Abson, V. (1990). 'Lost and found': Some logical and methodological limitations of self-report questionnaires as tools to study cognitive ageing. *British Journal of Psychology, 81,* 1–16.

References

Rabbitt, P., & Abson, V. (1991). Do older people know how good they are? *British Journal of Psychology, 82,* 137–151.

Rabinowitz, J. C. (1989). Age deficits in recall under optimal study conditions. *Psychology and Aging, 4,* 378–380.

Rabinowitz, J. C., Ackerman, B. P., Craik, F. I. M., & Hinchley, J. L. (1982). Aging and metamemory: The roles of relatedness and imagery. *Journal of Gerontology, 37,* 688–695.

Rafal, R., Smith, J., Krantz, J., Cohen, A., & Brennan, C. (1990). Extrageniculate vision in hemianopic humans: Saccade inhibition by signals in the blind field. *Science, 250,* 118–120.

Rea, C. P., & Modigliani, V. (1985). The effect of expanded versus massed practice on the retention of multiplication facts and spelling lists. *Human Learning, 4,* 11–18.

Read, J. D., & Bruce, D. (1982). Longitudinal tracking of difficult memory retrievals. *Cognitive Psychology, 14,* 280–300.

Reason, J. T., & Lucas, D. (1984). Using cognitive diaries to investigate naturally occurring memory blocks. In J. Harris & P. E. Morris (Eds.), *Everyday memory, actions, and absent mindedness* (pp. 53–70). London: Academic Press.

Reder, L. M. (1979). The role of elaborations in memory for prose. *Cognitive Psychology, 11,* 221–234.

Reder, L. M. (1982). Plausibility judgments vs. fact retrieval: Alternative strategies for sentence verification. *Psychological Review, 89,* 250–280.

Reder, L. M. (1987). Strategy selection in question answering. *Cognitive Psychology, 19,* 90–138.

Reder, L. M. (1988). Strategic control of retrieval strategies. In G. Bower (Ed.), *The psychology of learning and motivation* (Vol. 22). San Diego, CA: Academic Press.

Reder, L. M., & Anderson, J. R. (1982). Effects of spacing and embellishment on memory for the main points of a text. *Memory & Cognition, 10,* 97–102.

Reder, L. M., Charney, D. H., & Morgan, K. I. (1986). The role of elaborations in learning a skill from an instructional text. *Memory & Cognition, 14,* 64–78.

Reder, L. M., & Klatzky, R. L. (1993). The effect of context on training: Is learning situated? In D. Druckman and R. A. Bjork (Eds.), *Learning, remembering, believing: Enhancing team and individual performance,* Washington, DC: National Academy Press, in press.

Reder, L. M., Richards, D. R., & Stoffolino, P. (1993). A simulation model of feeling of knowing, in preparation.

Reder, L. M., & Ritter, F. E. (1992). What determines initial feeling of knowing? Familiarity with question terms, not with the answer. *Journal of Experimental Psychology: Learning, Memory, and Cognition, 18,* 435 –452.

Reder, L. M., & Ross, B. H. (1983). Integrated knowledge in different tasks: The role of retrieval strategy on fan effects. *Journal of Experimental Psychology: Learning, Memory, and Cognition, 9,* 55–72.

Reder, L. M., & Wible, C. (1984). Strategy use in question-answering: Memory strength and task constraints on fan effects. *Memory & Cognition, 12,* 411–419.

Reitman, W. (1970). What does it take to remember? In D. Norman (Ed.), *Models of Human Memory.* New York: Academic Press.

Resnick, L. B., & Glaser, R. (1976). Problem solving and intelligence. In L. B. Resnick (Ed.), *The nature of intelligence.* Hillsdale, NJ: Erlbaum.

Richardson-Klavehn, A., & Bjork, R. A. (1988). Measures of memory. *Annual Review of Psychology, 39,* 475–543.

Roediger, H. L. (1991). They read an article? *American Psychologist, 46,* 37–30.

Roediger, H. L., & Blaxton, T. A. (1987). Retrieval modes produce dissociations in memory for surface information. In D. Gorfein & R. R. Hoffman (Eds.), *Memory and cognitive process: The Ebbinghaus Centennial Conference* (pp. 349–379). Hillsdale, NJ: Erlbaum.

Roediger, H. L., & McDermott, K. B. (1993). Implicit memory in normal human subjects. In F. Boller & J. Grafman (Eds.), *Handbook of neuropsychology* (Vol. 8) (pp. 63–131). Amsterdam: Elsevier.

Rouse, W. B., & Morris, N. M. (1986). On looking into the black box: Prospects and limits in the search for mental models. *Psychological Bulletin, 100,* 349–363.

Rubens, A. B. (1979). Agnosia. In K. M. Heilman & E. Valenstein (Eds.), *Clinical neuropsychology* (pp. 233–267). New York: Oxford University Press.

Rubens, A. B., & Benson, D. F. (1971). Associative visual agnosia. *Archives of Neurology, 24,* 305–316.

Rumelhart, D. E., & McClelland, J. L. (1986). *Parallel distributed processing* (Vol 2). Cambridge, MA: MIT Press.

Rumelhart, D. E., Hinton, G. E., & Williams, R. J. (1986). Learning representations by back-propagating errors. *Nature, 323,* 533–536

References

Rundus, D. (1971). Analysis of rehearsal processes in free recall. *Journal of Experimental Psychology, 89,* 63–77.

Rundus, D. (1973). Negative effects of using list items as recall cues. *Journal of Verbal Learning and Verbal Behavior, 12,* 43–50.

Ryan, E. B. (1992). Beliefs about memory changes across the lifespan. *Journal of Gerontology: Psychological Sciences, 47,* 41–46.

Ryan, M. P., Petty, C. R., & Winzlaff, R. M. (1982). Motivated remembering efforts during tip-of-the-tongue states. *Acta Psychologica, 51,* 137–157.

Salthouse, T. A. (1991). *Theoretical perspectives on cognitive aging.* Hillsdale, NJ: Erlbaum.

Sanders, R. E., Murphy, M. D., Schmitt, F. A., & Walsh, K. K. (1980). Age differences in free recall rehearsal strategies. *Journal of Gerontology, 35,* 550–558.

Schacter, D. L. (1983). Feeling of knowing in episodic memory. *Journal of Experimental Psychology: Learning, Memory, and Cognition, 9,* 39–54.

Schacter, D. L. (1987). Implicit memory: History and current status. *Journal of Experimental Psychology: Learning, Memory, and Cognition, 13,* 501–518.

Schacter, D. L. (1990). Perceptual representation systems in implicit memory: Toward a resolution of the multiple systems debate. In A. Diamond (Ed.), *Development and neural bases of higher cognitive function* (pp. 543–571). New York: Annals of the New York Academy of Science.

Schacter, D. L., Cooper, L. A., Tharan, M., & Rubens, A. B. (1991). Preserved priming of novel objects in patients with memory disorders. *Journal of Cognitive Neuroscience, 3,* 118–131.

Schacter, D. L., & Worling, J. R. (1985). Attribute information and the feeling of knowing. *Canadian Journal of Psychology, 39,* 467–475.

Schley, C., Chauvin, Y., Henkle, V, & Golden, R. (1991). Neural networks structured for control application to aircraft landing. *Advances in Neural Information Processing Systems, 3,* 415–421.

Schmidt, R.A. (1991). Frequent augmented feedback can degrade learning: Evidence and interpretations. In G.E. Stelmach & J. Requin (Eds.), *Tutorials in motor neuroscience* (pp. 59–75). Dordrecht: Kluwer.

Schmidt, R. A., & Bjork, R. A. (1992). New conceptualizations of practice: Common principles in three paradigms suggest new concepts for training. *Psychological Science, 3,* 207–217.

References

Schmidt, R. A., Young, D. E., Swinnen, S., & Shapiro, D. C. (1989). Summary knowledge of results for skill acquisition: Support for the guidance hypothesis. *Journal of Experimental Psychology: Learning, Memory, and Cognition, 15,* 352–359.

Schmitt, F. A., Murphy, M. D., & Sanders, R. E. (1981). Training older adults free recall rehearsal strategies. *Journal of Gerontology, 36,* 329–337.

Schneider, W., & Pressley, M. (1989). *Memory development between 2 and 20.* New York: Springer.

Schreiber, T. A., & Nelson, D. A. (1993). *Feelings of knowing and retrieval processes.* Unpublished manuscript.

Schwartz, B. L. (1992). Cue priming influences feeling-of-knowing judgments. Poster session at American Psychological Society Convention, June 1992.

Schwartz, B. L., & Metcalfe, J. (1992). Cue familiarity but not target retrievability enhances feeling-of-knowing judgments. *Journal of Experimental Psychology: Learning, Memory, and Cognition, 18,* 1074–1083.

Seamon, J. G., & Virostek, S. (1978). Memory performance and subject-defined depth of processing. *Memory & Cognition, 6,* 283–287.

Searle, J. R. (1992). *The rediscovery of the mind.* Cambridge, MA: MIT Press.

Sehulster, J. R. (1981). Structure and pragmatics of a self-theory of memory. *Memory & Cognition, 9,* 263–276.

Sergent, J. (1987). A new look at the human split brain. *Brain, 110,* 1375–1392.

Serpell, R. (1976). Strategies for investigating intelligence in its cultural context. *Quarterly Newsletter of the Institute for Comparative Human Development,* 11–15.

Shallice, T., & Burgess, P. (1991). Higher-order cogntiive impairments and frontal lobe lesions in man. In H. S. Levin, H. M. Eisenberg, & A. L. Benton (Eds.), *Frontal lobe function and dysfunction* (pp. 125–138). New York: Oxford Univeristry Press.

Shallice, T., & Evans, M. E. (1978). The involvement of the frontal lobes in cognitive estimation. *Cortex, 14,* 294–303.

Shapere, D. (1971). The paradigm concept. *Science, 172,* 706–709.

Sharp, G. L., Cutler, B. L., & Penrod, S. D. (1988). Performance feedback improves the resolution of confidence judgments. *Organizational Behavior and Decision Processes, 42,* 271–283.

Shaw, R. J., & Craik, F. I. M. (1989). Age differences in predictions and performance on a cued recall task. *Psychology and Aging, 4,* 131–135.

Shea, J. B., & Morgan, R. L. (1979) Contextual interference effects on the acquisition, retention, and transfer of a motor skill. *Journal of Experimental Psychology: Human Learning and Memory, 5,* 179–187.

Shepard, R. N. (1992). The advent and continuing influence of mathematical learning theory: Comment on Estes and Burke. *Journal of Experimental Psychology: General, 121,* 419–421.

Sherman, S. J., Judd, C. M., & Park, B. (1989). Social cognition. *Annual Review of Psychology, 40,* 281–326.

Shimamura, A. P. (1986). Priming in amnesia: Evidence for a dissociable memory function. *Quarterly Journal of Experimental Psychology, 38,* 619–644.

Shimamura, A. P. (1989). Disorders of memory: The cognitive science perspective. In F. Boller & J. Grafman (Eds.), *Handbook of Neuropsychology* (pp. 35–73). Amsterdam: Elsevier Science Publishers.

Shimamura, A. P. (1993). Neuropsychological analyses of implicit memory: Recent progress and theoretical interpretations. In P. Graf & M. E. Masson (Eds.), *Implicit memory: New directions in cognition, development, and neuropsychology* (pp. 265–286). Hillsdale, NJ: Erlbaum.

Shimamura, A. P., Janowsky, J. S., & Squire, L. R. (1991). What is the role of frontal lobe damage in amnesic disorders? In H. S. Levin, H. M. Eisenberg, & A. L. Benton (Eds.), *Frontal lobe function and dysfunction* (pp. 173–195). New York: Oxford University Press.

Shimamura, A. P., Jernigan, T. L., & Squire, L. R. (1988). Korsakoff's Syndrome: Radiological (CT) findings and neuropsychological correlates. *Journal of Neuroscience, 8,* 4400–4410.

Shimamura, A. P., & Squire, L. R. (1984). Paired-associate learning and priming effects in amnesia: A neuropsychological study. *Journal of Experimental Psychology: General, 113,* 556–570.

Shimamura, A. P., & Squire, L. R. (1986a). Korsakoff syndrome: A study of the relation between anterograde amnesia and remote memory impairment. *Behavioral Neuroscience, 100,* 165–170.

Shimamura, A. P., & Squire, L. R. (1986b). Memory and metamemory: A study of the feeling-of-knowing phenomenon in amnesic patients. *Journal of Experimental Psychology: Learning, Memory, and Cognition, 12,* 452–460.

Skinner, B. F. (1974). *About behaviorism.* New York: Knopf.

Slamecka, N. J., & Graf, P. (1978). The generation effect: Delineation of a phenomenon. *Journal of Experimental Psychology: Human Learning and Memory, 4,* 592–604.

Smith, M. L., & Milner, B. (1984). Differential effects of frontal-lobe lesions on cognitive estimation and spatial memory. *Neuropsychologia, 22,* 697–705.

Smith, S. M. (July 1991). *The TOTimals method: Effects of acquisition and retention factors on tip of the tongue experiences.* Paper presented at the proceedings of the first International Conference on Memory, Lancaster, England.

Smith, S. M. (November 1991). *Tip-of-the-tongue states and blockers with imaginary animals as targets.* Paper presented at the annual meeting of the Psychonomic Society, San Francisco, CA.

Smith, S.M. (1993). Getting into and out of mental ruts: A theory of fixation, incubation, and insight. In R. Sternberg & J. Davidson (Eds.), *The nature of insight,* Cambridge, MA: MIT Press, in press.

Smith, S. M., Brown, J. M., & Balfour, S.P. (1991). TOTimals: A controlled experimental method for observing tip-of-the-tongue states. *Bulletin of the Psychonomic Society, 29,* 445–447.

Smith, S. M., Glenberg, A. M., & Bjork, R. A. (1978). Environmental context and human memory. *Memory & Cognition, 6,* 342–353.

Smith, S. M., & Rothkopf, E. Z. (1984). Contextual enrichment and distribution of practice in the classroom. *Cognition and Instruction, 1,* 341–358.

Sokolov, E. N. (1963). *Perception and the conditioned reflex.* Pergamon Press: Oxford.

Sokolov, E. N. (1975). The neuronal mechanisms of the orienting reflex. In E. N. Sokolov & O. S. Vinogradova (Eds.), *Neuronal mechanisms of the orienting reflex* (pp. 217–238). Hillsdale, NJ: Erlbaum.

Spellman, B. A., & Bjork, R. A. (1992). When predictions create reality: Judgments of learning may alter what they are intended to assess. *Psychological Science, 3,* 315–316.

Spiro, R. J. (1977). Remembering information from text: The "state of schema" approach. In R. C. Anderson, R. J. Spiro, & W. E. Montague (Eds.), *Schooling and the acquisition of knowledge.* Hillsdale, NJ: Erlbaum.

Squire, L. R. (1982). Comparisons between forms of amnesia: Some deficits are unique to Korsakoff's syndrome. *Journal of Experimental Psychology: Learning, Memory, and Cognition, 8,* 560–571.

Squire, L. R. (1986). Mechanisms of memory. *Science, 232,* 1612–1619.

Squire, L. R., Amaral, D. G., & Press, G. A. (1990). Magnetic resonance measurements of hippocampal formation and mammillary nuclei distinguishes medial temporal lobe and diencephalic amnesia. *Journal of Neuroscience, 10,* 3106–3117.

Squire, L. R., Shimamura, A. P., & Amaral D. G. (1989). Memory and the hippocampus. In J. H. Byrne & W. O. Berry (Eds.), *Neural models of plasticity* (pp. 208–239). Academic Press: New York.

Sternberg, R. J. (1977). *Intelligence, information processing, and analogical reasoning: The componential analysis of human abilities.* Hillsdale, NJ: Erlbaum.

Sternberg, R. J. (1981). Intelligence and nonentrenchment. *Journal of Educational Psychology, 73,* 1–16.

Sternberg, R. J. (1985). *Beyond IQ.* Cambridge, England: Cambridge University Press.

Sternberg, R. J., & Davidson, J. E. (1983). Insight in the gifted. *Educational Psychologist, 18,* 51–57.

Sternberg, R. J., & Gardner, M. K. (1983). Unities in inductive reasoning. *Journal of Experimental Psychology: General, 112,* 80–116.

Sternberg, R. J., & Ketron, J. L. (1982). Selection and implementation of strategies in reasoning by analogy. *Journal of Educational Psychology, 74,* 399–413.

Sternberg, R. J., & Nigro, G. (1980). Development patterns in the solution of verbal analogies. *Child Development, 51,* 27–38.

Sternberg, R. J., & Rifkin, B. (1979). The development of analogical reasoning processes. *Journal of Experimental Child Psychology, 27,* 195–232.

Sternberg, R. J., & Weil, E. M. (1980). An aptitude-strategy interaction in linear syllogistic reasoning. *Journal of Educational Psychology, 72,* 226–234.

Stoerig, P. (1987). Chromaticity and achromaticity: Evidence of a functional differentiation in visual field defects. *Brain, 110,* 869–886.

Stuss, D. T. (1991a). Interference effects on memory function in postleukotomy patients: An attentional perspective. In H. S. Levin, H. M. Eisenberg, & A. L. Benton (Eds.), *Frontal lobe function and dysfunction* (pp. 157–172). New York: Oxford University Press.

Stuss, D. T. (1991b.) Distrubance of self awareness after frontal system damage. In G. P. Prigatano & D. L. Schacter (Eds.), *Awareness of deficit after brain injury* (pp. 63–83). New York: Oxford University Press.

Stuss, D. T., & Benson, D. F. (1986). *The frontal lobes.* New York: Raven Press.

Sunderland, A., Harris, J. E., & Baddeley, A. D. (1983). Do laboratory tests predict everyday memory? A neuropsychological study. *Journal of Verbal Learning and Verbal Behavior, 22,* 341–357.

313

References

Sunderland, A., Watts, K., Baddeley, A. D., & Harris, J. E. (1986). Subjective memory assessment and test performance in elderly adults. *Journal of Gerontology, 41,* 376–384.

Suppe, F. (1977). *The structure of scientific theories* (2nd ed.). Urbana, IL: University of Illinois Press.

Swets, J. A. (1986). Indices of discrimination or diagnostic accuracy: Their ROCs and implied models. *Psychological Bulletin, 99,* 100–117.

Thomson, R. (1959). *The psychology of thinking.* Baltimore: Penguin Books.

Towle, V. L., Heuer, D., & Donchin, E. (1980). On indexing attention and learning with event-related potentials. *Psychophysiology, 17,* 291.

Treat, N. J., Poon, L. W., Fozard, J. L., & Popkin, S. J. (1978). Toward applying cognitive skill training to memory problems. *Experimental Aging Research, 4,* 305–319.

Tulving, E. (1962). The effect of alphabetical subjective organization on memorizing unrelated words. *Canadian Journal of Psychology, 69,* 344–354.

Tulving, E. (1983). *Elements of epsiodic memory.* Oxford: Oxford University Press.

Tulving, E. (1993). What is epsiodic memory? *Current Directions in Psychological Science, 2,* 67–70.

Tulving, E., & Madigan, S. A. (1970). Memory and verbal learning. In P. H. Mussen & M. R. Rosenzweig (Eds.), *Annual review of psychology.* Palo Alto, CA: Annual Reviews.

Tulving, E., & Pearlstone, Z. (1966). Availability versus accessibility of information in memory for words. *Journal of Verbal Learning and Verbal Behavior, 5,* 381–391.

Tulving, E., & Schacter, D. L. (1990). Priming and human memory systems. *Science, 247,* 301–306.

Tversky, A., & Kahneman, D. (1973). Availability: A heuristic for judging frequency and probability. *Cognitive Psychology, 4,* 207–232.

Tversky, B., & Tuchin, M. (1989). A reconciliation of the evidence on eyewitness testimony: Comments on McCloskey & Zaragoza (1985). *Journal of Experimental Psychology: General, 118,* 86–91.

Underwood, B. J., & Postman, L. (1960). Extraexperimental sources of interference in forgetting. *Psychological Review, 67,* 73–95.

VanLehn, K. (1989). Problem solving and cognitive skill acquisition. In M. Posner (Ed.), *Foundations of cognitive science.* Cambridge, MA: MIT Press.

Vesonder, G. T., & Voss, J. F. (1985). On the ability to predict one's own responses while learning. *Journal of Memory and Language, 24,* 363–376.

Victor, M., Adams, R. D., & Collins, G. H. (1989). *The Wernicke-Korsakoff Syndrome* (2nd Ed.). Philadelphia: F. A. Davis.

Vurpillot, E. (1968). The development of scanning strategies and their relation to visual differentiation. *Journal of Experimental Child Psychology, 6,* 632–650.

Wagenaar, W. A. (1988). Calibration and the effects of knowledge and reconstruction in retrieval from memory. *Cognition, 28,* 277–296.

Wagner, D. A. (1978). Memories of Morocco: The influence of age, schooling and environment on memory. *Cognitive Psychology, 10,* 1–28.

Wagner, R. K., & Sternberg, R. J. (1986). Tacit knowledge and intelligence in the everyday world. In R. J. Sternberg & R. K. Wagner (Eds.), *Practical intelligence* (pp. 51–83). New York: Cambridge University Press.

Warrington, E. K. (1982). The double dissociation of short and long-term memory deficits. In L. S. Cermak (Ed.), *Human memory and amnesia* (pp. 61–76). Hillsdale, NJ: Erlbaum.

Warrington, E. K., & Weiskrantz, L. (1968). New method of testing long-term retention with special reference to amnesic patients. *Nature (London), 217,* 972–974.

Warrington, E. K., & Weiskrantz, L. (1982). Amnesia: A disconnection syndrome? *Neuropsychologia, 20,* 233–248.

Wason, P. C., & Johnson-Laird, P. N. (Eds.) (1968). *Thinking and reasoning: Selected readings.* Hardsmonds, England: Penguin Books.

Wason, P. C., & Johnson-Laird, P. N. (1972). *Psychology of reasoning: Structure and content.* London: B. T. Batsford.

Watson, J. B. (1913). Psychology as the behaviorist views it. *Psychological Review, 20,* 158–177.

Weaver, C. A. (1990). Constraining factors in calibration of comprehension. *Journal of Experimental Psychology: Learning, Memory, and Cognition, 16,* 214–222.

Weingardt, K. R., Toland, H. K., & Loftus, E. F. (1993). Reports of suggested memories: Do people truly believe them? In D. F. Ross, J. D. Read, & M. P. Toglia (Eds.), *Adult eyewitness testimony: Current trends and developments.* Cambridge: Cambridge University Press, in press.

Weiskrantz, L. (1986). *Blindsight: A case study and implications.* Oxford: Oxford University Press.

References

Weiskrantz, L. (1988). *Thought without language.* Oxford: Clarendon Press.

Weiskrantz, L. (1989). Blindsight. In F. Boller & J. Grafman (Eds.), *Handbook of neuropsychology* (Vol. 2; pp. 375–385). Amsterdam: Elsevier.

Weiskrantz, L., Warrington, E. K., Sanders, M. D., & Marshall, J. (1974). Visual capacity in the hemianopic field following a restricted occipital ablation. *Brain, 97,* 709–728.

Wellman, H. M. (1977). Tip of the tongue and feeling of knowing experiences: A developmental study of memory monitoring. *Child Development, 48,* 13–21.

Wellman, H. M. (1983). Metamemory revisited. In M. T. H. Chi (Ed.), *Trends in memory development research* (pp. 31–51). Basel: Karger.

Wells, G. L. (1978). Applied eyewitness testimony research: System variables and estimator variables. *Journal of Personality and Social Psychology, 36,* 1546–1557.

Wells, G. L., Ferguson, T. J., & Lindsay, R. C. L. (1981). The tractability of eyewitness confidence and its implications for triers of fact. *Journal of Applied Psychology, 66,* 688–696.

Wells, G. L., & Murray, D. M. (1984). Eyewitness confidence. In G. L. Wells & E. F. Loftus (Eds.), *Eyewitness testimony: Psychological perspectives.* Cambridge: Cambridge University Press.

Wells, G. L., & Turtle, J. W. (1987). Eyewitness testimony research: Current knowledge and emergent controversies. *Canadian Journal of Behavioral Science, 19,* 363–388.

Wertheimer, M. (1959). *Productive thinking.* New York: Harper & Row.

Wertheimer, M. (1984). The experimental method in nineteenth- and twentieth-century psychology. In A. Parducci & V. Sarris (Eds.), *Perspectives in psychological experimentation: Toward the year 2000.* Hillsdale, NJ: Erlbaum.

West, R. L., Boatwright, L. K., & Schleser, R. (1984). The link between memory performance, self-assessment, and affective status. *Experimental Aging Research, 10,* 197–200.

Whipple, G. M. (1909). The observer as reporter: A survey of the "Psychology of Testimony." *Psychological Bulletin, 6,* 153–170.

Whitbourne, S. K. (1976). Test anxiety in elderly and young adults. *International Journal of Aging and Human Development, 7,* 201–210.

Wickelgren, W. (1980). Human memory. In P. H. Mussen & M. R. Rosenzweig (Eds.), *Annual review of psychology.* Palo Alto, CA: Annual Reviews.

References

Wickens, D. D. (1972). Characteristics of word encoding. In A. W. Melton & E. Martin (Eds.), *Coding processes in human memory* (pp. 191–215). Washington, DC: Winston.

Wiener, N. (1948). *Cybernetics, or control and communication in the animal and the machine.* Cambridge, MA: MIT Press.

Wilkinson, T. S., & Nelson, T. O. (1984). FACTRETRIEVAL2: A Pascal program for assessing someone's recall of general-information facts, confidence about recall correctness, feeling-of-knowing judgments for nonrecalled facts, and recognition of nonrecalled facts. *Behavior Research Methods, Instruments, and Computers, 16,* 486–488.

Winocur, G. (1982). The amnesic syndrome: A deficit in cue utilization. In L. S. Cermak (Ed.), *Human memory and amnesia.* Hillsdale, NJ: Erlbaum.

Winocur, G., Kinsbourne, M. , & Moscovitch, M. (1981). The effect of cuing on release from proactive interference in Korsakoff amnesic patients. *Journal of Experimental Psychology: Human Learning and Memory, 7,* 56–65.

Winstein, C. J., & Schmidt, R. A. (1990). Reduced frequency of knowledge of results enhances motor skill learning. *Journal of Experimental Psychology: Learning, Memory, and Cognition, 16,* 677–691.

Wiser, M., & Carey, S. (1983). When heat and temperature were one. In D. Gentner & A. L Stevens (Eds.), *Mental models* (pp. 267–298). Hillsdale, NJ: Erlbaum.

Woodworth, R. S., & Schlosberg, H. (1954). *Experimental psychology.* New York: Holt.

Yaniv, I., & Meyer, D. E. (1987). Activation and metacognition of inaccessible stored information: Potential bases for incubation effects in problem solving. *Journal of Experimental Psychology: Learning, Memory, and Cogninition, 13,* 187–205.

Yarmey, A. D. (1973). I recognize your face but I can't remember your name: Further evidence on the tip-of-the- tongue phenomenon. *Memory & Cognition, 1,* 287–289.

Yates, J. (1985). The content of awareness is a model of the world. *Psychological Review, 92,* 249–284.

Yates, J. F. (1990). *Judgment and decision-making.* Englewood Cliffs, NJ: Prentice-Hall.

Yavutz, H. S., & Bousfield, W. A. (1959). Recall of connotative meaning. *Psychological Reports, 5,* 319–320.

References

Zacks, R. T. (1969). Invariance of total learning time under different conditions of practice. *Journal of Experimental Psychology, 82,* 441–447.

Zaragoza, M. S., & Koshmider, J. W., III (1989). Misled subjects may know more than their performance implies. *Journal of Experimental Psychology: Learning, Memory, and Cognition, 15,* 246–255.

Zarit, S. H., Cole, K. D., & Guider, R. L. (1981). Memory training strategies and subjective complaints of memory in the aged. *The Gerontologist, 21,* 158–164.

Zelinski, E. M., Gilewski, M. J., & Anthony-Bergstone, C. R. (1990). Memory functioning questionnaire: Concurrent validity with memory performance and self-reported memory failures. *Psychology and Aging, 5,* 388–399.

Zihl, J. (1980). 'Blindsight': Improvement of visually guided eye movements by systematic practice in patients with cerebral blindness. *Neuropsychologia, 18,* 71–77.

Zimmerman, B. J., & Schunk, S. H. (1989). *Self-regulated learning and academic achievement.* New York: Springer.

Contributors

Robert A. Bjork
Department of Psychology
University of California, Los Angeles
Los Angeles, California

Janet E. Davidson
Department of Psychology
Lewis & Clark College
Portland, Oregon

Rebecca Deuser
Department of Psychology
Carnegie-Mellon University
Pittsburgh, Pennsylvania

Roger A. Dixon
Department of Psychology
University of Victoria
Victoria, British Columbia

Christopher Hertzog
Department of Psychology
Georgia Institute of Technology
Atlanta, Georgia

Kimberly A. Jameson
Department of Psychology
University of California, San Diego
San Diego, California

Asher Koriat
Department of Psychology
University of Haifa
Haifa, Israel

V. A. Lee
Department of Psychology
University of California, Irvine
Irvine, California

R. Jacob Leonesio
Department of Psychology
University of Washington
Seattle, Washington

Elizabeth F. Loftus
Department of Psychology
University of Washington
Seattle, Washington

Janet Metcalfe
Department of Psychology
Dartmouth College
Hanover, New Hampshire

Ann C. Miner
Department of Psychology
Carnegie-Mellon University
Pittsburgh, Pennsylvania

Louis Narens
Department of Psychology
University of California, Irvine
Irvine, California

Thomas O. Nelson
Department of Psychology
University of Washington
Seattle, Washington

Lynne M. Reder
Department of Psychology
Carnegie-Mellon University
Pittsburgh, Pennsylvania

Bennett L. Schwartz
Department of Psychology
Florida International University
Miami, Florida

Arthur P. Shimamura
Department of Psychology
University of California, Berkeley
Berkeley, California

Steven M. Smith
Department of Psychology
Texas A&M University
College Station, Texas

Robert J. Sternberg
Department of Psychology
Yale University
New Haven, Connecticut

Kenneth R. Weingardt
Department of Psychology
University of Washington
Seattle, Washington

Author Index

Author Index

Subject Index

6, 10, 47, 45 TOT
48 Harts RJR
65, 117
139
A block on a specific name.

STM would be overload if arbitrary
chains of association put data in STM.
~~Certain kinds~~ Therefore, items ~~are~~ matching
certain patterns are blocked from
entering STM. Blocking on Roberts's
name was the result of a malfunction of
that inhibition process.

———

People smooth out what they see
and also smooth what they
remember of events. Must AI
programs do this? Seems not.

185 Ineffectiveness of training